Voices of the People

Merlin Press Chartist Studies
Series editor: Owen R. Ashton

The Chartist Legacy
Edited by Owen Ashton, Robert Fyson & Stephen Roberts

Images of Chartism
by Stephen Roberts & Dorothy Thompson

The People's Charter
Democratic Agitation in Early Victorian Britain
Edited by Stephen Roberts

Friends of the People
'Uneasy' Radicals in the Age of the Chartists
by Owen R. Ashton & Paul A. Pickering

Papers for the People
A Study of the Chartist Press
Edited by Joan Allen & Owen R. Ashton

Chartism After 1848
The Working Class and the Politics of Radical Education
by Keith Flett

Forthcoming

Feargus O'Connor
by Paul A. Pickering

VOICES OF THE PEOPLE

Democracy and Chartist political identity
1830-1870

Robert G. Hall

MERLIN PRESS

First published 2007 by The Merlin Press Ltd.
96 Monnow Street
Monmouth
NP25 3EQ
Wales

www.merlinpress.co.uk

ISBN 9780850365573 paperback
ISBN 9780850365641 hardback

Chartist Studies Series No. 8
ISSN Chartist Studies Series 1478-7296

British Library Cataloguing in Publication Data
is available from the British Library

Printed in Great Britain by Cromwell Press, Trowbridge, Wiltshire

CONTENTS

List of Tables

For Carolyn

Acknowledgements

Although the act of writing is a solitary pursuit, the creative process is not. Over the past two decades, the advice and friendly criticism of friends, family members, and fellow labourers in the field have shaped my approach to and understanding of Chartist political identity. In many ways, this book, like Chartism itself, is the product of many different voices.

At Vanderbilt Michael Hanagan and David Goodway introduced me to the study of social and labour history; they later provided much-needed guidance during the early stages of work on the dissertation. David Carlton, Dale Johnson, Matthew Ramsey, and Margo Todd read the dissertation carefully and critically and made valuable suggestions for its improvement. While the footnotes gave some indication of the contribution of Jim Epstein to the dissertation, footnotes alone cannot, of course, tell the whole story. His book on Feargus O'Connor and the Chartist movement, *The Lion of Freedom*, sparked my original interest in the movement for the Six Points and transformed me into a Chartist enthusiast; over the years, he has generously passed along as well many references from his own research.

This work obviously owes a great deal to the skill and energy of the staffs of the National Archives at Kew; the British Library of Political and Economic Science; the departments of printed books, manuscripts, and newspapers of the British Library; the Bishopsgate Institute; the Institute of Historical Research; Manchester Central Library; the John Rylands University Library; Chetham's Library; the Tameside Local Studies and Archives Unit; and the Lancashire Record Office. In the United States, the staffs of the Interlibrary Loan Services of the Jean and Alexander Heard Library of Vanderbilt University and the John C. Hodges Library of the University of Tennessee have tracked down innumerable obscure requests. For financial support I owe a special thanks to the Ethel Mae Wilson programme at Vanderbilt and to the American Council of Learned Societies. The technical expertise of Wayne Cutler and the keyboard skills of Michelle Christopher and Joshua Burress were crucial to the final stages of this project; Michael Joseph Hradesky, of the Geography Department at Ball State University, created the map of the cotton district.

Chapter 2 contains a much-abbreviated version of an essay from *The Chartist Legacy*, an earlier title in the Chartist Studies series. Chapter 4 and the Conclusion originally appeared, in somewhat different forms, respectively in the *Journal of Social History* 38 (Fall 2004) and the *Journal of British Studies* 38 (October 1999). I wish to thank Merlin Press, the editors of the journals, George Mason University Press, the University of Chicago Press, and the North American Conference on British Studies for permission to reproduce them here. I am especially grateful to Adrian Howe and Anthony Zurbrugg of Merlin Press for their insightful commentary and timely advice during the copy editing process.

Over the years I have benefited from the advice and suggestions of scholars on both sides of the Atlantic and beyond. Owen Ashton, Jim Epstein, and Carolyn Malone have read all of the chapters of the manuscript, sometimes several times, with great care. Abel Alves, Richard Blackett, Jamie Bronstein, Jim Connolly, Bob Fyson, Phil Harling, Martin Hewitt, Paul Pickering, Stephen Roberts, and Chris Thompson have mulled over and have commented on individual chapters. I have also gained new perspectives on Chartism from conversations and correspondence with John Bohstedt, Malcolm Chase, Wayne Cutler, Ian Dyck, Nev Kirk, Alice Lock, John and Diana Poole, Iori Prothero, Jim Rogers, Marc Steinberg, and Dorothy Thompson.

Of equal importance to the creative process has been the love and support of my parents, Bob and Helen Hall. They instilled in me, at an early age, a love of history and respect for the life of the mind. Without a doubt, though, my greatest debt is to Carolyn Malone. Throughout our years together, she has been a source of warm and affectionate encouragement and inspiration (as well as good humour). And, of course, her patience is legendary.

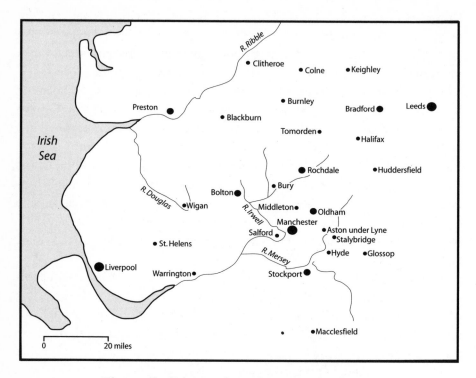

The textile districts of Northwest England, 1841

Introduction

Locality and Nation:
Democracy and Chartist Political Identity

For the most part, book-length studies of Chartism have focused on atypical communities; historians have usually studied networks of activists and associations in London or in one of the large provincial cities. As a mass movement, however, Chartism was always strongest in the small and medium-sized towns of the manufacturing and mining districts of South Wales, the Midlands, Lancashire, Yorkshire, the Northeast, and the Lowlands of Scotland. Unlike London or even Manchester, the small-scale, intimate world of these 'smaller towns, where the inhabitants do not number more than thirty or forty thousand' made possible, J.C. Coombe argued, a thorough and 'business-like' organization of the movement.[1] In these towns, the presence of one or two major industries, like textiles or coal, and common leisure and recreational activities, Dorothy Thompson has pointed out, 'made for speed of communication, common concerns in work and in political action and the kind of mutual knowledge and trust which was essential for the maintenance of organisations which were always on the very frontiers of legality'.[2]

One such Chartist town was Ashton-under-Lyne. Built on the banks of the Tame River, 'a stream rising in the Yorkshire moors', Ashton was situated about seven miles east of Manchester, in the heart of the cotton district of northwest England.[3] It was, at the time of the American Revolution, a small weaving hamlet of about three thousand persons; in the early 1790s, Ashton was in appearance still 'partly rural and partly town-like'.[4] With industrialization and the rise of the cotton industry, Ashton grew dramatically, more than doubling in size between 1821 and 1841 (see Table 1). The 1832 Reform Act in effect acknowledged the growing 'importance, wealth, population, and commerce' of the town and created the parliamentary borough of Ashton-under-Lyne.[5] In the early 1840s the responsibility for maintaining the peace and governing this industrial boom town rested with a hodgepodge of local governmental bodies: the justices of the peace, the court leet, and the police commissioners. A classic example of the Chartist town where 'slack religious and moral supervision' and the 'unpoliced public street and meeting-place' were the rule, Ashton had in 1840 a police force of three constables and a few watchmen; at this point, the population of the rapidly growing town came to almost 23,000 souls.[6]

The rapid industrialization and urbanization of the 1820s and 1830s, with all of the attendant problems and changes that followed in their wake, formed the immediate background to the coming together of Chartism in Ashton and the other mill towns of the cotton district. The impact of this dual revolution, together with the town's tradition of democratic politics, helped to make Ashton, as Dorothy Thompson has put it, 'the most radical and Chartist of all the factory towns'.[7] Between 1838 and 1848, its 'sturdy democrats' were among the most militant of the movement's rank and file and kept alive a local insurrectionary tradition which stretched back at least to the days of the Blanketeers and the Peterloo massacre.[8] 'The most ultra-political and theological opinions,' Angus Reach noted about Ashton, 'run riot amongst the population'; its working men and women, he added, were well-known for 'being turbulent and fanatical'.[9] During the 1839 and 1848 campaigns for the People's Charter, the town's 'sturdy democrats' certainly lived up to this reputation; they supported the strategy of mass arming and the call for a general strike and stood at the forefront of the struggle in 1842 for the Charter and a fair day's wage. The 14,200 signatures that the town contributed to the 1842 petition, a total that represented about 62 per cent of its population, demonstrated the extent to which Chartist ideas had touched the hearts and minds of 'the people' in Ashton.[10]

In his ambitious attempt to rethink nineteenth-century politics, Jon Lawrence has emphasized the multiplicity of ways in which the locality shaped popular politics after 1850; this study of the most 'Chartist of all the factory towns' also seeks to pay close attention to the 'politics of place'.[11] This is not, however, a traditional local history. Nor do I attempt to write a total history of this mill-town community in the style of the *Annales* school. In this study, I approach Ashton instead from the micro-history perspective and attempt to utilize the local to investigate some new perspectives on the movement. This approach allows me to use this militant locality as a way of examining the relationship between the local and the national in the movement and as a point of entry into wider issues about Chartist democracy and identity.[12] In approaching Chartism in this way, I try, above all, to explore how local political traditions and cultures at once reflected and shaped the national politics of this mass movement and its visions of democracy.

I

In an influential essay, Stedman Jones has emphasized the potential dangers of this sort of study of an individual locality or area. Too often these studies of 'local differences', he has argued, have simply delved into 'local or occupational peculiarities' of the movement and have overlooked what really mattered—namely, its national and political character.[13] In making this case, Stedman Jones has perhaps underestimated the emotional ties and loyalties to locality and contemporary concerns about centralization and over-powerful national authorities; moreover, this emphasis on Chartism as a national movement has obscured the extent to which the interplay between 'locality and centre' shaped the movement.[14] Linked up nationally by speaking tours, the *Northern Star*, and later by the convention, Chartism also came together as a national movement as a result of the actions and beliefs of radical activists and plebeian intellectuals in communities of all sizes all across England, Scotland, and Wales. Throughout its twenty year existence Chartism remained, in many ways, a decentralized, loosely organized movement, one that relied heavily on the energy and commitment of the 'sturdy democrats' in Ashton and hundreds of local associations and organizations.[15] 'For the most part,' Paul Pickering has argued, 'Chartism was a creed that flourished among kin, friends, neighbours, workmates and members of the local district Chartist associations.'[16] Independent and proud of its own traditions and history, the Chartist locality exerted a powerful and lasting influence on the process of defining and redefining the movement and its democratic programme and forms of action.

With a few exceptions, historians have only occasionally given serious consideration to the democratic ideas of the movement or to the nature and practice of Chartist democracy in the localities. 'The Chartist call for the reform of the representative and electoral system,' Miles Taylor has noted, 'comes a long way down the list of historians' interests in the movement.'[17] At the other end of the list is a rather different set of issues. For over a century and a half, the perspective of the young Frederick Engels has shaped how historians have conceptualized and understood the movement; he saw Chartism primarily as 'a class movement', one that embodied 'all the struggles of the proletariat against the bourgeoisie'.[18] From Mark Hovell onward, this portrayal of Chartism, and the issues that it has raised, have exerted a powerful (and long-lived) influence over Chartist historiography. To a considerable degree, despite all the attention to Stedman Jones' approach to language and his emphasis on the primacy of politics, even the debate over 'Rethinking Chartism' has turned on the issues of class and class consciousness.[19]

Looking back over the previous 'decade of disagreement', Taylor lamented in the mid-1990s the effects of this controversy; it was, in his opinion, this on-

going debate that was responsible for 'the current impasse in chartist historiography'. In an attempt to define a new agenda for the field, Taylor suggested
that historians consider four areas of future research; these are changes in the
relationship between Chartism and the state, the geography of the movement,
Chartist ideology and democratic practices, and the decline of the movement.[20]
In recent surveys of the literature, Andrew Messner and the editors of *Papers
for the People* have also emphasized the need to move beyond this interpretative
cul-de-sac and have considered some new areas of research for Chartist studies. Together, they have identified half a dozen new directions—the role of the
newspaper press in the movement, orality and print culture in Chartist politics,
the Land plan, the later career of Feargus O'Connor, the changing nature of the
post-1848 movement, and the overseas impact of Chartism in Australia (and
North America).[21]

This micro-history of the 'sturdy democrats' of the Ashton and Stalybridge
area also seeks to move beyond the 'Rethinking Chartism' debate. In doing so,
it pursues a number of these new directions but also considers a different way
of looking at the movement. It takes seriously the Chartists' commitment to
democracy and tries to explore, above all, the ways in which democratic ideas
and practices shaped and defined Chartist political identity. This was something
that neither Stedman Jones nor his critics examined in a systematic way; more
recently, John Garrard and other democratization scholars have continued to
downplay the significance of Chartist democracy and have also minimized the
contribution of the Chartist challenge to the advance of democratic politics.
'What made Parliament increasingly sympathetic,' Garrard has argued about the
situation after 1852, 'owed nothing to outside pressure. Rather it was increasing
perceptions that many working men were rendering themselves acceptable by
their willingness to pass through an agenda-fixing gateway of political fitness:
by abandoning Chartism; rioting rather rarely; and by embracing rationality,
self-improvement, self-help and thrift through participation in saving banks,
retail co-ops and friendly societies.'[22]

In their accounts of the coming of democracy, Garrard and like-minded
scholars have chosen to emphasize this tendency toward compromise and accommodation and to celebrate the enlightened self-interest of Liberal and Conservative elites; they have also downplayed the role of contention and conflict in
creating a more open and democratic system as well as the depth and extent of
the opposition to democracy in the nineteenth century. Well aware of the wealth
and influence 'arrayed against us', Chartist true believers viewed, of course, the
attitude of the ruling classes toward reform in a much less favourable light. They
emphasized the central importance of unanimity and determination within the
movement and urged all to 'be up and doing'; otherwise, defeat was certain.

In militant localities, like Ashton, leaders and activists certainly took, at best, a very sceptical view of the motives and principles of 'the base, bloody, and brutal Whigs' and the 'villainous Tories'.[23]

For all their optimism about the power of 'a united people' to overcome these problems, the Chartists had few illusions about the challenges that they faced. With the notable exceptions of classical Athens and Rome and the 'ancient democratic institutions' of the mythical Anglo-Saxon past, there were in the 1830s few models, real or imagined, of working democracies for the Chartists to draw on for inspiration or ideas.[24] The American and French Revolutions, two more recent (and very famous) attempts to establish democratic self-rule, only re-enforced and intensified contemporary fears and suspicions about democracy; they summoned up in 'the minds of millions' images of anarchy, violence, and mob rule. 'The impression,' recalled Joseph Barker, 'that was made on my own mind in early life, by the tales which I heard respecting the French Revolution, was, that hell with all its horrors had been let loose, to revel in blood, and to torture mankind, and blast and blight the creation of God. My impression for years was, that the Democrats of France had proved themselves the cruellest and most unprincipled of mankind.'[25] For Baron Abinger, lord chief baron of the exchequer, the creation of a democratic political system would lead inevitably to 'the destruction of the monarchy and aristocracy' and to an end of 'the security of property'.[26] Even John Stuart Mill viewed democracy with a deep and profound sense of unease; however, his objection to democracy took a somewhat different form. 'The real danger in democracy,' he mused in 1840, 'the real evil to be struggled against ... is not anarchy or love of change, but Chinese stagnation & immobility.'[27]

The Chartists also ran into a problem that was and is common to all political movements and parties, both then and now—the changing and conditional nature of identity itself. One way of understanding this problem is to consider the most basic question that one can ask, 'Who am I?' Depending on personal outlook and history and the social and political context, the same individual might answer this question in a variety of ways. Under different circumstances, a woman in late twentieth-century England might see herself, to borrow an example from E.P. Thompson, as a Labour party activist, an 'occasional' Anglican communicant, a textile worker, or a wife and mother.[28] The ebb and flux of these kinds of collective identities over time underscore their instability and malleability and the extent to which identities, like class and gender, overlap and shape the making of one another. The shifting, volatile nature of identity also points to the role of imagination and empathy, as well as material reality, in the creation of identity. To quote but one example, class was and is, as Margot Finn has argued, an 'imagined' construction, 'not in the sense that [it] lacked any material basis, but in that it required an heroic act of imagination for workers to regard their own existence primarily from [its] standpoint'.[29]

II

This study approaches the making of identities in Ashton and its environs from three different but interrelated perspectives. The first of these is from the factory floor. In the 1790s, the decision to move Samuel Crompton's spinning mule from the cottage into the factory and to attach his invention to the steam engine led to the creation of the new trade of mule spinning. In Chapter One, I examine the spinners' attempts to define themselves as members of a craft of skilled male workers. In their work place struggles to defend this sense of identity, they fought to exclude women from the 'mysteries' of their craft and to control the introduction of the self-acting mule and other new technologies. Nowhere in the cotton district was technological change of greater concern than in the Ashton and Stalybridge area. 'The system of employing women and lads to the essential exclusion of men,' Lieutentant-General Thomas Arbuthnot noted about the impact of the new technologies, 'prevails most at Stockport, and in a great degree at Ashton-under-Lyne [and] Stalybridge.'[30] The introduction and spread of these new technologies threatened not only their jobs and status as skilled workers but also their sense of manhood and respectability. 'Fifteen years ago,' recalled a Hyde man, 'spinners used to earn more, but with double deckers and self actors they have nearly done away with spinners. I want to get my living by the sweat of my brow; I have no inclination to go into a bastile, you may depend upon that.'[31]

On a number of occasions, like the 1818 strike wave, the spinners tried, however, to transcend craft boundaries and to present themselves as 'the voice of the people', the bearer of a wide-ranging critique of the new industrial order. Many spinners also embraced radical reform and came out in favour of 'pulling up the corrupt tree, root, and branch, that all might live comfortably'.[32] In the late 1830s, mule spinners brought with them into Chartism some of their democratic forms of organization as well as some of their concerns about 'overgrown capitalists' and the gender division of labour.[33] In the cotton district, the Chartist leadership included quite a few mule spinners (and ex-spinners), such as Timothy Higgins, William Aitken, and James Duke, all of Ashton; Charles Davies, James Mitchell, and John Wright, of Stockport; William Butterworth, of Manchester; and Daniel Ball, of Bolton.[34]

Over the course of Chapters Two through Five, I take up the second of these perspectives and explore the making (and unmaking) of a new kind of political entity—the democratic mass movement. In the late 1830s, against the background of overlapping crises in the political world and the economy, radical leaders and activists all across the country joined together to bring scattered enclaves of democrats into a national 'bond of union'.[35] By relating the cause of democratic reform to the 'bread-and-cheese' questions of everyday life, they were able to draw in ordinary men and women who knew 'nothing of Political principles' and to make Chartism a mass movement.[36] To distinguish themselves from the other political parties and groups of the day, they drew on myths about the past and historical figures and episodes to create their own version of English history and to position Chartism within a centuries-old struggle by 'the people' for liberty and equality. National and local leaders also committed themselves to an ambitious programme of democratic reform, one that ultimately came to emphasize universal male suffrage, and identified the cause of democracy with the working classes and the mass politics of the platform.[37] At the heart of this new political identity was a set of principles and practices that emphasized participation and the face-to-face politics of direct democracy. 'To understand Chartism,' as Clive Behagg has pointed out, 'we must enter a world where the represented surrendered none of their authority to the representative.'[38] Of equal importance to Chartist democracy was the myth of 'the people'; this set of stories emphasized the oneness of leaders and followers and affirmed the optimistic belief that 'the voice of the people cannot be withstood'.[39]

Through their own actions and their use of the spoken and printed word, the leaders and activists of the movement thus drew on nationality, gender, class, and other collective identities to create a new political identity. In the end, though, there was no single 'voice of the people'. Within the movement, divisions had always existed along the lines of ethnicity, gender, and craft. Chartism was also made up of individuals who brought to the movement different goals and ideologies and varying levels of literacy and political knowledge and commitment. From the mid-1840s on, the experience of defeat, together with the passing of the crises of the previous decade, heightened these divisions and forced national and local leaders of the movement to re-evaluate and eventually to abandon many of the core beliefs and defining features of Chartist political identity. Over time Chartism itself faded way; however, the beliefs and methods of the movement lived on in a multitude of small communities of democrats all across England, Scotland, and Wales. In former militant Chartist towns, like Ashton, the integration of the plebeian intellectuals and activists of the movement into the world of Liberal and Conservative party politics transformed and radicalized, moreover, the nature and practice of local and parliamentary politics. Chartism also acted as a source of inspiration (and tactics) for later mass movements. 'Later demands for an expanded franchise, female suffrage, disestablishment of the Anglican Church, and home rule in Ireland,' Charles Tilly has noted, 'all followed some of the patterns set in place by Chartism.'[40]

The third and final way of viewing the making of identity is from the perspective of the plebeian intellectual. In Chapter Four and in the Conclusion, I try to look at Chartism and its democratic beliefs and practices through the eyes of this new type of individual. For over thirty years, the most well-known local example of the plebeian intellectual was William Aitken. 'As one who sprung from the people,' the *Ashton News* noted in its obituary notice, 'he knew intimately their feelings and their wishes, and could express what the many felt with fullness and point.'[41] His energy and superior abilities as a speaker and writer made Aitken a natural leader and a crucial go-between in the bond of 'democratic friendship' that joined the locality to national organizations and leaders; however, these same qualities set apart this passionate autodidact, intellectually and culturally, from the majority of the working classes.[42]

The social and political circumstances of his life also pointed to a more complicated relationship to 'the people'. As a young man, Aitken left the world of mule spinning, with few regrets, for the more congenial (and profitable) livelihood of schoolmaster; however, he continued to think of himself as 'a working man' and to identify with the rights and wrongs of working men and women.[43] In his autobiography, despite the recent passage of the 1867 Reform Act, Aitken also continued to identify democracy as the people's cause and to remind his readers of the deep-seated opposition of 'the higher and middle classes' to democratic reform. At the same time, he distanced himself, however, from his youthful confidence in the power of 'the united voices and determination of the people' to overcome all obstacles and to bring about immediate social and political change.[44] In telling the story of his life, Aitken the autobiographer chose instead to give the myth of 'the people' a rather different twist and to emphasize the role of the radical hero or patriot as the true agent of change. 'Without men of that stamp,' he concluded, 'no great measure for the improvement of mankind was ever yet carried to a successful issue.'[45]

Chapter I

The Art and Craft of Mule Spinning:
Masculinity, Skill and the Gender Division of Labour,
1790-1860

Several weeks after the collapse of the Manchester spinners' strike near the end of the summer of 1818, a 'Journeyman Cotton Spinner' lamented the sad decline of this once honourable trade. Looking back to the closing decades of the eighteenth century, he penned an idyllic description of mule spinning:

> When the spinning of cotton was in its infancy, and before these terrible machines for superseding the necessity of human labour, called steam engines, came into use, there a great number of what were … called *little masters*; men who with a small capital, could procure a few machines, and employ a few hands; men and boys (say to twenty or thirty)…. the master spinner was enabled to stay at home and work, and attend to his workmen. The cotton was then always given out in its raw state, from the bale to the wives of spinners at home, where they beat and cleansed it ready for the spinners in the factory. By this they could earn eight, ten, or twelve shillings a week, and cook, and attend to their families.

To tell this story, the 'Journeyman Cotton Spinner' drew upon still vivid memories of the early days of the trade to create a myth of a bygone golden age. In this preindustrial world, master spinners and their men worked together in harmony; wives and children were able to stay at home. With the coming of the steam engine and large-scale factory production, all this passed away. The triumph of 'the overgrown capitalists', he argued, reduced the spinners to mere 'instruments' and 'bondsmen' and forced their wives and children to go to work in the factory.[1]

In his 1840 prison interview, Timothy Higgins also evoked this myth of a golden age as a way of highlighting the harsh realities of the present. Deeply concerned about the future of his trade, he blamed the self-acting mule for the decline of his 'calling' and emphasized how this new technology undermined his own sense of self-identity both as a skilled worker and breadwinner and as a man:

I was brought up a cotton spinner—it was a very agreeable calling when I first followed it, but they have got into the habit of applying self-acting machinery, and
man is of no use. I know some of the most intelligent in Society who cannot get
bread. They take a man now for his muscular appearance not for his talent. Machines have become so simple that attending to them is common place labour.[2]

His description of this technological challenge to his 'independence' and 'respectability' underlined the intimate link, in his mind and others, between skill
and masculinity and the uncertain, precarious nature of both in the 1830s and
1840s.

Among Higgins' contemporaries as well as later historians, there has been, at
times, a heated debate over the spinners' claim that mule spinning was a 'calling', or craft. On the one hand, I.J. Prothero and E.P. Thompson have pointed
to the close ties between the values, institutions, and work practices of the artisan and the mule spinner. On the other hand, mule spinners were clearly not,
in the strictest sense of contemporary usage, 'craftsmen' or 'mechanics'. After
all, they did not work in the small-scale, intimate surroundings of the all-male
workshop; nor did they rely solely upon their own tools and labour power to
produce goods. For the most part, certainly by the early 1800s, they instead
worked side by side with young women and children in steam-powered factories, where they spun yarn on a pair of mules, a highly developed and complex
piece of machine technology. Lacking a historically-based handicraft tradition
and a formal system of apprenticeship, the spinners also failed to meet, according to the definitions of Michael Hanagan and Richard Price, two of the other
crucial features of a nineteenth-century trade or craft.[3]

The question of how to define the term 'skill', something that most labour
historians and sociologists have avoided, lies at the heart of this dispute. One
who has not dodged this difficult question is Charles More. 'Manual facility',
together with specialized knowledge that requires training to acquire, consti-
tute what More calls 'genuine skill'. An alternative way of acquiring skill, the
social construction of skill, 'leads, via perhaps a strong union which upholds
high wages among certain groups of workers, to a differentiation of workers
into grades, some of which are better paid and are regarded as more skilled'.[4] In
recent years, several feminist scholars and historians have given a distinctly different twist to this notion of the social construction of skill. Far from being an
objective fact, skill is, Phillips and Taylor have stressed, too often an ideological
category that is imposed on certain types of work by virtue of the gender of the
worker who performs it. 'In all that the men are saying about skill and status,'
Cythnia Cockburn has added, 'they are saying something, too, about sex and
gender ... [and] their self-definition as *men*.'[5]

In many ways, this kind of hard and fast distinction between objective and subjective ways of defining skill is, of course, misleading. In the first half of the nineteenth century, skill was, certainly in the case of mule spinning, at once genuine and socially constructed. During the early years of their trade, especially the 1780s and 1790s, the journeymen spinners successfully established themselves as independent producers and members of a respectable trade; above all, the spinners possessed the most important attribute of the artisan—skill. Their status as craftsmen was a product of the nature of work in the spinning rooms, where their skill, knowledge, and strength formed the basis of the labour process.[6] While their work on the hand mule and later the self-acting mule continued to require genuine skills, the spinners quite self consciously chose to exclude women from their trade and to portray themselves as members of a thoroughly respectable, thoroughly male craft. From their perspective, the possession of skill, 'their only property', was central to setting up and maintaining a household and family and their sense of 'manly' independence.[7] In the cotton industry, these kinds of assumptions about masculinity influenced and contributed to the emergence of a gender division of labour that defined men's work as skilled and women's work as unskilled.

In his prison interview, Higgins alluded to (and clearly agreed with) these contemporary beliefs about the link between masculinity and skill; however, his interview also underscored how his sense of identity as a skilled craftsman intertwined with other concerns and sources of identity. 'A man of considerable intelligence, not devoid of feeling', he worried about his wife and four children and the near destitute state of his family; in fact, at the time of the interview, they were 'about to be thrown upon the Parish'. An outspoken freethinker, physical-force Chartist, and Irishman, this devoted family man was also a classic example of the radical autodidact, a self-educated working man who burned with a fierce passion for books and knowledge. His love of his family, and his intellectual and political convictions, inevitably shaped his sense of his 'calling' and his concerns about the future of his trade; this intertwining of identities meant that Higgins and his fellow spinners were able on occasion to transcend craft boundaries and to integrate their work-place struggles into a broader critique of the social and political oppression of 'the people'.[8]

I

On a very basic level, masculinity and femininity were and are deeply rooted in sexual and biological difference. These identities do have a real and immediate connection to the physical and material world, in the differing body shapes, genitalia, and secondary sexual characteristics of adult men and women. In other words, the starting points for how societies define masculinity and femininity are often these physical signs of difference; they serve as the most common, widely accepted way of differentiating between men and women. By the early 1800s a sort of paradigm shift had occurred in the ways in which people understood these kinds of sexual differences. 'The dominant, though by no means universal, view since the eighteenth century,' Thomas Laqueur has argued, 'has been that there are two stable, incommensurable, opposite sexes and that the political, economic, and cultural lives of men and women, their gender roles, are somehow based on these "facts". Biology—the stable, ahistorical, sexed body—is understood to be the epistemic foundation for prescriptive claims about the social order.'[9] But, as Laqueur is careful to point out, biology is not destiny. In and of themselves, these biological and sexual differences carry no meaning; it is society itself that creates or constructs what masculinity and femininity 'mean'.

Of course, these meanings vary and can and do change over time. Dynamic and changeable, masculinity and femininity were also, as Michael Kimmel has stressed, 'relational constructs; the definition of either depends on the definition of the other'. In a similar fashion, Sonya Rose has pointed to 'the way femininity was constituted and connected to masculinity'.[10] Of these two identities, masculinity was especially unstable and conditional. 'Masculinity,' Kimmel has observed, 'was something that had to be constantly demonstrated, the attainment of which was forever in question.'[11] This crucial insight certainly applied to the mule spinners, who had few doubts about how at least some of their contemporaries regarded them and their aspirations as craftsmen. Throughout the industrial North, many coal miners and metal workers viewed 'the men of the loom and the mule' as somehow unmanly, 'as a set of spiritless milksops—as soft and pliable as the woolly fibre which they twist'.[12] The red hot infidel and Ten Hours advocate Charles Aberdeen shared this less than flattering estimation of the manliness of the mule spinners. 'The strength and vigour of a farmer's man in the country,' he claimed, 'is equal to the strength of three of these men.'[13] Those who recruited for the military in fact preferred men from the agricultural counties and regarded male factory workers as 'less robust' in terms of their health and physical strength and stamina. 'They are generally,' noted one recruiting sergeant, 'very thin, and very delicate-looking; many are rejected for their delicate appearance by the surgeons.'[14] Quite a few mill owners, as well as political economists, likewise challenged the claim that spinning on the hand mule required physical strength and skill; rather it was, in their opinion, fit work only for women or young boys.[15] Well aware of their insecure position, the mule spinners struggled to protect their craft and sense of manhood in the face of the threats of unemployment, technological change, and displacement by women and adolescents. In doing so, they tried to put forward the image of themselves as 'freeborn Englishmen', skilled and independent, and to distinguish themselves from the ultimate Other: women.

In the first half of the nineteenth century, the acquisition of skill was a crucial step toward adulthood and independence and in becoming a man in the fullest sense of the word. For a young boy, 'the choice of a trade,' noted W.E. Adams, 'was a serious question', one that profoundly shaped his future earning power, status, security, and marriage prospects.[16] Apprenticeship in a skilled trade, to the hatmaker James Burns, represented 'the grand turning point in my existence'. It was, he added, 'the half way house between the desert of my youth, and the sunny lands of my manhood'.[17] In the 1820s and 1830s the great transition for the young piecer typically came during his late teens or early twenties. With a little luck he left behind forever his days of piecing 'for children's wages' and graduated to what one former spinner called 'men's work' as the 'master' of his own pair of wheels.[18] After working for around eight years as a 'learner' and then as a scavenger and little and big piecer in various spinning rooms, the young William Aitken decided, at age nineteen, to leave his *master* and to strike out on his own. 'I could make,' he recalled, 'as good a cop and do as much work as the most of spinners that ever doffed a jacket. I was receiving the very *handsome* sum weekly of eight shillings and sixpence a week, spinning the most of my time, whilst *my master* was doing something else, so I resolved to *"give over"* and look out for a pair of wheels for myself.'[19]

Certainly, at this point, the late 1820s and early 1830s, Aitken and his fellow spinners took the view that a craft, like their own, quite naturally consisted of adult males. They made this assumption, even though there were a number of young boys and women who worked as spinners on smaller mules.[20] One reason why they made this assumption was the widely-held view that skill was a form of property. During the 1818 strike wave the handloom weavers had quoted John Locke in a classic statement of this line of argument. Mr Locke, they pointed out in one of their addresses, 'said that "every man that possesses his natural powers, has a property in himself, viz. *in the work of his hands and labour of his body"*'.[21] John Doherty likewise emphasized in 1829 that the object of forming a national association of the mule spinners of England, Scotland, and Ireland was 'simply to prevent any farther depreciation of the value of their only property, labour'.[22] An unspoken assumption that underlay Doherty's comment was that skill, like other forms of property, could be owned or possessed only by an adult male. After all, as Doherty and the other delegates knew, women, especially married women, had at best very limited rights in the late 1820s to enter into contracts or to own property or even their own earnings.[23]

Whether a journeyman spinner or hatter, the skilled artisan believed that his property in skill gave him the right to respectable status for himself and his family and a fair day's wage. 'To be respectable, in his judgment,' claimed Doherty, 'it was not neccessary that they should wear black coats or white handkerchiefs; for there were many of those who were so clad, that were in no way entitled to the appellation; but honest industry, however humble, was the best title to that distinction that could be found.'[24] Their skill and 'honest industry' entitled the spinner and other craftsmen, Doherty believed, to a fair day's wage, one that enabled them 'to get plenty of good wholesome food, decent clothing, comfortable lodgings, and education for their children'.[25] One other aspect of respectability that was crucial to an artisan's sense of manhood and self-dignity was the ability to support himself and family without recourse to charity or to the workhouse. 'I want to get my living by the sweat of my brow;' declared a Hyde spinner, 'I have no inclination to go into a bastile, you may depend on that.'[26]

Property in skill also bestowed on its possessor 'independence', an attribute or quality that was central to nineteenth-century notions of manhood. For mule spinners and other craftsmen, independence stood in stark contrast to the 'docility' of women and meant, among other things, a 'manly' lack of subservience that was the birthright of every 'freeborn Englishman'.[27] 'We can spin with greater pleasure than you,' a journeyman spinner in the United States noted, 'for we are quite our own masters. We do not go to our employer with our hats in our hand,… but talk to him the same as to any other man.'[28] Responding to a letter to the editor from an unemployed fine spinner, Doherty brought out another of the attributes of independence—the ability to set up and maintain a household. In his response Doherty was careful to stress how years of labour to acquire a skill gave the the spinners a 'generous glow of conscious pride and independence' and the means of fulfilling their natural and God-given responsibilities as husbands and fathers; however, the loss of their pair of wheels, through the practice of replacing adult males with young women or boys, threatened all of this:

> After labouring for years to acquire a knowledge of a business by which they hoped to maintain their families, they find themselves deprived of all means of subsistence. Instead of feeling that generous glow of conscious pride and independence, which animated them when they could provide the necessaries of life for their families by their own exertions, they are forced to depend on that family for what is barely sufficient to keep body and soul together. Instead of being what both God and nature intended them for, the chief providers for, and protectors of their own tender offspring, they are forced to see that offspring deserted, as it were, by their mothers, who are forced by the avarice of some greedy employer, to beg for permission to toil where they have been driven from. Thus the miserable father has to take the place of the mother.[29]

Doherty, in this editorial, also highlighted the centrality of work to a man's sense of self identity and pointed as well to some of the ways in which unemployment threatened to invert the 'natural' order of gender roles and to undermine the spinner's sense of manhood.

For Doherty and most of his male contemporaries, there were, of course, no such links between femininity and property or skill; women were, by their very nature, unskilled. Lacking the strength and natural facility for working with 'complicated and cumbrous' spinning mules and other machines, women were seen as incapable of keeping up the pace and turning off high-quality yarn. Female spinners, Doherty claimed, simply did not have the 'physical strength' and stamina that was necessary for the arduous task of spinning, especially on large or double-decked mules.[30] Consequently, as a Glasgow spinner argued, 'Women do not throw off the quantity, neither is the quality for their work so good'.[31] In the 1840s a like-minded tendency to dismiss women's work as unskilled came through clearly in discussions about the impact of the technical improvements of James Bullough and William Kenworthy on the powerloom. With the creation of this fully automated powerloom in the early 1840s, neither skill nor strength, two technical writers argued, were necessary; the only requirements of the weaver were attentiveness and a certain limited dexterity, all of which made women the ideal weavers. 'The business of the weaver in attendance on the powerloom,' noted George White, 'is not labourious; nor do the duties require much time in aggregate for their performance; nor skill, but rather a nimbleness of hand; hence young women are almost universally the weavers by power in the factories.'[32] Decrying this common habit of mind in 'manufacturing towns', the Owenite feminist Frances Morrison bitterly attacked such attitudes toward women's work. 'The contemptible expression is,' she observed, 'it is made by woman, and therefore cheap? Why, I ask, should woman's labour be thus undervalued?'[33]

One of the most striking features of work in the cotton industry was the way in which these views about gender and skill shaped the division of labour; these assumptions were, as Sonya Rose has pointed out, common among both masters and men.[34] Although adult males represented a minority of the workforce in cotton, they filled all of the high paying occupations, both in the weaving sheds and the spinning mills (see Tables 2 and 4). The bulk of the women and children who found work in the spinning branch of the industry were concentrated in low paying, casualized jobs. With the exception of the carding overlookers and the strippers and grinders, occupations which were usually held by adult males, women and children made up most of the workforce in the cleaning and carding departments, where 'not more than one male in four persons is required'.[35] While women spinners were common on throstle frames, few women in the 1830s had their own pair of wheels, despite the widespread practice of hiring female piecers and the system of employing young boys and women on small mules.[36] Throughout this period, in fact, the spinning room remained a distinctly male preserve. Over the course of the crucial decade of the 1840s, the age, gender, and ethnicity of the mule spinners in Ashton-under-Lyne remained virtually the same. Although in 1851 the Ashton spinners were slightly older and included a higher percentage of married men than in 1841, they were still almost exclusively adult Englishmen (see Table 3).

Well aware that the employment of women and children was central to the organization of work in the spinning mill (and their privileged position within the labour process), the mule spinners accepted this gender-based hierarchy of work as necessary and even as 'natural'. Francis Place, master tailor, found the spinners' acceptance of this state of things an affront to his sensibilities as a member of an 'honourable' trade:

> If, then, the men refused to work in mills and factories with girls, as they ought to do, as other trades have done, in workshops, and for those masters who employ women and girls, the young women who will otherwise be degraded by factory labour will become all that can be desired as companionable wives, and the whole condition of factory workers would soon be improved, the men will obtain competent wages for their maintenance.[37]

But, almost without exception, the spinners drew the line, no doubt with Place's approval this time, at allowing women into the 'trade' of mule spinning. The practice of certain Manchester firms of employing women as operative spinners, Doherty noted, was 'a source of mortification and dislike to the whole body of spinners, from the first hour of their introduction'. The spinners feared, above all, that the influx of 'boys and women' into their craft would force down piece rates and earnings and would lead ultimately to 'the total ruin of the trade'.[38]

II

Just as the mule spinners of the early nineteenth century still had ties to the attitudes and values of the workshop, like independence, they also adopted many of the artisans' methods for protecting their skill in property.[39] Beginning during the 1780s and 1790s and lasting into the next century, a stream of hatters, shoemakers, smiths, tailors, and other journeymen left their trades for the high wages of mule spinning and brought with them into the factory many of the institutions and customs of the skilled trades.[40] Although the spinners never developed a formal apprenticeship system or a tramping network, two of the classic artisan institutions, they were able to use the subcontract system to exer-

cise some control over entry into the trade, the grand object of formal apprenticeship, and occasionally took out a tramping card from a friendly society, like
the Odd Fellows, to go on the road in search of a pair of wheels.[41] In addition
to providing a wide range of benefits, like tramping allowances, and social activities, friendly societies also protected the spinner and his family against the
hardships arising from accident, illness, and old age and served as a nucleus for
the organization of their trade, especially during the years before the repeal of
the Combination Acts.[42]

From the mid-1820s on, the spinners were able, however, to pursue more
formal and open forms of organization to protect the interests of their trade.
While they tried, on several occasions, to create a national organization and
even a general union of all trades, the spinners were careful to exclude women
and typically focused on local or 'district' societies.[43] Wary of strong national
organizations, spinners generally opposed any attempt to undermine the ability
of local societies to manage their 'own affairs'. What did Manchester have to do,
queried one delegate, 'with Bolton, or any other district'; or, for that matter, he
added, what did Bolton have to do with Manchester?[44] This approach to organizing their trade emphasized local control and autonomy and frequent elections
of officials, usually on 'a sort of universal suffrage system', as well as strict accountability and economy. With the exception of a secretary, the societies of
this period usually had no paid officials and cost its members but 'very little'.[45]
Unwilling to turn control of their societies over to a cadre of trade union professionals, the operative spinners watched their leaders closely for any signs of
dictation or suspect behavoir. These suspicions on the part of the rank and file
contributed to the already difficult lives of Doherty and the other leaders of the
spinners. 'The working man who takes upon him to advise and direct his fellow workmen,' Doherty wearily concluded, 'must be prepared to be suspected,
abused, and calumniated aboard, harassed and persecuted by his employer, and
annoyed and pestered even by the "partner of his griefs and joys".'[46]

From the very beginning, then, the spinners borrowed and adapted to their
own ends two of the distinctive institutions of the artisans' world—the friendly
society and later the trade union. They also observed St. Monday as well as many
of the drinking customs of the workshop. This was especially true during the
first generation of hand mule spinning in the 1780s and 1790s, when the spinners frequently spent the early part of the week in 'idleness and drinking' and
then worked 'desperately,' night and day, toward the end. 'They were not controlled to time,' noted a contemporary about the spinners, 'and they were very
irregular.'[47] Like 'almost very trade and profession', the mule spinners also had,
a temperance advocate noted with distaste, their 'own code of strict and well-
observed laws' on the times and occasions of drinking.[48] One such occasion,

the payment of 'footings', a practice which had existed, as one spinner put it, 'time out of mind', provided spinners with an opportunity to meet together and to discuss trade matters. 'When assembled on these occasions,' a journeyman spinner observed, 'nothing could be more natural than to talk over and discuss the various matters which more particularly affected them as workmen.'[49] For the spinners, the paying of a 'footing', however, was also simply an occasion for conviviality and fellowship. William Chadwick described a typical spinners' 'footing' at the Pack Horse, Mottram during the first half of the century:

> It was a custom among the operatives for every one who commenced spinning in the mills to pay a footing of 5s. or more, as the case might be, and the other spinners paid a shilling each to it. The whole of the money was spent at some public house, when a potatoe pie was provided out of the funds, and the remainder spent in drink.[50]

By this point, drinking customs, like 'footings' and St. Monday, were clearly on the decline among the spinners. But, as late as the 1860s, the spinners at Baxter's Park Mill in Hollinwood still stepped outside during the day for an occasional 'fuddle'. Many years later, a local man recalled about his early days as a piecer at Baxter's mill, 'Often have I seen four or five minders sitting in the steps having a bit of a fuddle together'.[51]

What ultimately enabled the spinners to establish themselves as a group of male craftsmen was the role of skill, the most important attribute of an artisan, in the labour process. In this sense, their skill was indeed genuine, not merely a social construction. During the early years in cottages and 'private rooms in dwelling houses', the skill and physical strength which mule spinning required enabled the spinners to establish themselves as independent artisans and to define mule spinning as a male craft. Throughout the entire cycle of operations, from drawing out the spindle carriage to winding on the yarn and returning the carriage, the spinner controlled and provided the moving power for all the motions of the mule. Drawing out the yarn to the precise thickness was a delicate operation and called for a deft, sure touch and a thorough understanding of the different kinds of cotton fibers; putting up the mule, however, was an even more complex and arduous task. Turning the fly wheel with his right hand, the spinner returned the wheeled mule carriage along the rails and wound the yarns on to the spindles by working the faller with his left hand.[52] During the decade after the invention of the mule, when it was still a crude piece of wooden machinery, spinning required, in addition to skill in spinning and physical strength, skill in maintaining, repairing, and, in some cases, constructing mules. The artisans who left their original trades and became mule spinners in the 1780s and 1790s brought with them a variety of different craft skills and made, as John Kennedy pointed out, a very real contribution to the evolution of the mule:

> If in the course of their working the machine, there was any little thing out of gear, each workman endeavoured to fill up the deficiency with some expedient suggested by his former trade; the smith suggested a piece of iron; the shoemaker a welt of leather etc. all of which had a good effect in improving the machine. Each put what he thought best to the experiment, and that which was good was retained.[53]

In the early years of mule spinning, the piece rate system and the spinners' dislike of 'regular hours of work' likewise highlighted their independence. Paid by the piece, typically per pound of yarn, the spinners in turn paid their assistants, usually children, out of these earnings and indulged their fondness for irregular hours and St. Monday. 'Sometimes none at all,' recalled an Ashton spinner, 'for a Day or two at the beginning of the week, and then at latter end of the week they made long days.'[54]

With the application of water and then steam power to the mule during the 1790s, mule spinning made the transition from the cottage to the mill. This led, of course, to changes in the nature of work in the spinning room. And yet, during the early years of hand mule spinning in the factory, between the 1790s and the 1830s, the spinners' physical strength, skill, and specialized knowledge still formed the basis of the labour process. At the jennygate the basic unit of organization was the adult spinner and his piecers, a system which had emerged during the 1790s in conjunction with the rise of the practice of pairing mules.[55] Because of the slippery floors and the close, humid atmosphere of the spinning rooms, where the temperature stayed in the upper 80s and 90s, the spinners and piecers always took off their shoes to get a better grip on the floor and wore a minimum of clothing. Barefoot and dressed only in light shirts and trousers, they stationed themselves on the oily patch of floor between their pair of mules. A factory inspector described how the motions of the two machines were carefully coordinated: 'One is always advancing while the other is retreating, and he [the spinner] turns from one to the other at regular intervals. The one which is advancing draws out the cotton (roving) from the back, and moves slowly towards the spinner, spinning the thread the while.'[56] Although the spinner had little to do during this first series of movements, 'the draw', except to piece broken threads, he performed himself the arduous, difficult task of putting up the mule. While pushing the fifteen hundred pound spindle carriage home along the rails, the spinner used one hand to work the faller wire and, with the other hand, turned 'a rim or wheel, which ... turns, by means of bands, the whole of the spindles, drums, and pulleys in the carriage'. Relying on his experience and knowledge of his mules, he carefully worked the wheel to maintain the necessary degree of tension on the threads and manipulated the faller to build the thread on the spindle in the form of a cylindrical shaped cop.[57] The building of a superior cop represented the pinnacle of the spinners' art, a point of pride as well as a mark of distinction; no two spinners in fact ever made a cop in precisely the same shape or in precisely the same way. 'Joshua's cops,' noted an admirer, 'were always in great demand .... His work had a voice of its own. It recommended itself.'[58] What made these tasks even more difficult by the 1830s was the intensity of work at the jennygate. In the course of a twelve hour work day, a coarse spinner put up each mule somewhere around 1800 to 2500 times and also pieced, with the aid of his assistants, several broken threads during each draw, an activity which demanded constant attention and activity.[59]

In addition to physical stamina and dexterity, mule spinners possessed a body of specialized knowledge about cotton and about their pair of wheels and drew upon this knowledge to carry out basic repairs and maintenance tasks and to fine tune and adjust the motions of their mules. Cotton varied according to the length, strength, and fineness of its fibres, or staples. Short, soft staples were typically used for spinning weft yarns, while warp yarns required cotton with long, strong fibres. Coarse and fine counts likewise used different types of cotton. An understanding of the relative merits of short and long staples, or of the different qualities of Surat cotton and Orleans cotton, enabled the spinner to make the necessary adjustments in his mules and thus to avoid faulty work. James Mawdsley, general secretary to the Spinners' Amalgamated Association, recalled that his father, a hand mule spinner, had attributed his ability to produce superior yarn to his knowledge of the different qualities of short and long staples:

> He spun under the old hand mule system, where they had a very large range of counts. They ranged from 60 twist to 160 weft, a rather large range of counts for one mule to produce; and he attributed his success ... to the fact that he thoroughly understood how to set his steel rollers and the distances apart between them in accordance with the length of the staple he was spinning.[60]

Apart from this sort of tinkering with the mule, Mawdsley's father, like the other hand spinners of his generation, devoted considerable time to basic repairs and maintenance work. Several times a week, with the aid of his piecers, the spinner cleaned and oiled his mules and periodically adjusted and repaired pulleys, straps, and rollers to reduce wear and tear and to prevent any falling off in the quality and quantity of yarn. Joshua Bradley, who spun on hand mules in the 1830s and 1840s, carried these duties to the point of obsession:

His mules were kept constantly clean, well oiled, and in good working condition; and, with these facilities, they produced the best quality of yarn possible in all respects. As his dinner was always taken to him into the mill "warmed up" … he had every facility afforded to him to spend some little time during the dinner recess, day by day, in keeping the mule in good working order. The various pulleys and ropes were all set in such a way as to work with perfect freedom …. His straps or belts, too, were constantly kept at the proper tension, in order that there would be no unnecessary friction in any part of the mule, or upon the engine that drove it.[61]

The spinners' role as subcontractors of labour under the piece work system re-enforced their position as the key figures in the labour process of the spinning mill and, in many cases, freed the spinners from direct supervision. Many spinning rooms in fact had no overlookers or supervisors. In mills where overlookers were employed, they generally received a straight time wage and consequently had no vested interest in 'driving' their spinners. By relying on the piece rate system to encourage their spinners to maximize earnings, mill owners actually used the subcontracting system as a way of avoiding the difficulties of supervising and managing the production process.[62] At the jennygate the supervision of work often ended up as the responsibility of the spinner because of his role in hiring and supervising his piecers, a role which gave the spinner a certain amount of control over the division of labour and entry into the trade. While gradually learning how to piece, the scavenger, the youngest and most inexperienced of the assistants, cleaned dust and flue off of the mules. The older piecers helped out with the piecing of broken threads during the draw and also performed a variety of other tasks which ranged from putting on rovings to oiling and cleaning the mules. In addition to these routine tasks, piecers on occasion ran the mules, while the spinner stepped out for breakfast, or a 'fuddle', or, in some instances, to read.[63] Although the spinner in some cases hired his own children or 'near relations', both boys and girls, the subcontract system never served as a means of reconstituting within the factory the family division of labour which had existed under the domestic system. 'They don't so much work,' observed an overlooker, 'under the eyes of the parents and relations, as under the eyes of those who have children of their own.'[64] But, the subcontract system nevertheless clearly bore some resemblance to the family economy of domestic manufacture, where young children and adolescents of both sexes worked under the supervision of the adult male. The piece rate system, the prevailing method of payment for mule spinning, likewise reflected the trade's origins in the cottages of late eighteenth-century Lancashire, where working by the piece was the usual practice. Under the piecework system, the spinner was not paid directly for his labour or his time, but for a product, yarn. 'So much weight of prepared cotton is delivered to him,' a factory inspector noted, 'and he has to return by a certain time in lieu of it a given weight of twist or yarn of a certain degree of fineness, and he is paid so much per pound for every pound that he so returns.'[65] Out of these earnings, the spinner in turn paid a straight wage to his two or more piecers and frequently had to pay for oil, banding, and candles as well.[66]

III

From the late 1820s onward, the introduction and spread of new technologies, like double decking and the self-acting mule, threatened to turn upside down the spinners' world and to open up the trade to an influx of adolescents and women. With a few exceptions, most notably Mary Freifeld, historians have generally assumed that the self-actor led to the de-skilling of mule spinning and reduced the spinner by the late 1840s to a mere machine minder.[67] And yet, on the factory floor, the immediate effect of this revolutionary innovation was never so dramatic or so clear; there was, moreover, a considerable time lapse between the initial introduction of the self-actor and its widespread adoption in the cotton industry. Because the self-actor in fact failed to eliminate the role of 'special knowledge' and skill in mule spinning, the struggle between labour and capital over technological change took the form of a protracted, halting process of compromise and conflict, a process that continued for decades after its initial introduction.

In the beginning, however, the likely outcome of the introduction of 'improved machinery' often looked rather different. The rapid increase in the size of spinning mules certainly represented a very real threat to the craftsmen status of the spinners.[68] The dramatic growth in the number of spindles occurred both in Manchester, where mules of a thousand spindles were in use by the late 1830s, and in the outlying towns and villages of the cotton district. In the course of this decade, Joshua Bradley of Hyde went from a pair of mules, the 'Royal Georges', of around 320 spindles each to a pair of 'extraordinary' wheels with around 600 to 720 spindles each.[69] What also contributed to this trend and made it particularly disturbing to the spinners was the introduction of the practice of paying a progressively reduced price to spinners who had 'large wheels'. This practice, the spinners feared, would encourage further 'alteration of the machinery' and would open the way for a continuous round of wage reductions.[70] One such widely adopted 'alteration' was double decking, or 'yoking the wheels together', of small mules. For the spinner, who was now in effect responsible for *two* pairs of mules, double decking dramatically increased his workload (but not his earnings) and raised the spectre of mass unemployment. 'Whilst the men are doing double labour by this alteration,' complained one spinner, 'they are absolutely netting to themselves less real wages.'[71] Double decking also frequently led to a loss of jobs. Pointing to a Manchester fine spinning mill, where eighty spinners had been employed, the Chartist James Leach charged that double decking had reduced the number of spinners by three-quarters. '60 out of 80,' he claimed, 'have been thrown upon the streets, or compelled to go "piecing" for children's wages.'[72] Double decking and the increase in mule size placed, however, a premium on physical strength and stamina and made it difficult, in the years before the widespread adoption of the 'putting up motion', to replace adult males with women. The decline in the number of female spinners during the 1830s, Doherty noted, was in fact the product of this trend toward large wheels which required 'more physical power'.[73]

Of even greater concern to the mule spinners was the creation of the self-acting mule by Richard Roberts.[74] Almost immediately mill owners and political economists hailed the invention with great enthusiasm and extolled the merits of what James Montgomery called 'one of the most beautiful specimens of mechanical combination that is to be found'. E.C. Tufnell praised Roberts' self-acting mule as 'a death blow to the Spinners' Union'. While also applauding the self-actor as a means of taming the 'refractory conduct' of the spinners, Andrew Ure quoted with approval Roberts' claim that his invention made possible 'the saving of a "spinner's" wages to each pair of mules, piecers only being required'.[75] In the early 1830s, a Glasgow mill owner reported in fact that he had already begun to introduce this new system on the self-actors at his mill.[76]

In the late 1830s and 1840s, the initial impact of the self-acting mule on skill, jobs, and the gender division of labour appeared to confirm these predictions. For the spinners, the self-actor threatened to reduce their trade to a 'slavish and degraded condition' and themselves to mere 'ciphers'.[77] But, beyond the degradation of the trade, the self-acting mule forced down prices for spinning and threatened not only to eliminate jobs but also to displace the adult male altogether. A former mill worker predicted in the early 1830s that the ultimate result of the self-actor would be 'to dispense with adult labour, and either to call for a greater proportion of juvenile labour, or to leave its amount pretty much where it is'.[78] A group of coarse spinning mills in Manchester offered an ominous confirmation of this prophecy. At these mills the introduction of the self-acting mule during the 1830s led to a substantial drop in piece rates and threw out of work over half of the spinners.[79] An ex-spinner recalled its devastating impact on the traditional division of labour in the spinning rooms at Chorlton-upon-Medlock, a small town near Manchester:

In 1837, the "self-actors" … had come into common use. One girl can mind three pairs—that used to be three men's work—getting 15s. for the work which gave three men 7£ 10s …. We had a meeting of the union, but nothing could be done, and we were told to go and mind the three pairs, as the girls did, for 15s. a week. We wouldn't do that. Some went for soldiers, some to sea, some to Stopport (Stockport) to get work where the "self-actors" weren't agait.[80]

Although in some cases, like that of the mill at Chorlton-upon-Medlock, the introduction of the self-actor took the form of a sudden and ruthless subjugation of labour, technological change in the spinning industry was often a gradual, protracted process. The self-acting mule, the very symbol of the Lancashire spinning industry in the second half of the century, was introduced in a piecemeal fashion over a forty to fifty year period, first on coarse counts and later on fine counts. In the late 1830s, when fear about the effects of the self-actor was running high, it was still very much the exception, not the rule.[81] Many mill owners shared John Kennedy's concern about the risks of 'over-ambitious changes' and also had their doubts about the high initial cost of Roberts' self-acting mule and its appetite for coal.[82] 'Before the cotton famine,' as Samuel Andrew pointed out, 'some hesitancy existed in people's minds as to whether the self-actor mule was a complete success, and it was only the more adventurous spinners who would order a complete concern of self-actors.'[83] Even at his new coarse spinning mill in Mossley, John Mayall continued to install both kinds of mules in the mid-1850s, sometimes in the same spinning rooms, and in fact relied on hand mules for around 80 per cent of his spindles.[84] By the 1870s the hand mule had become, however, the exception in the coarse spinning centre of Oldham and in the Ashton area. But, as late as the 1870s, it remained the preferred technology for spinning 80s and above and held its own in the fine spinning town of Bolton well into the 1880s.[85]

The spread of the self-actor and double decking clearly placed the spinners in a vulnerable position; however, the introduction of new spinning technology nonetheless involved a certain amount of give-and-take between masters and men. A classic example of this occurred in the early 1840s in Oldham, where double decking and other 'improvements' threatened to destroy the traditional system of one spinner per pair of mules. Deeply disturbed about the implications of this new practice, a group of Oldham spinners formed a committee to investigate the problem and then met with the master spinners and argued, 'one man spinner to each pair of mules could do more work, and better work than could be done by there being one spinner to several pairs of mules.' To convince the mill owners, many of whom had their doubts, the spinners' committee set up an experiment and carefully instructed the spinners who took part, 'on your doing good work, and plenty of it, depends the success of the Spinners' Union, and the one spinner system'. The experiment succeeded, and the traditional organization of work at the jennygate survived.[86] As this example suggests, the adult male and the 'one spinner system' survived in part because the system offered certain benefits to the master spinners. It allowed them to continue to evade the problems of recruiting and supervising piecers and also served to ensure that only hard workers graduated from piecer to spinner. 'Employers have had,' noted James Mawdsley, 'a splendid selection and they select the giants—I do not mean the giants in stature, but the giants in working capacity.'[87] But, the example of the Oldham spinners also demonstrates that the 'one spinner system' survived because of the spinners' determined support. With the revival of spinner trade unionism in the mid-1840s, a revival which culminated in the formation of the powerful Amalgamated Association in 1870, the spinners were increasingly able not only to bargain from a position of strength but also to use their trade union strength to uphold the traditional subcontract system.[88]

Partly through these kinds of negotiations, and partly through the influence of widely-held beliefs about the link between masculinity and skill, the self-actor minders were able to assert successfully their claim that they were members of a craft. What strengthened this claim was the continued role of skill in the labour process.[89] Roberts' invention, like many other new forms of technology, undermined and destroyed some skills; but, at the same time, it transformed old skills into different forms and created new skills as well. By making the whole cycle of operations on the mule automatic, the self-actor eliminated the need for physical strength to put up the heavy mule carriage; in theory the quadrant nut likewise made the complex process of winding on completely automatic. For some fifty years after the first introduction of Roberts' invention, persistent technical flaws continued, however, to plague the quadrant nut and prevented in particular the proper working of the strapping and nosing motions, both of which were crucial to cop formation. While downplaying such problems, Marsden acknowledged their continued existence in the 1880s:

> The governing arrangement of the quadrant nut was neither sufficiently sensitive nor reliable for the performance of good work.... The backing off motion was also defective in its arrangement, and this often caused "snarls"* or kinks to be produced in the yarn, a fault which it was highly desirable should be avoided if possible, as it seriously depreciated the value of the yarn.... A defect in the winding motion, arising from the peculiar form of the spindle, was a long standing trouble to spinners, and an almost unsurmountable difficulty to inventors.[90]

For many years, because of these technical problems, the spinner turned by hand the quadrant nut during the crucial early stages of forming the bottom of the cop and later manually delayed the rise of the winding faller during the tricky final stages of cop formation. This was certainly still the case in the 1860s, when the master spinner Kurt Neste discovered that few spinners actually used the strapping motion:

> The screw for moving the quadrant nut is turned by hand; various apparatus have been employed to make this regulation self-acting, but according to inquiries made of a great number of workmen in different mills, the workman always has still to correct this regulation; so that until now nothing else has been achieved by the self regulating motions, but that the workman has to turn the screw a few times less.[91]

Just as the spinners were able to transfer their skill in cop building from the hand to the self-acting mule, they likewise retained their monopoly of 'special knowledge' about yarn production and about the operation of their mules. 'A long apprenticeship has to be served,' noted a Hyde man, 'to the working of the self-acting mule before a person can be considered to be master of that wonderful and complicated machine.' Even the overlooker Joshua Bradley, a man with years of experience on the hand mule, never fully understood the new spinning technology. When he had to make the necessary adjustments to switch from one count to another, or to spin weft yarn on twist mules, he relied on the expertise and knowledge of his self-acting spinners.[92] The spinners' habit of tinkering with the motions of the mules added to their unique understanding of the mechanical idiosyncrasies of their pair. Always anxious to prevent any drop in the quality or quantity of the yarn, the spinners constantly adjusted the motions of their self-actors often 'with little respect for the intentions of the maker or the principles of engineering' and had in particular a tendency to fine tune the nosing and strapping motions during the building of the cop. 'Before very long, no two mules ever were alike', noted Catling about this predilection to tinker.[93] The price lists of the late nineteenth century in fact recognized this unique relationship between the spinner and his mules. 'When the machinery is being repaired,' a contemporary study of these lists noted, 'the presence of the minder is necessary, owing to his special knowledge of the mule.'[94] Apart from helping out with major repairs, the spinners were also solely responsible for a variety of maintenance tasks and routine repairs. Spinners constantly monitored the performance of their mules' complex systems of levers, springs, and bands and replaced from time to time worn drafting rollers and straps. To keep their mules in top working condition, they regularly oiled and cleaned the mules and applied varnish to the rollers and unguents to the crucial rim band; these varnishes and dressings were often prepared from 'secret recipes' which had been handed down from father to son.[95]

IV

For all the efforts of the spinners and later the minders to define and to protect their status as members of an honourable trade, their sense of identity as craftsmen was shot through with ambiguities; they often regarded mule spinning simply as a way of making a living, not as a 'calling'. This perspective on work was a common one among other trades as well. 'For my own part,' declared a Manchester machine maker, 'I perceived very early that labour was not a thing to be liked for its own sake, but merely for the rewards or comforts that it brings.'[96] Known and respected in his mill as 'an excellent hand at his wheel', Joshua Bradley clearly took pride in his work, but after a few years, he wearied of spinning and seriously considered a shift over to dressing, 'knowing, as he did, that by this means he would be able to realise much higher wages'.[97] To a certain extent, Aitken shared this perspective on the trade; he left the spinning room at an early age and never looked back.[98] There was, in fact, an inherent lack of stability to the craft identity that Aitken and others shared; for most men, mule spinning was not, certainly in the 1830s or 1840s, a life long 'calling'. In some cases, it even marked the first step in upward social mobility. In the first half of the nineteenth century, Thomas Mason, Abel Buckley, and John Mayall took advantage of the 'space and turning' system to get their start in the cotton trade, and all three of these former journeymen spinners went on to become leading members of the Ashton 'steamocracy'.[99] Of course, this was not what happened for most spinners. Forced to leave mule spinning, because of either the blacklist or old age, a number of ex-spinners, like James Duke, who ran the Bush Inn in the late 1830s, became publicans or tradesmen. An investigation of the occupations of former mule spinners living in the Ashton area revealed that in the early 1840s this group included fourteen master spinners and manufacturers, sixty-one shopkeepers, forty-two publicans and beer sellers, and eleven grocers and tea dealers.[100]

Unstable and conditional, the craft identity of the spinners did not exist in some sort of social and political vacuum; it was profoundly shaped by struggles in the workplace and political arena and by its imbrication with other identities. What shaped Timothy Higgins' sense of belonging to an honourable trade were the ways in which craft influenced and was influenced by his political identity as a Chartist and his ethnic identity as an Irishman.[101] Over the course of the nineteenth century, the spinners had developed their own distinctive approach to social relations in the mill and trade unionism that emphasized the image, if not the reality, of 'manly' independence and a decentralized and participatory form of organization. In many ways, Chartism embraced very similar forms of democratic organization, ones that stressed the link between masculinity and citizenship and local control and direct participation.[102] Throughout the cotton district, there was also a very real association, in the minds of many people, between Englishness and the craft of mule spinning. With the exception of a very few spinners, like Higgins and Doherty, the Irish generally worked in the 1830s in 'the roughest departments of the mill, the blowing hole, card room, etc'.[103] Sneered at as feckless and improvident, the Irish were regarded by many of the English as strikebreakers and as unskilled labourers who 'will work for less wages than themselves'.[104] It is not clear how exactly all this affected Higgins and his sense of self-identity. A freethinker, with 'his own ideas upon the subject of religion', he had no apparent ties to the Catholic church, a crucial source of Irish identity, and only rarely identified himself as an Irishman.[105]

Over the course of his public career as a radical and trade unionist, Doherty, like Higgins no doubt, struggled to work through and perhaps to reconcile somehow these tensions between ethnicity and craft. Often referred to in the press as 'O'Daugherty' and 'Dogherty' he was once described by an opponent as an 'impudent and conceited ape'. Even among the mule spinners, his election to office in their society supposedly 'caused a great scandal'.[106] And yet, perhaps because of his frequent encounters with ethnic bigotry, Doherty repeatedly urged his fellow spinners to move beyond differences 'as to nations' and to recognize their common interests as a craft. 'They were,' he argued at the 1829 Isle of Man meeting, 'but one trade, and he could not see why they should attempt to create, or perpetuate distinctions as to nations, while they were all bound by the same laws, injured by the same means, or benefitted by the same cause. Their interests were all bound together.'[107]

This tendency to look upon Irishness, like femininity, as the polar opposite of the industrious and skilled 'free born Englishman' points to just how easily a strong sense of craft identity could lead, under certain circumstances, to what Pollitt called 'the snobbery of the craftsmen' and a heightening of divisions among members of the manual working classes.[108] 'Social distinctions', Alexander Somerville shrewdly observed in the 1840s, existed not only between the bishop and curate, or the lord and tenant farmer. 'Look for them,' he added, 'also between the artizan who has long tails to his coat, and the humble labourer who has short tails to his coat; between the engine-maker, who is a free member of his trade, and the blacksmith, who has not been apprenticed to engine-making.'[109] Without a doubt, the spinners were guilty, on occasion, of adopting this kind of attitude. 'Very particular as to the class of company he kept', Joshua Bradley had, as his biographer was quick to point out, a habit of paying little attention to his neighbours and acquaintances 'in humbler stations in life' or to the poor. 'He sometimes carried', it was further noted, 'this rather objectionable spirit to an unwarranted extent.'[110]

The cotton industry's reliance on the labour of women and children, together with the impact of new technologies on other skilled trades, meant, however, that the struggle of the spinners to defend their position as skilled craftsmen went beyond the narrow confines of their trade to touch the lives of other working men and women and even to shape a broader sense of class identity. In the mill towns of the cotton district, most working men and women, even those who went on to other occupations, had worked at some point in their lives either in the spinning mill or in the weaving shed. In the village of Denton, near Ashton, many parents relied on their children's wages from the mill to supplement earnings from hatmaking.[111] In a similar fashion, the teenage sons of the shoemaker John Davies and the tailor Patrick McGuire, two of Aitken's neighbours, went into the mill, not the workshop, and took up the art of piecing.[112] Even 'aristocratic' smiths and machine makers frequently worked in the spinning rooms during their early years; before his apprenticeship to the wheelwright Samuel Buckley, young Joseph Radcliffe spent time at Mellor's mill as a piecer.[113]

The shared experience of factory work promoted a sense of class unity among the journeymen artisans and factory workers of the town and also introduced them to a force that cast a shadow across many of the trades of the cotton district—technological change. During the 1830s and 1840s new technology hastened the demise of the handloom weavers and threatened to revolutionize not only the already highly mechanized spinning industry but also the 'aristocratical' engineers and smiths and even building trades, like the sawyers. After describing the loss of spinning jobs through the introduction of the self-acting mule, a Manchester man went on to emphasize how improvements in machinery affected a wide range of skilled trades:

> Again, there are hundreds of our fellow-countrymen in other trades that are suffering from the same causes. Mechanics for instance. In machine shops we find self-acting slide-laithes, self-acting slotting machines, self-acting boring machines, and self-acting plaining machines that perform as much work in one day as fifty men. We have machines for sawing timber by power. Engraving is done in part by machinery; and in the "Mechanics' Magazine", I read of an Iron Mason.[114]

On the subject of the origin and spread of the 1842 strike, James Leach chose to emphasize how technological change and its impact on piece rates and employment led to 'a oneness of action' among workers in different trades. 'Could it be believed for a moment,' he asked at his trial, 'that a few people coming from the mills where they were half-sweated to death, could stop the mills, mechanics' shops, iron founders, and cause every description of labour to stand still in that line of industry, as you were told by one of the learned counsel who addressed you? No, the real truth is this; discontent and penury created a oneness of action among the working classes.'[115] Drawing on these kinds of common experiences and concerns, as well as the shared values of the artisan, the spinners' struggles were able, on certain occasions, to transcend a narrow craft outlook and had the potential to create, if only for a passing moment, a vision of 'the Working Class of Society' in opposition to 'their avaricious Employers'.[116]

Chapter II

What Is a Chartist?
Defining a Democratic Political Identity, 1838-1842

Mr. Doubtful. Good morning to you, friend; I understand you profess Chartist principles, and as I confess, in common with many others, my ignorance of what Chartism means, I should be obliged by your informing me what is the meaning of the term 'Chartist'.

Radical. It is one who is an advocate for the People's Charter.

Mr. D. The People's Charter, pray what is that?

Rad. It is the outline of an act of parliament, drawn up by a committee of the London Working Men's Association, and six members of parliament; and embraces the six cardinal points of Radical Reform.

Mr. D. What are these points?

Rad. They are as follows: 1. *Universal Suffrage* - 2. *Annual Parliaments*- 3. *Vote by Ballot*- 4. *Equal Representation*- 5. *Payment of Members*- 6. *No Property Qualifications.*[1]

Produced by the Finsbury Tract Society in 1839 for sale to a national audience, this fictional conversation between 'Mr. Doubtful' and a 'Radical' turned on the latter's attempt to answer the question 'what is the meaning of the term "Chartist?"'[2] The dialogue that ensued was significant for its omissions as well as its emphases. Patient and reasonable in tone, 'Radical' described the People's Charter primarily as a way of reforming the parliamentary system by eliminating corruption, bribery, and intimidation and by making the system of representation more fair and equitable and more responsible to the electorate. He never failed to defend this democratic agenda against the charge of introducing 'un-English' reforms, like the ballot, and always pointed to continuities with the constitutional past and its traditions.[3] Throughout their conversation 'Radical' was careful to assure 'Mr. Doubtful' that the People's Charter represented no threat to the family or to property. After assuaging fears about Chartist intentions to extend the suffrage to women and children, he went on to portray 'universal adult male suffrage' as a form of security against bad laws and bad government and as the birthright of the freeborn Englishman. 'Possession of the franchise,' he argued, 'is the only difference between a free man and the Russian serf, who is sold with the land and the cattle, as part of the farm stock; or the slave of South Carolina, where it is punishable to teach a slave to read.'[4] Of a more controversial nature was the query of 'Mr. Doubtful' about 'the clause for the distribution of property'. This evoked, really for the only time in their conversation, a very warm and passionate response from 'Radical':

> That is a base and slanderous calumny, which those who profit by things as they are have forged to damage our cause. There never was the slightest foundation for such a charge, although judges on the bench and parsons in the pulpit have not scrupled to give currency to the falsehood.[5]

In the end, by carefully stressing the strictly political (and constitutional) nature of the People's Charter and the cross class reform alliance that produced 'this outline of an act of parliament', 'Radical' succeeded in convincing 'Mr. Doubtful' that 'Chartist principles' seemed 'reasonable'. But, in doing so, he passed over in silence some of the other features of the movement, its reliance on the mass platform and its identification of 'the people' with 'the working classes', that defined the meaning of the term 'Chartism' for many of its leaders and activists.

Both then and now, definition is central to the creation of political identity. An extended exercise in self-definition, this piece of Chartist propaganda points to the crucial role of language in this process. Almost effortlessly, 'Radical' slipped into the constitutionalist language of the day and turned to keywords, like 'slave' and 'corruption', to frame his answers to 'Mr. Doubtful'.[6] Consciously or unconsciously, the Chartists also employed the language of popular constitutionalism and drew on contemporary political terminology and party labels to create a separate and distinct political identity and to set themselves apart from 'Whigs', 'Sham Radicals', 'Tory Radicals' and the other parties and movements of the day. In many ways, then, language provided the intellectual and cultural framework and even the political terminology for Chartist attempts to define political identity.

Language is not, however, a free-floating system of communication, static and entirely autonomous and self-referential. After all, it is men and women who also create, in a particular place and at a particular time, meaning through and with language. If the speaker or the time and place change, the meaning of phrases and words, like 'Chartist', undergoes shifts in emphasis and sense; context is crucial.[7] Meaning is also a product of struggle and conflict between different individuals and groups, each with their own definitions and their own emphases and omissions. In the first half of the nineteenth century, the terms 'patriot' and 'the people', as James Epstein has observed, 'had a wide range of meanings within radical discourse, but, more important, these meanings were constructed in opposition to the accent given by other social and political groups'.[8] What shaped in turn the possible range of meanings of 'Chartist' was the interplay between national and local contexts. The defining of 'Chartism', or any other collective identity, occurs as men and women build networks that link together nationally individuals, even though they are dispersed spatially; as Miles Taylor has pointed out, 'the complex dynamics between locality and centre' has too often been overlooked.[9]

As a national movement, Chartism emerged out of a convergence of crises in the late 1830s in the world of politics, the economy, and the work place; this was the immediate political and social context in which radical leaders and activists all across the country articulated their demands and set out to define and to give meaning to a new political identity. In the world of politics, disillusionment with the 1832 Reform Act began to grow within radical political circles almost from the moment of its passage. From that point on, the 'exclusive' legislation, like the New Poor Law, of the Whig governments of Grey and Melbourne confirmed the worst suspicions of radicals and trade unionists about the far-reaching social and political consequences of Whig 'tyranny' and dramatically underscored the relationship between the monopoly on political power and the poverty and oppression of the working classes.[10] In the late 1830s, against a backdrop of trade depression and a fierce struggle in the cotton industry between labour and capital over technological change and the organization of work, these radical concerns took on new meaning.[11] This series of overlapping crises together raised fears about what the spinner David M'Williams saw as an emerging alliance between 'the government and the manufacturing and commercial interests' against 'the working classes' and focused attention on the central importance of democratic political power as the solution to, as the Chartists typically put it, 'class legislation'.[12]

This perspective on the crises of the late 1830s, developed by M'Williams and R.J. Richardson in their speeches at a public meeting in Manchester on behalf of the Glasgow spinners, points to some of the ways in which the interplay of national and local contexts affected the creation of political identity. Though national, and on occasion international, in their perspective, Chartists in Ashton and other localities drew upon at the same time 'the politics of place' in their struggles to define the movement.[13] To set themselves apart from the emerging Liberal and Conservative parties as well as from 'Sham Radicals' and Owenite Socialists, Chartists chose to narrate their own radical version of history and to stress the unique democratic programme and vision of the movement. In doing so, they ultimately decided, however, to emphasize the association between citizenship and masculinity and to pass over in silence the question of women's

suffrage and their contribution to the history of 'the people'; they likewise chose
to privilege the history and traditions of England at the expense of other nationalities. Ashton Chartists also sought to create a separate and distinct political
identity through identifying the movement with the cause of labour and 'the
working classes' and through advocating the confrontationalist (and potentially
insurrectionary) style of the 'mass platform'.[14] From the outset, then, the defining of Chartist political identity intertwined with gender, class, and other collective identities.

I

For the Chartists, their efforts to create a clearly defined political identity almost
inevitably led them to construct their own distinctive view of history as a coun-
ter-statement to the prevailing interpretations of the day and as a way of posi-
tioning themselves within contemporary debates over the constitutional past;
the language and concepts of this popular constitutionalism profoundly shaped
Chartist politics as well as Tory and Whig politics. In this period, celebrations of
certain dramatic episodes, like the 1688 Revolution, and historically-based arguments that drew on constitutional and legal documents and precedents were,
as James Epstein has pointed out, 'the very stuff of politics'.[15] The depth and
intensity of contemporary political debates over the nature of the constitutionalist past underscored the lack of consensus about the meaning and trajectory
of English history and pointed to the role of partisan politics and the emerging
party system in these historical controversies. This was hardly surprising; after
all, political programmes and activities have typically involved, in the words of
the Popular Memory Group, 'a process of historical argument and definition'
and contention over interpretations of the past.[16] In the 1830s, this was all the
more the case, because at that point history was typically the province of members of the legal profession, clergymen, journalists, politicians, and men (and
women) of letters, not of university-trained, 'professional' historians.[17]

Deeply rooted in partisan politics, the various Whig and Conservative interpretations of the past were crucial to the making of these different political identities. Looking back to their struggles with George III and to the Glorious Revolution and beyond, the Whigs chose to emphasize the unfolding of the cause of
civil and religious liberty. In doing so, they upheld the right of resistance against
corrupt and tyrannical governments, but they preferred to point to the role of
moderate, incremental reform in dealing with what Lord Grey referred to as
'those abuses which have crept into the Constitution, and into the various institutions of the Country'.[18] From the perspective of most Conservatives, however,
history demonstrated instead the need to conserve and protect 'the throne, the
altar, and the constitution' from innovation and change and foreign influences:

democracy, popery, and revolution. During the 1830s, speakers at Conservative dinners in Manchester and other towns of the cotton district embraced this historical outlook with a passion; through toasts and speeches they celebrated the military victories and heroes of the wars with revolutionary France and commemorated a version of the English past that was at once thoroughly Protestant (and Anglican) and monarchist in its sympathies.[19] There also emerged, in the decade or so after 1832, a trend in historical writing that cut across these kinds of partisan interpretations. This was the tendency to see the history of England, and other Western societies as well, in terms of the rise of what John Stuart Mill called 'the trading and manufacturing classes'.[20]

Sceptical about the historical reliability and truth of these interpretations, radicals and later Chartists knew only too well that the rich and powerful, and the victors, wrote history. 'If Washington had been defeated,' John Snowden told a Heyhead Green meeting, 'he would have been hung on Bunkers Hill as a rebel, but the tools of tyranny were defeated by him, and his name is one of the brightest spots in the History of Freedom.'[21] Chartists were also quick to point out how party biases shaped the writing of history. While acknowledging Thomas B. Macaulay's obvious talents, a notice in the *People's Paper* described his best seller, not as history, but as a partisan 'apology':

> Its purpose is unequivocal—being plainly an hypothesis of aristocratic liberalism—a deification of that base and cold blooded oppressor Prince of Orange—and a depreciation of anything that does not chime in with the existing political and social institutions of our country…. It is only the apology and defence of a party and a system.[22]

Radical critics countered this kind of 'apology and defence' in a variety of ways. By choosing to emphasize the role of 'the great mass of the population', or the working classes, in history, they tried to move beyond the narrow definitions of historical causation and 'the people' in Whig and Conservative accounts. In a similar fashion they also challenged the tendency to reduce history to what William Cobbett dismissed as 'narrations relating to battles, negotiations, intrigues, contests between rival sovereignties, rival nobles, and to the character of kings, queens, mistresses, bishops, ministers, and the like'.[23]

Drawing on speeches and toasts, commemorative rituals and ceremonies, music, songs and drama, the leaders and activists of Ashton Chartism developed their own radical version of history, one that typically took a public form and relied, not on the printed word, but on the spoken word. They turned to this kind of history as a way of instructing and inspiring 'the people' and as a way of forging a sense of unity and common struggle that cut across and broke down ethnic differences and animosities and divisions between the literate and illiterate and between Chartists and old radicals 'from the school of Cartwright and Hunt'.[24] Creating a people's history was also at the centre of their attempt to build a distinct political identity and to distinguish themselves from the emerging 'liberal' and 'tory' political parties in Ashton. Sympathetic to the American and French Revolutions as well as to suffering Ireland, these people's historians tried to place English history within a broader, more universal history of liberty and challenged the portrayal of democracy as something foreign and alien and the loyalist emphasis on the relationship between monarchy, the Established Church, and the constitution in God's Elect Nation; their interpretation of the past stressed instead the historical roots of their democratic programme and the right of resistance and vigorously criticized, especially in the case of recent history, the Whigs and Tories for oppressing 'the people' and for, as Aitken put it, 'undermining the ancient foundations of British freedom'.[25]

For the Ashton Chartists, the hustings of 'an old English meeting of the people' served as a natural forum for expounding their version of the past.[26] Tracing many of the evils of the 1830s back to 'the aristocracy of the country, founded by that tyrant, William the Robber—or, if they would rather, William the Conqueror', Charles Walker told a meeting in the marketplace that William had stolen the land from 'the people' and had abolished all the free institutions of the country; the only way to regain power from the aristocracy was through parliamentary reform.[27] In a similar fashion, John Deegan took up the theme of monarchical and aristocratic robbery and lost rights in his depiction of the Reformation; here he chose to underscore how members of the nobility, like the family of Lord John Russell, had benefited, at the expense of the poor, from the plunder of the church during Henry VIII's reign.[28] Looking back into the distant past, he described universal suffrage as 'the birthright of Englishmen' and defiantly asserted the right of 'the people' to 'those constitutional rights which were gained for us not by moral but by physical force'; he also defended the right to bear arms and the calling of a convention by pointing to specific historical precedents, like Magna Carta and the Glorious Revolution.[29] 'How was James compelled to abdicate—to resign his throne,' Deegan asked at a mass meeting in May 1839, 'and who called in the Prince of Orange? Why, it was what was termed in those days a National Convention, assembled in London.'[30]

In November 1839 a small band of radical veterans and activists gathered at the house of Mr. Walker in Ashton to celebrate the birthday of Henry Hunt; they met to reassert their political presence and beliefs in public and to begin the process of reviving and rebuilding the movement in the aftermath of the abortive national holiday in August. To do so, they turned to the conventions of elite political dining and modified them to their own political ends. The very setting for the dinner, as well as the songs that they sang and the speeches and toasts that they gave, placed the Chartist struggle within the historical context of 'the great and sacred cause of freedom'. Mrs. Walker, 'the woman of the house', had been wounded by a saber 'on the blood-stained field of St. Peter'. Decorated with evergreens and portraits of radical heroes and patriots, the room itself where the dinner took place stirred up memories of past defeats and victories in the history of liberty. The evening's songs, like 'The Birth of Paine' and 'Peterloo', and dramatic readings from the poetry of Robert Burns and Volney's 'New Age' likewise encouraged those who were present to try to understand recent events from a broad, historical point of view.[31] One of the many toasts that was given that evening explicitly underscored these kinds of associations:

> The immortal memory of Thomas Paine, William Cobbett, Major Cartwright, Robert Emmett, John Knight, Julian Hibbert, Hampden, Wat Tyler, Sidney, Thomas Hardy, Horne Tooke, Volney, Voltaire, Elihu Palmer, Mirabeau, Robespierre, William Tell, Andreas Hofer, Washington, Wallace, and all the illustrious dead of every nation, who by their acts and deeds have contributed to the cause of liberty.[32]

This toast positioned Chartism within a radical tradition that stretched back to John Horne Tooke and Thomas Hardy in the 1790s and beyond to Major John Cartwright's *Take Your Choice* in 1776, a tradition that had survived many setbacks and defeats. This historical roll call of England's contributions to 'the cause of liberty' also brought together local heroes, like Oldham's John Knight, and the well-known national figures John Hampden and Algernon Sidney as well as Wat Tyler, one of the leaders of the 1381 Peasant Revolt. By linking these English 'patriots' to the struggles of Scottish and Irish radicals and nationalists and to other European and American champions of liberty, the Ashton Chartists took an international perspective on the people's history; by including gentlemen and members of the landed classes, like Julian Hibbert and Hampden, they also chose, on this occasion, to expand their definition of 'the people'.

The evergreen-draped portraits, songs, and toasts at the 1839 dinner also demonstrated how 'invented traditions' and rituals, based on local history, contributed to the making of the Chartists' alternative history.[33] Of all the events that the Ashton Chartists chose to commemorate through the use of ceremony and symbolism, the one that cast the longest shadow was the fateful day of August 16, 1819. On that day, parties of men, women, and children marched, with flags and banners flying and the Stalybridge band playing, to Manchester for what Samuel Bamford called 'the most important meeting that had ever been held for Parliamentary Reform'; the Ashton contingent also proudly displayed a cap of liberty.[34] Soon after the meeting began, the Manchester magistrates ordered local yeomanry and troops to arrest Henry Hunt and the other radical leaders on the hustings. In the ensuing panic, at least eleven died, and around four hundred were wounded or injured in some way; at least eighteen men and women from Ashton and environs sustained injuries, some as the result of blows or sabre cuts, others as the result of being 'knocked down and trampled'.[35]

Outraged by the events of that day, James Higson and some of his friends organized in August 1820 an 'immense' crowd to commemorate the first anniversary of Peterloo. Bearing white wands, surmounted with black crepe, they gathered to sing Samuel Bamford's 'Song of the Slaughter' and later to march in procession through the town, 'headed with the well known black flag, as a symbol of mourning to the murdered ones'.[36] By turning upside down some of the conventions of elite politics, like the coronation parade, this ritual act of remembrance allowed radicals to assert the right of assembly and to critique and challenge local and national authorities.[37] Their practice of keeping 'sacred' the anniversary of 'the never-to-be-forgotten, never-to-be-forgiven, blood-stained 16th of August' placed Peterloo at the centre of their people's history and also re-enforced the tendency to view the events of that day from a class perspective.[38] 'The bitter feeling which that brutal attack created amongst the operatives of Lancashire,' recalled Robert Cooper in 1868, 'is transmitted to this generation.'[39] Over the course of the 1820s and 1830s, the Ashton radicals continued to hold dinners and processions to keep alive memories of Peterloo, until, as they put it, the 'authors and abettors of the deeds … are arraigned before a tribunal'.[40] For the young William Aitken, 'a Radical banquet of potato pies and home brewed ale' at 'Owd Nancy Clayton's' in Charlestown marked his initiation into radical culture in Ashton and its symbolic rendering of this crucial episode in the history of 'the people'. Wounded on 'that memorable day' at St. Peter's Field, Nancy Clayton, he recalled years later, had worn 'a black petticoat, which she afterwards transformed into a black flag, which, on the 16th of August, used to be hung out and a green cap of liberty attached thereto'.[41]

Through the use of music and songs, the Ashton Chartists tried to dramatize these rituals of remembrance and their version of history and to draw in and include men and women who had at best a rather limited ability to read or to write. Early on, Samuel Bamford had recognized the potential gains of introducing music and the 'heart-inspiring song' to radical meetings. 'As it was a custom to sing hymns and psalms in the Church,' Samuel Bamford urged a Saddleworth crowd, 'he would advise the reformers to sing hymns to Liberty; & the French patriots at the dawn of Liberty in that country sung the Marseillois Hymn and so could the English Patriots with the same enthusiasm to rend the air with Hymns to Liberty.'[42] One such 'patriot' who composed and sang his own 'Hymns to Liberty' was the 'Charlestown poet' John Stafford, 'who, though he never had the opportunity of learning either to read or write, has composed songs that would do honor to a Southey'.[43] On special occasions, like radical dinners to commemorate Hunt's birthday or the Peterloo massacre, this 'village Hampden' made his contribution to the evening's proceedings by singing, to the tune of one of the popular airs of the day, 'The Life and Death of Henry Hunt', 'Peterloo' or one of his other compositions.[44]

'At the most urgent request of a large circle of Friends,' Stafford eventually crossed over into the world of print and published, with the help of the Chartist printer and bookseller John Williamson, a collection of some of his poems in 1840.[45] The preface to this slim volume emphasized the close relationship between his sense of history and his political beliefs: 'The following collection of his Songs [was] composed at various times during the last twenty years on occasions of Public excitement; when the author had no other object in view, but the advancement of the great and glorious cause of the People.'[46] Filled with critical and often caustic references to 'middle class people', Whigs and Tories, 'parsons with lies', and 'police men and vampires', the printed versions of his songs recorded in verse the highlights of the history of Ashton's 'working people' from the 'Ludding Time' and Peterloo to the 1832 parliamentary election and the Ten Hours movement to 'The Welsh Patriots, Frost, Jones and Williams'.[47] Through his involvement in Chartist culture and its round of meetings, lectures, newspaper readings, and dinners, Stafford knew something about the key texts, the press, and national leaders of the movement and was well aware of the world beyond Manchester and the cotton district. In his collection of songs he mentioned by name William Cobbett, the *Black Dwarf*, Feargus O'Connor, and 'The Welsh Patriots' and in 'Miners', a pro-trade union song, reminded his audience of the example of the French Revolution.[48]

At about the same time, a group of young Ashton Chartists with an artistic flair turned to theatre as a way of enacting a version of the people's history that appealed to those who 'never had the opportunity of learning either to read or write' and also placed the local struggle within an international context. Of considerable popularity was their theatrical presentation of the trial of the Irish revolutionary Robert Emmet.[49] Executed for high treason in 1803, the young Emmet was one of the most romantic of the martyrs of radicalism; during the 1830s, reprints of his famous speech from the dock circulated, O'Brien claimed, in the tens of thousands at least.[50] 'Among the many portraits that were given with the *Northern Star*,' recalled William Farish, 'none was more popular than that of Robert Emmet. The fervour of his youthful patriotism, and the poetic passion of his sweetheart, Miss Curran; immortalised in the touching verses of Tom Moore … throw a halo around a memory which is always attractive to sentimental and sympathetic natures.'[51] The young Chartist players, dressed in 'full' costume, clearly tried to appeal to these feelings in their public performances of the trial of Emmet in Charlestown and Hyde and at the Hall of Science in Manchester. The play, a notice in the *Northern Star* reported, had a 'striking effect' on members of the audience, some of whom wept during the performance.[52]

This kind of reaction to Emmet's fate provides some sense of the potential of the Chartist approach to history to transcend narrow national and ethnic boundaries and to create a sense of unity and shared aspirations that brought together not only radicals of different generations and nationalities but also passionate autodidacts and barely literate factory workers. Their radical version of the past also allowed the Chartists to counter the contemporary tendency to dismiss democracy as foreign and 'unEnglish' and to make a case for the historical foundations of their political strategy and democratic programme. Through references to historical and legal precedents, Chartist militants were able to assert the sovereignty of 'the people' and the right of 'a free people' to take up arms to protect 'their ancient liberties' against a tyrannical state; this was, the Ashton radicals asserted, 'the last and most solemn step, which the constitution requires them to take'.[53] In a similar way, the Chartists presented on occasion the People's Charter itself as an attempt to regain lost rights and looked back to the distant (and sometimes mythical) past to discover the origins of their decentralized, participatory approach to democracy.

For all their efforts to take a broad, inclusive approach to creating a people's history, the Chartists also marginalized or left out altogether certain groups. Although they displayed a far ranging interest in the contributions of 'patriots' of other lands, like Andreas Hofer, to the history of liberty and regularly offered toasts to the memories of Emmet and Scottish radicals, the Chartists ultimately chose to emphasize England over the histories and traditions of other nationalities.[54] Africans and women, rarely, if ever, appeared in Chartist narrations of the struggle of 'the people' for liberty and freedom. Two of the most dramatic reforms of the early nineteenth century, the abolition of the slave trade and slavery, never figured very prominently in the attempts of the Ashton Chartists to create their version of the past. Nor did they refer to the well-known example of the Haitian revolutionary François Dominique Toussaint L'Ouverture or to the contributions of Robert Wedderburn, whose career was publicized in Richard Carlile's *Republican*, and the Spencean martyr William Davidson to early nineteenth-century radicalism.[55] The absence of women from the people's history, in spite of the role of Nancy Clayton and others in its creation, represented yet another silent omission, one that the Ashton Female Political Union hoped to correct:

We do not despair of yet seeing intelligence, the necessary qualification for voting, and then Sisters, we shall be placed in our proper position in society, and enjoy the elective franchise as well as our kinsmen. Remember, dear Sisters, what glorious auxiliaries the friends of the human race have had amongst our sex; ought we not to be proud, that we can point to Joan of Arc, Madam la Fayette, Margaret of Strafford, Charlotte Cordy, Flora McDonald, and a host of others too numerous to name?[56]

II

In his influential essay, 'Rethinking Chartism', Stedman Jones has made a compelling argument for the primacy of politics in Chartism. It was, in his opinion, first and foremost a political movement, one that drew on a sixty-year old tradition of radicalism for its programme and frame of reference and traced the oppression of 'the people' to 'a political source'.[57] And yet, even though leaders and activists turned to the People's Charter as a way of defining political identity, they went far beyond, in their views on political reform, the formally stated, public goals of rooting out 'Old Corruption', the traditional enemy of radical reform, and reforming parliament and the electoral system. For John Deegan and members of the Stalybridge Radical Association, the winning of political power meant 'independence' for labour from 'over-grown and all-devouring capitalists', higher wages and the Ten Hour day, happy and comfortable cottages, and even 'a more equitable distribution of wealth':

Without the Suffrage, you have been the toiling slaves of over-grown and all-devouring capitalists; with it you could procure a more equitable distribution of wealth—free the labourers from their hateful bondage; and elevate them to a state of independence and comparative affluence….What do we expect from reform? A diminution of the hours of labour—an augmentation of our wages—and, consequently, the means of securing a larger share of the substantial enjoyments of life, and increased happiness and comfort in our homes. Without these things reform would not be worth having,—to gain them, where is the man or woman who would not make the greatest sacrifices?[58]

The political and economic crises of the late 1830s clearly shaped this effort to define the meaning of Chartism. Drawing on keywords of the political vocabulary of the day, like 'slaves', and concerns about the working-class family and 'independence', Deegan and his fellow radicals struggled to situate the movement within the spectrum of competing party and ideological positions; to avoid the centrifugal pull of what O'Connor called 'Church Chartism, Teetotal Chartism, Knowledge Chartism, and Household Suffrage Chartism', they ultimately chose, however, to emphasize democratic political reform as the necessary first step and to pass over in silence women's rights, the 'social ends' of reform, and other controversial and potentially divisive questions.[59] The efforts of Deegan and others to translate the formal goals of the movement into a distinctive form of democratic politics also influenced the meaning of Chartist political identity.

Creating a separate and distinct political identity required the Chartists first to define themselves in opposition to the ideologies and political styles of the emerging Liberal and Conservative parties; the rise of party in Ashton and its neighbouring mill towns was, above all, a product of the 1832 Reform Act.[60] By making the town a single member borough, the Reform Act created a new arena of conflict for local political interests, and by excluding almost all 'labouring men' from the franchise, it divided 'the people' of Ashton into 'electors' and 'non electors' and placed political power firmly in the hands of the middle classes. 'The constituency of Ashton,' noted Joshua Hobson, 'is confided to the shopkeepers, and publicans, and tradesmen of the town; there not being more than thirty labouring men who will have the elective franchise.'[61]

During the 1830s and the early 1840s, a period of very real party differences in the House of Commons and great bitterness between Dissent and the Church, Ashton's two parties fought three contested parliamentary elections and engaged in an annual struggle over revisions of the borough and county lists of electors; they also clashed over a wide range of hotly debated political issues, especially the always controversial religious issues of disestablishment and church rates.[62] Passionate and outspoken in their opposition to popery and all 'promoters of anarchy and confusion', Ashton's Conservatives typically portrayed themselves as the loyal defenders of the monarchy and 'our glorious constitution in church and state'. And yet, for all their mistrust of the 1832 Reform Act and the spread of 'the principles of democracy and disorganisation', they tried to reach out to 'non-electors' through establishing newspaper reading rooms and an Operative Conservative Society.[63] Looking back over the political changes of recent years, Charles Hindley and his political 'friends', the 'reformers' or Liberals of Ashton, adopted a rather different perspective. Invigourated by the passing of the Reform Act, 'the great charter of English liberty', they confidently expected to see additional reforms to advance the cause of 'civil and religious liberty'. From the mid-1830s on Hindley's 'friends' regularly toasted 'the people, the legitimate source of all power' and pushed an advanced reform programme that embraced the ballot, suffrage extension, and the repeal of taxes on knowledge.[64] As an MP Hindley clearly tried to live up to his reputation as a radical reformer and to bridge, as he put it, the evergrowing gulf between 'the two great classes of society, rich and poor'.[65] After his election in 1835, he served briefly (and not very successfully) as the leader of the Ten Hours movement in the House of

Commons.[66] Besides regularly consulting with the Ten Hours men and the local reform committee of electors and non-electors, Hindley also appeared each year at a public meeting in the marketplace to give an account of his conduct and his votes in parliament.[67]

By the late 1830s the Rev. J.R. Stephens, renegade Methodist and 'political preacher', and the Stephenites had emerged in the Ashton and Stalybridge area as representatives of what contemporaries sometimes called 'Tory Radicalism'. This term was, however, a rather misleading description of his complex and often contradictory approach to politics in this period.[68] For much of the decade, Manchester's Conservative newspapers consistently attacked Stephens as a radical, and they did so for good reasons. During the 1830s, he had no connection with any Conservative groups or organizations,[69] and on several occasions he fiercely attacked the Anglican church for abandoning the people. Stephens had associated first with middle-class Dissenters and Liberals in the Ashton Church Separation Society and later with working-class radicals. By the late 1830s, as a result of his frequent denunciations of local 'Whigs' and 'steam lords', Stephens had broken all ties with his friend Hindley and the middle-class reformers in Ashton and Stalybridge. With the secession of the middle-class members of his chapels, his only remaining sources of support were the men and women of the working classes.[70]

A powerful open air orator and fierce critic of the 'millocracy' and the factory system, Stephens lent his support, from 1836 on, to the Ten Hours movement and took up the causes of the striking Preston spinners and the Glasgow spinners; he also quickly emerged as one of the most popular and outspoken leaders of the anti-Poor-Law campaign.[71] Focusing on the connection between the tyranny of the factory system and the introduction of the New Poor Law, J.R. Stephens virulently condemned the new law as an unchristian and inhuman violation of the rights of the poor and charged that this new system, especially the emigration scheme, aimed to reduce wages and to replace 'MAN, the only proper operative' with the cheap, abundant labour of women and children; in turn, he drew upon scriptural teachings and referred to English constitutional traditions to justify and indeed to urge the people to take up arms and resist, through physical force, the introduction of the New Poor Law.[72] These views struck a resonant chord among the leaders and activists of the emerging Chartist movement. Between autumn 1838 and the summer of 1839, relations between Stephens and the movement were friendly but distant. Although he never opposed the People's Charter in principle and always supported the people's right to universal suffrage, he was not an enthusiastic advocate of the Six Points and only occasionally appeared on the hustings of Chartist meetings.[73] Nevertheless,

Ashton Chartists elected him, at a public meeting, to serve as their delegate to the convention.[74]

In the late 1830s, republican infidels, Owenite Socialists, and Spenceans represented the other end of the spectrum of political positions and ideologies. Of these, only the Owenites had any sort of institutional presence in Ashton, in the form of a branch of the national organization, the Association of All Classes of All Nations; this branch consisted of about sixty members and candidates, most of whom belonged to 'the most intelligent portion' of the working classes.[75] Fiercely abused by local clergy and other 'mental slaves to superstition' and often denied a place to meet, Ashton's Owenites nonetheless carried on their struggle to offer an alternative to organized religion. Together with lectures on women's rights and the marriage system, they set up their own Sunday School and friendly society and held 'social festivals' at Christmas and Easter.[76] In this period the Owenites were repeatedly attacked from the pulpit and hustings and in the press for their attempts to challenge the world of church and chapel; they also were regularly denounced as enemies of private property and the family and marriage and were stigmitized as advocates of sexual immorality and promiscuity. One such critic, John Brindley, declared in a public debate that Owen regarded marriage, religion, and private property as 'the great trinity of causes of crime and immorality'. At one point, Brindley offered his own decidedly unsympathetic answer to the rhetorical question, 'What is Socialism?':

> It was, in his opinion, a system that aimed at the destruction of all our institutions that are now in existence.... It was a system that would throw down every moral standard, and declare that man ought to have full, unbounded liberty to think, speak and do as he liked on all occasions.... It was a system that went a step higher: it positively denounced every kind of marriage in principle and practice, and it denounced all religion, of every kind and sort; and then it positively denied the existence of one personal, intelligent Being, which we call God.[77]

Although O'Connor admired the courage and energy of Robert Owen, he was well aware of the prevalence of these sentiments and consequently opposed any kind of close association of the movement with Owenite Socialism. 'Because,' he explained, 'the Socialists themselves had mixed the social with the religious question, and I feared that the adoption of the one might taint our cause with the prejudice of the other.'[78]

It was within this spectrum of competing parties and ideologies that Chartists set out to create a political identity for the new movement in the late 1830s. To distinguish themselves from Liberals and Conservatives and Stephenites and Owenite Socialists, they identified the People's Charter, from the very beginning, with the sixty year old cause of radicalism. There was, argued Feargus O'Connor, 'no earthly difference between the principles of a Radical and of a Chartist'; to underscore this association, the delegates who drew up plans for a national organization chose in the early 1840s to define formally the objects of the National Charter Association (NCA) as 'a "Radical Reform" of the House of Commons'.[79] Dismissive of the Whigs and Tories as 'the positive and declared enemies of the rights of man', the Ashton Chartists cast themselves as the true political heirs of the radical tradition that reached back in time to Henry Hunt and Peterloo and beyond to Thomas Paine and Major Cartwright and the revolutions of the late eighteenth century.[80] In doing so, they took particular care to exclude all 'Sham Radicals', 'rotten' Whigs, and 'Malthusian Radicals' and to reject the claims of Charles Hindley and the Lord Broughams of the world to the term 'radical'.[81] Their emphasis on the central importance of democratic reform as the solution to 'class legislation' also set the Chartists apart from the programmes and outlooks of Rev. Stephens and Robert Owen, neither of whom had much faith in politics or democratic reform.

Chartism was one of a wave of social and political 'agitations' that swept through Britain between 1828 and 1838; its leaders and activists defined their political identity as separate and distinct from these other movements but also borrowed some of their tactics and strategies and learned from their successes and mistakes. Of these 'agitations', Catholic Emancipation (1829) and the Reform Bill campaigns (1830-32) served as influential models of how the Chartists might try to organize a successful national movement for radical reform. In both cases, mass campaigns mobilized public opinion outside of parliament around a single set of political goals and used the threat of violence and insurrection to win concessions from the governments of the day.[82] In a similar fashion, the advocacy of physical force by Stephens and his passionate defence of the sanctity of the working man's cottage during the Ten Hours and anti-Poor Law movements clearly prepared the way for the Chartist mass arming strategy and shaped how the Ashton and Stalybridge Chartists articulated concerns about the working-class family and gender roles. The influence of Stephens' rhetoric was apparent in July 1839, when the placard 'Dear Brothers' mysteriously appeared on the walls of buildings throughout the neighbourhoods and public areas of Ashton-under-Lyne; authorities later discovered a copy among the papers and correspondence of Timothy Higgins, who had a small arsenal in his house at the time of his arrest. Shot through with apocalyptic and revolutionary overtunes, the placard adopted themes, images, and phrases from Stephens' 'political' sermons and put them to Chartist ends. Drawing a stark contrast between the passivity of 'slaves' and the vigour of 'freemen' bearing arms, the anonymous author appealed to his 'Dear Brothers' to give their support to the Chartist strategy of mass arming and warned them that their very identities as freeborn Englishmen and breadwinners depended upon the strength of their 'own right arms'. He justified the mass arming strategy as a means not only of protecting the working-class family but also of securing 'a fair day's wage', a wage that would allow the working man to support his family by his own labour.[83] What was also striking about 'Dear Brothers' was that for all its militancy on labour and family issues, it framed its insurrectionary call to action without any explicit references to Owenite views on private property or family and marriage. Determined to build a mass movement, the Ashton and Stalybridge Chartists had taken to heart and had learned from the plight of the Owenite Socialists in their towns.

Although the Chartists typically took care to distance themselves from 'levelling' and attacks on respected institutions, like the monarchy and marriage, they advocated a programme of radical reform that represented a revolutionary challenge to the political establishment of the day. It was the ambition and extremism of their political demands, not their moderation and caution, that most impressed (and disturbed) their contemporaries. Sir Robert Peel certainly regarded the 1842 national petition in this way; it represented, he charged, 'an impeachment' of the constitution and society itself:

> The petition tells me that it is wrong to maintain an Established Church—it says that 9,000,000£ of money are annually abstracted from the people for the purpose of maintaining the church. The petition tells me that the people of Ireland are entitled to the repeal of the union. The petition draws a most invidious comparison between the expenses of the sovereign and those of a labourer. I say that the petition is altogether an impeachment of the constitution of this country, and of the whole frame of society.[84]

There were sound reasons for this perspective on the People's Charter; after all, it called for a new democratic definition of citizenship and a far-reaching reform of the principle of representation and the House of Commons itself. By stripping citizenship and the office of MP of all connections to wealth and property, the Chartists redefined a citizen as 'every person' who was able to produce 'proof of his being 21 years of age' and opened up the corridors of power at Westminster to poor men of talent and ability.[85] Of course, their definition of citizen ultimately narrowed the meaning of 'universal suffrage' and underscored the association between citizenship and masculinity; but, at the same time, the logic of their argument about citizenship as 'the universal political right of every human being' left open the possibility of extending the franchise to women.[86] Their emphasis on the ballot and annual parliaments sought to transform in turn the relationship between citizen and representative. 'If the representative did make mistakes,' argued a Bolton Chartist, 'they should be properly brought to account every twelve months'; the ballot, he went on to stress, was necessary to ensure that 'no tyrannical power could be used over them in the exercise of the franchise'.[87] These two points of the People's Charter, together with additional reforms to prevent party manipulation of the electoral register and to eliminate bribery and intimidation during elections, were thus intended to make the MP less independent and more accountable to constituents, an important step toward the realization of the radical and later Chartist goal of making MPs the delegates, not the representatives, of 'the people'. The People's Charter also stipulated a redistribution and reduction, by at least 50 per cent, of the seats in the House of Commons.[88] All in all, it represented at once a radical alternative to and a thoroughgoing critique of the 1832 Reform Act and the electoral system that it had created.

For the Chartists, this emphasis on democratic reform was crucial to the defining of political identity in the late 1830s. It gave the movement a sense of coherence and unity and delineated the boundaries that separated them from their political enemies and from 'Sham Radicals' and other would-be allies; it also served as the means of avoiding a diffusion of political energies. In autumn 1838, a crucial moment in the coming together of Chartism, these were very real problems for activists and leaders in Ashton and other localities. John Wilde warned an Ashton crowd to beware of parties that tried to divert 'the people' with 'the repeal of the corn laws, peerage reform, the ballot, and other questions of minor importance'.[89] Motivated by similar concerns, a group of Ashton Chartists urged their 'brother Radicals' to avoid, above all, 'the smooth-tongued, hypocritical thieves, the Sham-Radicals', and their attempts to direct energy and attention away from the Charter:

> And now brother Radicals, be not led astray by any … leaders that would direct your attention to any other question either in the shape of a repeal of the Corn Law, the New Poor Law, Free Trade, the Malt Tax, the Church Question, the Pension List, the National Debt, the Factory Question, the Canadas, Russia, France, or any other clap-trap that may be held out to distract your councils and divide your efforts in the accomplishment of your object, as the Suffrage is the grand levee that will lift this damnable incubus from off your shoulders, and without it you are slaves in reality.[90]

In the late 1830s, these kinds of concerns about political focus and unity shaped the twists and turns of the Chartist approach to the always controversial and divisive issue of women's suffrage. This issue was closely associated, in the minds of many, with the 'atheism' and 'immorality' of the best known advocates of women's rights, the Owenite Socialists, and with the 'very wicked book' of Mary Wollstonecraft, *A Vindication of the Rights of Woman*.[91] Within the movement itself, there were varying shades of opinion that ranged from the qualified opposition of Feargus O'Connor to the open support of R.J. Richardson to shades of difference between these two extremes.[92] In many ways, this varied mix of Chartist opinions paralleled quite closely Marion Reid's point about contemporary views on woman's proper sphere: 'There is at present, we believe, almost every variety of sentiment on this subject, from the narrowest and most bigoted to the most extended and liberal.'[93]

By portraying the shortcomings of the Chartists on this crucial question as primarily a case of the pervasive influence of 'the fatal flaws of misogyny and patriarchy', Anna Clark and Jutta Schwarzkopf have downplayed this diversity of opinion and have underestimated the extent to which these concerns about focus and unity affected the Chartist handling of women's suffrage.[94] The most well-known account of the decision to concentrate on universal (male) suffrage explained the decision as a matter of strategy and practical politics. 'I may here state,' William Lovett noted in his autobiography, 'that the first draft of the Bill, afterwards called the People's Charter, made provision for the suffrage of women, but as several members thought its adoption in the Bill might retard the suffrage of men, it was unfortunately left out.'[95] Here the memory of Lovett the autobiographer was not entirely reliable; the proposal for women's suffrage probably came from provincial radicals who had received advance copies of the People's Charter. The response of the London Working Men's Association was a revealing one:

> Against this reasonable proposition we have no just argument to adduce but only to express our fears of entertaining it, lest the false estimate man entertains for this half of the human family may cause his ignorance and prejudice to be enlisted to retard the progress of his own freedom.[96]

Worried about the potential consequences of this 'ignorance and prejudice', the Chartists dropped the issue of women's suffrage and thereafter tried, for the most part, to avoid the question altogether; instead, they chose to define citizenship in distinctly masculine terms but usually stopped short of ruling out other definitions. In some instances, Chartists turned to very general and gender neutral terms to define the meaning of universal suffrage and thus left open the possibility of including women as well as men. 'Universal Suffrage,' James Taylor told a Middleton meeting, 'was the undoubted right of every adult of mature age and sound mind, with a character untainted by crime.'[97] On other occasions, Chartists took a more direct (and positive) approach to the issue of women's suffrage. A short review in the *Northern Star* praised R.J. Richardson's *The Rights of Woman* for its able demonstration of woman's right to equality on the basis of scriptural and civil law; the same issue ran an account of the South Lancashire delegate meeting at which delegates called on its lecturers to recommend Richardson's work.[98]

More typical of the Chartist approach to the question was the position of Bronterre O'Brien and James Leach. They defended the emphasis on universal male suffrage by pointing to the 'identity of interests' between husband and wife but then promptly conceded that women had, of course, 'the same right to the franchise as adult males'.[99] Even O'Connor came out, on one occasion, in favour of extending the vote to all widows and spinsters who were at least twenty-one years of age; on another, more well-known occasion, he admitted that women certainly possessed the intelligence and honesty to use their votes wisely; but, he worried that women's suffrage would lead to divisions and conflict within the family and the movement itself. 'IT WOULD LEAD,' he argued, 'TO FAMILY DISSENTIONS, *while it would not advance or serve the cause of democracy one single bit.*'[100] Although O'Connor's stance on this occasion clearly narrowed, in his case, the meaning of democratic reform, his position on the controversial question of women's suffrage was consistent with his often-stated determination to protect *'the cause of democracy'* from the divisiveness of 'Church Chartism, Teetotal Chartism, Knowledge Chartism, and Household Suffrage Chartism'.

And yet, despite the emphasis in official addresses and propaganda on democratic reform and universal male suffrage, the Chartists never saw the People's Charter as an end in itself, but rather as 'a means to an end' and 'a stepping-stone to greater improvements'.[101] They were, however, usually circumspect on the subject of the precise nature of these changes. 'I have never desired,' O'Connor noted, 'a too close investigation into the various results likely to spring from Universal Suffrage, and for this reason; one section of society would object to one measure, and another to another measure.'[102] On certain occasions, Chartists set aside this reticence to reveal a diversity of opinions about the 'ends' of democratic reform. The list of additional reforms that 'Radical' produced for 'Mr. Doubtful' was reasonable and moderate: the repeal of bad laws and the passage of good laws, reduction of taxes and the civil list, legal reform, and a system of national education.[103] The hopes and aspirations of others went beyond this programme and foresaw far-reaching changes in the political world and society. For the members of the Ashton Female Political Union, a logical next step was votes for women. 'We do not despair,' they declared in their address, 'of yet seeing intelligence, the necessary qualification for voting, and then

Sisters, we shall be placed in our proper position in society, and enjoy the elective franchise as well as our kinsmen.'[104] *The Northern Star* reading group that met weekly in the home of Ben Brierley's father in Hollinwood dreamed of the abolition of the House of Lords and the monarchy and the creation of a republic.[105] Speaking in the Hall of Science, Manchester, John Deegan dismissed any programme of reform that limited itself to politics; political reform, without a transformation of society and 'an equitable distribution of wealth,' was not, in his opinion, worth 'a bunch of radishes':

> They had heard it often said, that all the working men wanted was a fair day's wages for a fair day's work; but he thought they ought to get all they earned, and he would not give a bunch of radishes for any reform which would not give something like what was represented on that canvass. [Here Mr. Deegan pointed to a representation of a Social Community, which adorns the hall.] He meant he would not value any reform which did not give them a comfortable home. (Cheers.) Let them not spend their time in denouncing Whig or Tory; but endeavour to convince every person opposed to them that the happiness and prosperity of the whole country depended on an equitable distribution of wealth. The working classes must be determined to enjoy all the wealth they themselves produced, or otherwise they would always be in a state of strife and dissatisfaction.[106]

This sort of Chartist admiration for the excellence of the 'economical arrangements' of the Owenites was hardly unusual.[107] 'As a Chartist,' wrote Peter McDouall, 'I wish for Universal Suffrage; but I wish it only as a means, not as an end. This Universal Suffrage, and the other principles of Chartism, are to me the key of the garden; the instrument to make a better social organization—the wall to protect the builder.'[108]

For all their emphasis on the People's Charter, then, the Chartists never regarded democracy as simply a radical reform of the House of Commons and nothing more. Nor did they regard democracy as strictly a matter of programmes or ideologies. It was also about the creation of new political institutions and styles of leadership and activism. When they set out to translate the formal political principles of the Charter into organizations and practices, they gave in turn new meanings to their definition of democratic political identity. Their attempts to build democratic institutions and to create their own version of democratic politics turned not only on their often adversarial relationship with local and national authorities but also on the complicated relationship between locality and centre in Chartist politics.[109] On the one hand, radical leaders and activists of the 1830s knew only too well the importance of establishing some kind of national organization. Before Chartism, John Bates recalled, the radicals in his West Riding village 'were without unity of aim and method, and there was but little hope of accomplishing anything'. The emergence of Chartism as a national movement changed all this and gave members of his association a sense of 'a real bond of union'.[110] Worried about the dangers that localism and isolation continued to pose for the movement, Chartists repeatedly returned to the importance of linking up the scattered communities of radicals into a truly national union of 'Englishmen, Scotchmen, Welshmen, and Irishmen'. To obtain their political rights, it was essential, Deegan told an Ashton crowd, that they joined with 'the people of Birmingham, Glasgow, and other parts of the country'.[111] On the other hand, Chartists typically viewed with suspicion 'a knot of men' off in London and continued to hold fast to their belief in the diffusion of political power and local autonomy.[112] 'The more you dispose and subdivide legislative authority,' argued Bronterre O'Brien, 'the better and safer for public liberty. The great merit of our ancient Saxon institutions consisted in this:—that they allowed every parish, and every tithing and every county to legislate exclusively for its own internal affairs; *alias* for such matters as concerned only such parish, tithing, or county. This is genuine democracy.'[113] Out of this tension between localities and national organizations emerged a Chartist version of direct democracy, one that emphasized decentralization and local control and participation.

Drawing on this set of democratic values and the examples of the parish vestry and the Methodist 'system of classes', Ashton and Stalybridge Chartists organized in the late 1830s and early 1840s a multiplicity of democratic associations in their area.[114] On the eve of the coming together of Chartism, radical associations existed in Ashton, Stalybridge, Dukinfield, Woodhouses, Mossley and Hyde.[115] In 1839 there were in Ashton alone at least three different Chartist bodies: a thriving women's association, the so-called 'Juvenile Radical Association' in Cricket Lane, and another radical association in Fleet Street.[116] The only one of these that apparently survived the collapse of the movement after the general strike of August 1839 was the 'Juvenile Radical Association'; it lingered on until October 1840, when its members voted to dissolve the society and to join the National Charter Association, the new national organization. In the early 1840s, however, this new society was only one of the five NCA localities within a four mile radius of the Ashton marketplace.[117] Membership in these localities was open to 'any person' who took out a card and paid a weekly subscription of one penny; apparently, it was not unusual for women to enroll as members.[118] For the entertainment and instruction of members and all interested parties, the NCA localities offered a steady round of tea parties, soirees, and a wide range of cultural and leisure activities. In Ashton, Chartists also met on a regular basis, usually on Sunday evenings in their room, to discuss the political issues of the day or to hear a lecture; at quarterly general meetings, they conducted locality business, like the reading of accounts, and elected officers.[119]

Based and conducted on the 'principles of democracy', this kind of political organization, argued R.T. Morrison, was of great value in spreading Chartist principles and preparing the public mind; however, he carefully pointed out to 'the people' the dangers of relaxing their vigilance and placing too much faith in leaders. This led inevitably to the rise of 'tyranny' and 'despotism' and the suppression of free discussion and differing opinions.[120] Morrison's warnings underscored the extent to which the Chartist approach to democracy turned on questions of accountability and the nature of representation ('virtual representation' versus 'delegation').[121] In 1839 the *National* explored, in some detail, this distinction, in an article, entitled 'Leaders?'; rejecting the idea and practice of the independent 'parliamentary' man, the editor W.J. Linton chose to emphasize the role of the leader as 'servant and interpreter' and challenged the very notion of a hard and fast distinction between leaders and followers:

> We want, not *leaders*, but *representatives*. We want, not parliament men to chalk out their own course for their own especial benefit, but men to do *our* work, under *our* direction, men who can honestly represent the people's wishes.... A representative has no right to act upon his own opinion in preference to that of his constituents, however opposite their opinions. If he cannot conscientiously follow *all* the wishes of a majority of those whom he is pledged to represent, whose servant and interpreter he is, let him throw up his office. *Else he is no honest man....* Our best leaders are those who most faithfully represent and strenuously *serve* us: who do not asked to be followed, but accompanied; who have our confidence *because they earn it*.[122]

In a similar fashion, the South Lancashire delegate meeting stressed the importance of annual parliaments and a close 'connection between the elector and the representative' and set up a committee to keep 'a continual correspondence' with members for Lancashire to the 1842 convention and to pass along the 'information and instruction' necessary for them to carry out their duties.[123]

On the local level, in their own associations, Chartists followed the practice of regular and frequent (often quarterly) elections for their officers. Between May 1841 and October 1842 there were, in Ashton, at least four such elections. Of the twenty-eight men who were elected to leadership positions, only eight held office more than once during this eighteen month period, a fairly high turnover rate.[124] When the Ashton Chartists elected someone to represent them at the regional or the national level, they clearly looked upon these individuals as delegates, not as independent or autonomous representatives; moreover, they firmly believed in, as John A. Stewart put it, 'the importance of the frequent intercourse between a member and his constituency ... in order that a full interchange of sentiments and views might take place'.[125] In 1839 Ashton and Stalybridge Chartists expected their delegates to the convention, McDouall and Deegan, to stay in close contact and to act and to vote in a manner that was satisfactory to 'the people'. If they were unable to do so, they were to resign.[126] In a similar fashion, the Chartists closely questioned Charles Hindley at a public meeting during the fiercely contested 1841 parliamentary election and demanded a series of pledges about the People's Charter and repeal of the New Poor Law and the Rural Police Act. Dissatisfied with his positive (but qualified) responses, they refused to endorse his candidacy and declared that he was unfit to represent their borough.[127]

This last and very public episode points to the crucial role of the mass meeting in Chartist democracy. In many ways, this was not a new development. Certainly, since the days of the Blanketeers and Peterloo, Lancashire radicals had relied on the open air meeting as a way of defining a distinctive political style and programme; this form of action had also served as a dramatic way of asserting their right to participate in the public sphere and of communicating their message to ordinary men and women, many of whom remained, to a large extent, outside of the print culture. Public meetings, the *Manchester Political Register* stressed in 1817, 'are not only useful in furnishing information to many who attend them, but they also exhibit that unanimity of sentiment and feeling which so generally prevail'.[128] Dismissive of 'hole and corner' meetings as cowardly and undemocratic, Ashton Chartists preferred public meetings and held up as their ideal the 'old English meeting of the people', where speakers met with and consulted the audience 'face to face'.[129]

In the late 1830s, turning these ideals into practice, however, was no easy task. Most churches and chapels, and the town's few public buildings, had closed their doors to the Chartists. On certain occasions, even the public streets were contested terrain. In May 1839, when Chartist feelings were running high, police and special constables harassed factory women on their way home in the evening as well as any person 'who dared to stand to talk to each other in the street'.[130] There were, moreover, in Ashton 'no open or convenient spaces for exercise, in the form of public parks, gardens, or walks'. Half a mile west of town was Ashton Moss, a popular spot in the past for open air meetings; but, in the 1830s, the lord of the manor was in the process of reclaiming this two hundred acre stretch of peat moss.[131] Together, all this meant that during the early years of the movement, most mass meetings took place in the new marketplace or in the large Charlestown meeting room; the latter was able to hold a crowd of around fifteen hundred persons. On occasion the Chartists also held meetings on a piece of vacant ground behind Thacker's foundry in Bentinck Street.[132]

Implicit in the Chartist emphasis on 'face-to-face' contact through frequent meetings and elections was a deep and abiding faith in the virtues of political activism and participation. 'The best test of every man's political principles,' argued William Lovett, 'is not what he will *profess*, but *what he will do* for the cause.'[133] Although Lovett chose here to portray political activism in masculine terms, the Chartists typically encouraged the participation of women in the public world of the movement; in 1839 the wide-ranging involvement of women pointed to the depth and extent of the Chartist ideal of participatory democracy. While they rarely appeared on the hustings or delivered speeches, Ashton and Stalybridge women were hardly passive bystanders. They formed their own associations, drew up and published addresses, and signed petitions; in August, in the aftermath of the general strike, they clashed with police in a street brawl.[134] Women also organized radical dinners and regularly attended mass meetings and demonstrations from the peaceful display at Kersal Moor in the fall of 1838 to the rowdy, tumultuous meeting in the marketplace in April 1839.[135] As their presence at the latter meeting suggested, Ashton's female Chartists showed a ready willingness to support the mass platform's strategy of confrontation and intimidation and even took part in the mass arming of the spring and summer of 1839. Quoting the Bible, they told their sisters in early 1839, 'Tis better to be slain by the sword than die with hunger'; in late May, at a meeting of almost one thousand female factory workers, the meeting resolved to organize an exclusive dealing campaign against opponents of the Charter, and twenty-four young women volunteered to collect money for the national rent.[136] Throughout all their exertions on the part of the movement ran the sense that they too were active agents in the struggle 'to emancipate our husbands and children and ourselves from the domination of the tyrants that have ruled our country so long with a rod of iron'.[137]

III

Apart from their advocacy of the radical programme of the Six Points and its distinctive approach to democratic politics, the Chartists also defined their movement through the association of the Six Points with the cause of labour and the working classes. In the early 1850s, R.G. Gammage, the future historian of the movement, emphasized this crucial feature of the coming together of Chartism:

The People's Charter is essentially a working-class measure; for although it includes in its provisions men belonging to every class, yet its real and palpable purpose is to establish justice for those millions whom the great conspirators against the bulk of society have regarded as political and social slaves; and in the commencement of the Chartist agitation, so strictly was it deemed a working-class movement, that men belonging to other classes were not allowed to be *bona fide* members of our association, lest they should seek to turn the current of popular agitation into a class channel.[138]

In the late 1830s the Chartists self-consciously chose to identify themselves and the emerging movement with 'the labouring classes' or 'the real "people"' and vigourously denounced 'the middle class', bankers and 'cotton lords' as enemies of 'the people'.[139] By defining 'the people' in this way, Chartists challenged Tory and Whig definitions of this crucial political term and drew a line that highlighted the social and ideological differences between themselves and Whigs, Tories and assorted 'Sham Radicals'.[140]

For all the controversy over Chartism and class, historians have not really challenged this Chartist definition of the movement's constituency; in fact, Miles Taylor has argued that Stedman Jones and Dorothy Thompson were essentially in agreement on the working-class 'character' of the movement.[141] This is true, but only in a limited sense. To use Marx's famous distinction between 'class in itself' and 'class for itself', Stedman Jones and Thompson have agreed that Chartism was, in terms of the socio-economic background of its rank and file, a class movement; however, they have disagreed over the extent to which the movement embodied a revolutionary awareness of 'class for itself'.[142] In the case of Ashton and other militant localities, Chartism clearly took the form of a mass movement of working men and women and at certain moments broke through to a broader and more revolutionary sense of itself as a class movement. But, at the same time, this vision was fleeting and elusive; moreover, from the very beginning, there was a constant tension in Chartist politics between class antagonism and a longing for class conciliation.

In the late 1830s, the Chartists and their critics agreed, more or less, about the social composition of the rank and file of the movement. Although some party politicians, like Lord Brougham, had their doubts about Peter Bussey's identification of 'the working classes' as the real 'people of this country', most members of the political establishment regarded Chartism primarily as a movement of the working classes.[143] 'No man —not even the members of the Convention—,' sneered Edward Baines, 'pretend that Chartists are to be found (in numbers worth mentioning) in any class except the working class.'[144] In terms of the social background of its leaders and followers, Chartism in the Ashton and Stalybridge area clearly confirmed this assumption of Baines and others; it was a movement of the working classes.[145] Of the forty leaders and activists whose occupations have been identified, 60 per cent were members of the manual working classes at the time of their involvement in the movement; moreover, almost one-third of the lower middle class members of the Chartist cadre were ex-factory workers. The list of Land Company subscribers, an invaluable (but rarely utilized) source of information on Chartism's mass following, likewise revealed that over 90 per cent of its subscribers came from the factories, mines and workshops of the town and its environs. (see Tables 5 and 6).

In 1839 the *Annual Register* went beyond contemporary assumptions about the social composition of Chartism and instead chose to identify Chartist hostility to 'the capitalists in general' and the middle classes as 'another remarkable feature' of the new movement; certainly, throughout that decade, a bitter strain of anti-capitalist rhetoric ran throughout radical and later Chartist rhetoric in the Ashton and Stalybridge area.[146] The spinners' leader J.J. Betts divided society into hostile classes, the factory 'slaves' and the mill owners. 'There seems to my eye's judgment,' he charged, 'hardly any proportion of the middle class of society in this community. The grinders and the ground make up the bulk of the inhabitants.'[147] The ownership of capital, William Clarke pointed out, had decisively shifted the balance of power in favour of 'the grinders' of society. 'Such is the power that capital confers on its possessors,' he added, 'that they are thereby enabled to dictate their own terms to the persons in their employ.'[148] Along with the suspicion and hostility with which they viewed the emerging capitalist order, Ashton's working men and women became increasingly aware of the basic, fundamental opposition of interests between labour and what a group of Stephens' followers called 'the avaricious capitalist'. Every day, indeed every hour, argued Robert Cunningham, the power of capital has increased. 'The working man,' he added, 'has no protection against the avarice and cruelty of the capitalist.'[149] The best means of defending 'the rights of labour against the encroachments of monopoly and capital', concluded a group of Stalybridge radicals, was for 'the people' to win political power. 'Labour,' they asserted, 'would never be efficiently protected until the people obtained universal suffrage; when they would have an opportunity of electing a legislative assembly, that would pass laws enabling the poor to defend their only property—their labour—against the ravages of capital.'[150]

'Where were the middle classes of society?' asked an Ashton Chartist in 1839. 'They had unfortunately left the people to themselves.'[151] Deeply disturbed by rhetoric about 'over-grown and all-devouring capitalists' and the mass arming strategy of the Chartists in the late 1830s, the wealthy and influential members of Ashton's middle classes avoided any and all contact with the movement; many shared, no doubt, Francis Place's dislike of the very word 'Chartist'. 'Under the name of Chartist,' he argued, 'well meaning inconsiderate men and other misled men have in very many cases, all over the country from the extreme west to the extreme east and from Brighton in the South to nearly the extreme north of Scotland, denounced every man who is not a working man, applied to him the grossest epithets and most atrocious intentions and conduct, have threatened them with vengeance, and in some places, have proposed plans for the seizure and division of their property.'[152] It was, above all, the events of autumn 1838 that had brought about this state of affairs. The physical force rhetoric and mass arming that accompanied 'the torch-light agitation' in the Ashton and Stalybridge area, together with the mysterious fire that destroyed Jowett's mill and rumours of night-time attacks on self-acting spinning mules, alarmed the middle classes and left the Hyde magistrates with 'a strong foreboding of impending Evil and of great danger to the best interests of Society'.[153] Haunted by memories of murder, assassination attempts, and homemade bombs during the violent 1830-31 strike of the mule spinners, Ashton's mill owners and men of property knew only too well the dangers of their isolated and vulnerable position in a factory boom town where the 'civil power' amounted to three constables and a couple of watchman.[154] Unlike their counterparts in Manchester and Salford, 'the operatives' in Ashton and other outlying towns, noted Charles Shaw about these troubled months, 'have a greater ascendency and have the millowners more in their power'.[155]

And yet, even in Ashton and Stalybridge, two of the most militant Chartist towns, a very real tension existed in the hearts and minds of leaders and activists between hostility toward 'the avaricious capitalist' and a desire for class conciliation. This came through clearly in a speech that William Aitken delivered in early 1842, about the time that the local Anti-Corn Law League (ACLL) had begun to make overtures to the Chartists. Although he had described, in the not so distant past, Ashton's 'cotton masters' as a 'bloodthirsty set of monsters' and had emphatically rejected 'the political opinions of the majority of Mr. Hindley's friends', he toned down the rhetoric at this meeting in Stalybridge Town Hall. After carefully drawing the distinction between 'the people' and 'manufacturers' and 'shopkeepers', he conceded, however, that 'the people' and the middle classes had common interests; he went on to read a resolution that called for 'an union of the two classes for their mutual defence' against the aristocracy.[156]

This tension between conflict and conciliation also ran throughout the recurring debate within the movement about a cross class reform alliance. Although the Chartists always insisted on the importance of maintaining the independence of the movement, even the most militant leaders, like Leach and McDouall, never entirely ruled out the possibility of such an alliance. Always willing to extend the right hand of fellowship to 'honest' members of the middle classes, Leach admitted at a meeting called by Manchester's middle-class reformers:

'He would unite with the devil himself, if he would give the people universal justice.'[157] Doubtful about a union with the middle classes, McDouall nevertheless kept an open mind on the question as long as it was 'a coalition on the broad principles of the Charter'; however, he warned Chartists to avoid turning over 'any power in directing the movement' to the middle classes. 'They must,' he told a Chartist audience in Manchester, 'look at the middle classes as men who would give them power in the day of battle, but never place confidence in them.'[158] An address of the South Lancashire delegate meeting used similar language to describe the possibility of a political alliance with the middle classes; once again, the delegates warned about the dangers of 'any union of expediency' and cautioned all Chartists to watch closely those who 'have no sympathy beyond pounds, shillings, and pence':

> Hold out the right hand of fellowship to all who are willing to join you, willing to join you on principle, but above all, be not juggled into any union of expediency with those who have so often betrayed your interests. These parties seek only their own ends; they have no sympathy beyond pounds, shillings, and pence. Watch them well.[159]

IV

Drawing on radical beliefs and tactics which stretched back to the end of the Napoleonic wars and beyond to the 1790s, the Chartists also sought to create a democratic political identity through their use of a distinctive method of mass mobilization, one that embodied their optimistic (and indeed romantic) belief 'that the people when united were irresistible'.[160] First brought into being by Henry Hunt during the days of the Blanketeers and Peterloo, the mass platform provided the people with a way of demanding their rights in a constitutional manner, 'peaceably if we may, forcibly if we must', and took the form of a steadily escalating national campaign of mass mobilization which sought to bring popular pressure from without to bear upon the authorities.[161] In hotbeds of Chartist support, like Ashton and Stalybridge, 'a constant state of agitation' existed during mass-platform campaigns; an almost nonstop round of meetings and processions provided the Chartist faithful with the latest news and kept spirits running high. 'These large meetings,' William Lindsay also emphasized, 'did much to weld the working classes together, and led them to see clearly wherein their common interests lay.'[162]

In the late 1830s, O'Connor and other leaders drew upon a familiar set of radical tactics and forms of action to launch the first great platform campaign. At the centre of the first (and the later two) national campaigns for the Six Points was the petition. At once novel in its scope and constitutional in its form, the national petition was an effective way of mobilizing 'the people' and linking together localities to form a truly national movement; it was also, as Harney pointed out to his fellow Chartists, 'a means of furthering their organization, and of annoyance to their oppressors' and gave the Chartists 'a legal excuse for assembling together'.[163] Through mass meetings and canvassing on behalf of the national petition, leaders and activists introduced men and women who 'have never heard of the agitation, and know nothing of Political principles' to democratic politics and were able to raise 'the spirit' of 'the People'.[164] To give the movement a sense of unity and direction and to coordinate activities, like petition campaigns, leaders and activists turned to the radical concept of a people's parliament, or a convention. Although the events of 1660 and 1688 gave the convention an aura of constitutional respectability, it also summoned up memories of the American and French Revolutions; moreover, some radicals clearly regarded the convention as a potential alternative to the corrupt institutions at Westminster.[165] Petitioning and the convention were, however, only two in a repertoire of radical measures at the disposal of Chartist leaders; others included withdrawal of savings, conversion of 'paper money into gold', boycotting 'any articles paying taxes to the present Government', the creation of 'a system of exclusive dealing' with shopkeepers and tradesmen who supported the People's Charter, simultaneous meetings, mass arming, and the general strike.[166]

Of these, the last was, according to Matthew Fletcher, 'a favourite project with the real friends of the people'.[167] Some, like O'Connor, ultimately came to regard this tactic as a peaceful and largely symbolic display of the unity and determination of the movement and its mass support. For many Chartist militants, however, the national holiday was a way to bring about a potentially revolutionary confrontation between the authorities and an armed and resolute people. 'Think together, act together,' Benbow enthusiastically predicted, 'and you will remove mountains— mountains of injustice, oppression, misery and want.'[168] The more historically-minded among the Chartists thought of the general strike as an updated version of the secessions of 'the Roman plebeians of old to the Aventine-hill'; they too had acted together to overcome patrician control of politics and the legal system.[169]

These distinctive methods of mass mobilization drew upon and gave expression to Chartist ideas about democratic politics and leadership; the mass platform also required certain things of its practitioners. Often forced to speak in the open air to 'a scratch crowd', radical and later Chartist speakers typically adopted a more informal and familiar approach, 'more conversational, not so serious', and tried to break down, rhetorically at least, distinctions between leaders and followers.[170] In Aberdeen, the Chartists 'conducted their agitation, to a great extent, in the open air in Castle Street, on the Inches, and under the shadow of the Broad Hill'; their speakers 'divested themselves of every form of conventionality, and spoke naturally and with vigour, using the most ordinary, simple, but always telling comparisons and illustrations. Sometimes splendid pieces of natural humour enlivened these great gatherings'.[171] In a similar fashion, Henry Hunt, one radical admirer recalled, 'spoke to the people in their own language; he knew their popular sayings—like old familiar melodies their words were re-echoed in his speeches'.[172] To be successful, a quick wit and a thick skin were also essential; *Northern Star* reports of meetings routinely recounted the give-and-take, sometimes quite heated, between speakers and their audiences—pointed questions, shouted comments (and accusations) as well as cheers and laughter and occasional groans.[173] But perhaps, the most striking quality of O'Connor and other effective platform speakers was their ability to sense the mood of their audience and to become, if only for a few minutes, 'one in feeling and desire' with their listeners.[174] The young German Georg Weerth vividly recalled his first exposure to O'Connor's oratory, a three-hour speech to an indoor meeting of fifteen hundred working men and women:

> The impression on the audience was indescribable. More than once the women who surrounded the speaker on the rostrum wiped the scalding tears from their cheeks, more than once they broke out into prolonged shouts of joy. On the faces of the men you could read what was going on in their hearts; the speaker's mood was mirrored there.[175]

Through the mass platform, then, distinctions between leaders and followers faded away (at least momentarily) as 'the sympathy of mutual feeling and mutual indignation' linked 'the speaker to his hearers'.[176] On these occasions, even gentleman leaders, like O'Connor and McDouall, seemed to transcend class boundaries and to complete their identification with their audience of 'men with fustian jackets, unshorn chins, and blistered hands, their wives, and children'.[177] The mass politics of the platform, Chartist true believers argued, also demonstrated the unity and determination of 'the people'. Of central importance to the mass platform, this myth of 'a united people' consisted of shared stories, some real, some imagined, about 'the people' and the democratic struggles of the past; these stories took a variety of forms.[178] In some stories, Chartist speakers and writers evoked the sacrifices of democratic marytrs and patriots and turned to personalities and episodes from the radical past for inspiration and legitimacy; they regularly claimed Henry Hunt as one of their own and praised him for his selfless and unshakeable dedication to the democratic cause.[179] In other stories, 'a united people' overturned all obstacles and triumphed over the enemies of reform and democracy; these victories confirmed their belief in the ability of 'the people' to bring about immediate social and political change.

Of course, there were precedents from the recent past, like the Catholic Emancipation movement and the 1832 Reform Bill agitation, that gave an air of plausibility to this optimism; the often-repeated (and reprinted) words of Lafayette from the summer of 1789 also underscored the potential of 'a united people' to usher in a new democratic age: 'For a nation to love liberty, it is sufficient that she knows it; and to be free, it is sufficient that she wills it.' A recurring theme in Chartist rhetoric, these words regularly appeared on banners and in the columns of the Chartist press and in speeches.[180] In 1848, the year of revolutions, Richard Pilling evoked Lafayette's lines as a way of explaining the events of that spring. 'Democracy,' he told an Oldham Edge meeting, 'was advancing throughout all Europe; and they had to thank the brave French for the manner in which they had carried their revolution. If the whole nation would act together, and determine to will it, as France had done, they might depend upon it they should see a great change in this country too.'[181] Perhaps here Chartist leaders also had in mind the famous confrontation between the 'Privileged Class' and the 'People' in chapter 15, of Volney's *Ruins of Empire*, a standard text for the well-read Chartist of deistical leanings. In this chapter, 'The New Age', the 'People' met and challenged members of the nobility, the priesthood, and other sections of the 'Privileged Class'. In the end, the 'People' used reason and the justice of their cause to refute the arguments of these elites and to overcome the threat of physical force; determined to create 'a new order of things', they cast aside their slavery and asserted their freedom and sovereign power. 'We will,' declared the 'People' triumphantly, 'henceforth manage our own affairs. And the little group said: "We are lost! the multitude are enlightened".'[182]

Inspired by this prospect, Chartist speakers frequently drew on Volney's vision during the mass platform campaigns of 1839 and 1842. 'The Government,' Aitken defiantly asserted in 1839, 'cannot put down the united voices and determination of the people of Great Britain.' If 'a free and enlightened people' stood united against 'tyranny', then 'the banner of democracy', he predicted, would soon wave in triumph.[183] 'It was his opinion,' declared John Campbell, 'in conjunction with thousands of his fellow-men, that if the people would be firm, united, consistent, and determined, the oppression of the millions, the hunger, starvation, and want which prevailed in society, would soon be banished. Truth and justice would combine to ensure the people success.'[184] In a similar fashion William Dixon greeted the 1842 general strike as an expression of the invincible will of 'the people' and alluded to Lafayette's speech. 'Union,' he told a meeting at Carpenters' Hall, Manchester, 'was the only thing necessary for their success. The cry was going from east to west, from north to south, "we will be free;" and for a nation to be free, it was sufficient that she willed it. (Hear.) The tyrant might attempt, by a glittering sabre or a dazzling bayonet, to intimidate the rising spirit of an inquiring nation seeking for liberty, but the day was gone by for that.'[185]

At certain moments and in certain places, this vision of 'a united people' seemed very real. For a few weeks, or even months, in 1839 and 1842, the 'oneness' of the working classes in militant localities, like Ashton and Stalybridge, appeared to turn myth into reality; on these occasions, it seemed as if all of the Chartist faithful were able to act together 'as one man, with one heart, one soul, and one strength'.[186] And yet, despite momentary successes here and there, members of the Chartist leadership were well aware of the difficulties in creating and maintaining this sense of oneness and unity. 'Let your watch-word be, "Unite",' David Ross exhorted a Chartist audience. 'There must be,' he added, 'no bickering; banish jealousy, encourage emulation; and work perseveringly, harmoniously, and determinedly, for the overthrow of injustice, and for the establishment of pure and unsullied democracy.... Do this, and victory is ours. (*Cheers.*) Divide, and we are powerless.'[187] The events of 1839 and 1842 underscored these words of warning and also stirred up doubts and misgivings within the movement about the irresistable force of a free and enlightened people.

Chapter III

Myth and Reality:
The Experience of Defeat, 1839-1842

In the late 1830s, Chartism came together in the midst of overlapping crises in politics, the economy, and the work place. In the political world, the 1832 Reform Act and the electoral system that it established came to represent, from the perspective of many radicals, a betrayal of all that they had hoped and struggled for during the Reform Bill campaign. Over the course of the 1830s, the 'tyrannical' and 'exclusive' legislation of the Whig governments deepened this sense of betrayal and made clear the dangers of an unrepresentative House of Commons. The Anatomy Act, the Irish Coercion Act, the New Poor Law, the hostility of the Commons to the Ten Hour day, and the prosecution of the Dorchester labourers and the Glasgow spinners dramatically illustrated the relationship between the monopoly on political power and the social and economic oppression of the working classes.[1] 'The Reform Ministry,' R.J. Richardson reminded labour leaders and activists, 'supported by the middle class, for whom you struggled to obtain votes, recklessly and unceasingly wage war against your interests, supporting the unholy influence of capital against the sacred rights of labour.'[2] These kinds of radical and trade concerns and grievances in turn coincided with a prolonged trade depression, one that hit the cotton district particularly hard, and struggles between labour and capital over technological change, falling piece rates, and the organization of work; these work place issues affected not only the highly mechanized sectors of the textile industries but also traditional crafts, 'aristocratical' engineers and smiths and even the building trades.[3]

This situation led to an intertwining of political, economic and social grievances and heightened concerns among working men and women about an emerging alliance between government and business. 'His opinion was,' declared David M'Williams, 'that the government and the manufacturing and commercial interest were determined to bring the working man down to the continental level in their wages.... The Whigs wanted to bring the working classes down to the level of the miserable pauper under the poor law amendment act.'[4] This set of crises, and the concerns that it raised, profoundly shaped the making of Chartist political identity. In creating their own version of history, Chartists placed recent examples of Whig 'tyranny' within a centuries-long process of excluding and oppressing 'the people' and turned to constitutional examples and precedents to emphasize the deep historical roots of their democratic programme and the right of resistance. The overlapping crises of the 1830s also intensified awareness of class in the late 1830s and suffused Chartism in the cotton district with a sense of labour's exploitation at the hands of the 'avaricious capitalist'; the nature and intensity of these crises focused attention, above all, on the Six Points as the solution to the 'class legislation' of the 1830s.[5] The object of this 'devouring monster—class-legislation', a group of Manchester delegates emphasized, was 'the aggrandisement' of the aristocracy and the 'moneyocracy' at the expense of the working classes. The only real solution, James Leach argued, was to destroy root and branch 'the power that made bad laws' through democratic reform. 'So long as capital alone was allowed to make the laws,' he added, 'the people would lie prostrate under its greedy avarice.'[6] This ability of Leach and his fellow Chartists to link the Six Points to the problems of everyday life, like low wages and the ever-present threat of the workhouse, in turn drew working men and women into the movement and made possible the mass politics of the platform. In the recent past, the successes of the anti-slavery and the Catholic Emancipation movements, together with the passing of the Reform Act, pointed to the potential of the mass platform and its strategy of bringing popular pressure to bear on the government at Westminister.

In the late 1830s and 1840s, the strength and stability of the state and the unwavering loyalty of the propertied classes and the military meant, however, that the Chartist quest for political power faced daunting, near impossible odds.[7] On the one hand, the unrepresentative and deeply conservative nature of parliament represented a serious obstacle to the Chartist strategy of working within the system to bring about democratic reform. There were in the House of Commons a few radical reformers, like Charles Hindley, who were genuinely sympathetic to the Six Points; however, they were able to muster only a handful of votes for the People's Charter.[8] On the other hand, Chartist attempts to pursue a more confrontational strategy inevitably unified their opponents and intensified divisions with the movement over ulterior measures, like the general strike, and the right of 'the people' to resort to physical force. In the end, moreover, the real physical force was firmly in the hands of the national and local authorities and the military. On the eve of the 1839 general strike, Sir Charles Napier reflected in his journal on the dilemma that the Chartists faced:

They have set all England against them and their physical force:—fools! We have the physical force, not they. They talk of their hundred thousands of men. Who is to move them when I am dancing around them with cavalry, and pelting them with cannon-shot? What would their 100,000 men do with my 100 rockets wriggling their fiery tails among them, roaring, scorching, tearing, smashing all they come near? And when in desperation and despair they broke to fly, how would they bear five regiments of cavalry careering through them? Poor men! Poor men! How little they know of physical force![9]

And yet, despite these obstacles and the strength and determination of the opposition, defeat still came as a shock. Devoted to the cause of 'the people', Chartist leaders and activists shared an optimistic set of beliefs about democracy and the power of ordinary men and women to bring about immediate social and political change. Urging 'every man, aye, and woman, too' to lend their support to the movement, they emphasized the virtues of political participation and activism and called on 'the producers of all wealth' to perform their 'great public duty'.[10] If only the people avoided 'divisions in our camp' and acted with 'determined perseverance', then 'soon the polar star of freedom shall shine resplendent o'er our land'.[11] The events of 1839 and 1842 brought myth and reality into direct conflict and dealt a shattering blow to this sense of self-confidence and optimism. 'The experience of defeat,' as Christopher Hill has pointed out for an earlier generation of radicals, 'meant recognizing the collapse of a system of ideas which had previously sustained action, and attempting to discover new explanations, new perspectives.'[12]

The collapse of the mass-platform campaigns of 1839 and 1842 forced leaders and followers to grapple with painful questions and to think critically about some of the defining features of Chartist political identity—its identification with the working classes, its reliance on the mass platform, its advocacy of mass arming, and its belief in the myth of 'a united people'. The political (and psychological) fallout of defeat hit militant localities the hardest. Although leaders and activists in Ashton and Stalybridge successfully mobilized thousands of working men and women behind the Six Points, they discovered in 1839 and again in 1842 that differing levels of commitment and preparation from one area to another and divisions over the physical-force strategy and the general strike left militant towns, like Ashton and Stalybridge, isolated and vulnerable. The obvious fact that 'the people' were not of 'one mind' represented a serious blow to the Chartist strategy for winning political power. 'It will be admitted by all,' as the *Operative* emphasized early on, 'that unless the Working Classes be perfectly united, we cannot obtain Universal Suffrage.'[13]

I

In the cotton district, the torchlight processions and meetings of the fall of 1838 marked the emergence of Chartism as a mass movement. Of these the most important was the great 'South Lancashire Demonstration' on Kersal Moor in late September. Working-class radicals and trade unions from all across south-east Lancashire, from Ashton and Oldham to Bolton and Bury, attended what the *Manchester Guardian* grudgingly called the largest political meeting in the Manchester area since 'the memorable meeting on the 16th of August, 1819'.[14] In the following weeks, throughout south-east Lancashire and West Riding, the Chartists launched 'the torch-light agitation' to organize support for the People's Charter and the convention. Apart from the talk of arming and the violent language of the speakers, the sheer size and daunting physical appearance of these meetings had a dramatic effect on the middle classes; R.G. Gammage later recalled:

> The people did not go singly to the place of meeting, but met in a body at a starting point, from whence, at a given time, they issued in huge numbers, formed into procession, traversing the principal streets, making the heavens echo with the thunder of their cheers on recognizing the idols of their worship in the men who were to address them, and sending forth volleys of the most hideous groans on passing the office of some hostile newspaper, or the house of some obnoxious magistrate or employer. The banners containing the more formidable devices, viewed by the red light of the glaring torches, presented a scene of awful grandeur. The death's heads represented on some of them grinned like ghostly spectres, and served to remind many a mammon-worshipper of his expected doom. The uncouth appearance of thousands of artizans who had not time from leaving the factory to go home...and whose faces were therefore begrimed with sweat and dirt, added to the strange aspect of the scene.[15]

On one such evening in November 1838, about ten thousand men and women marched into Hyde from all directions, bearing hundreds of torches and flags, banners, and 'transparent placards' with the inscriptions 'Liberty or Death', 'Remember the bloody Deeds of Peterloo', and 'For children and wife we will war to the Knife'. With bands of music playing, they paraded through the streets of the mill town until the meeting began around nine o'clock. During the speeches of O'Connor and Stephens, the Hyde magistrates noted with alarm, 'repeated cries of "We are ready now", "We are ready now", were uttered, accompanied with the frequent discharge of Fire Arms as proofs of their preparation'. After the speeches, the Chartists formed into processions and marched through the streets until after midnight 'to the great alarm of the peaceable and orderly In-habitants of the place'.[16]

The torchlight processions and mass meetings of the late fall coincided with and probably initiated the first round of arming in certain militant centres, like the Ashton and Stalybridge area. For the leaders and activists who participated in 'the torch-light agitation', mass arming and the people's right to resort to physical force were crucial parts of the Chartist strategy of pushing open, con-stitutional agitation to its limits; they saw no hard and fast distinction between 'moral' and 'physical force'. At a meeting in early December 1838, which con-demned the Birmingham Chartist George Edmonds for his attack on Stephens, the Ashton Chartists argued: 'This meeting hopes that their Brother Radicals of Birmingham will not censure Englishmen for what they commend in the French National Guards, viz.—the petitioning with arms in their hands, as we think that moral, unaccompanied by physical, force will prove as unprof-itable as heretofore—hence every man ought to be provided with the means of self-defense.'[17] Mass arming was also seen as a defensive measure, especially as a means of protecting their leaders from arbitrary arrest and of preventing another Peterloo massacre. 'In 1819,' Aitken reminded the jury at his trial, 'a peaceable meeting of the inhabitants of Manchester was held, when the peo-ple were attacked by the cavalry, and butchered in a most inhuman manner. This was the reason why the people went now to their meetings armed.'[18] But, above all, the right to bear arms was a constitutional right of all Englishmen. In December the Stalybridge Chartists defended in constitutional terms Stephens and his advocacy of arming but went on to assert the people's ultimate right to resort to physical force:

> The Law sanctions the possession of arms, and the people ought to have them for the purposes contemplated by the Constitution. *He does not recommend an appeal to physical force until every OTHER legal and constitutional means has been tried and found non-effective.* Daily experience confirms us in the belief that the time is fast approaching when an appeal to arms will be indispensible if the people are determined to be free. The blindness and fatuity of our rulers are hourly accelerat-ing that critical time.[19]

'Was it to be wondered at,' Robert Lowery later reflected about the situation in the manufacturing districts, 'that these men with the history of the Magna Charter, of the Commonwealth, of the revolution of 1688, and the threats of the Whigs during the Reform Bill agitation, all within their knowledge, should not hesitate to declare they would meet force with force if they were stopped in seeking a redress for their grievances?'[20]

Drawing on the rhetoric of the anti-Poor Law and Ten Hours movements, the Chartists also described the possession of arms as the dividing line between freedom and slavery and as a key attribute of manhood and citizenship.[21] 'It is my solemn conviction,' declared John Deegan, 'that you will never get anything worth having in the shape of political or social reform, until every man of you is well-armed, and ready to enter the field of battle, resolved to die freemen rather than live slaves.'[22] The anonymous Chartist author of the 'Dear Brothers' placard cast the mass arming strategy as a way of asserting the rights of 'free-men' and defending the working-class family; the melodramatic appeal of 'Dear Brothers' to physical force also drew on a sense of masculinity under siege from technological change and the cotton industry's growing reliance on the labour of women and children:

> Do you intend to be freemen or slaves? Are you inclined to hope for a fair day's wages for a fair day's work? Ask yourself these questions, and remember that your safety depends upon the strength of your own right arms. How long are you go-ing to allow your mothers, your wives, your children, and your sweethearts to be for ever toiling for other people's benefit? Nothing can convince tyrants of their folly but gunpowder and steel; so "put your trust in God, my boys, and keep your powder dry".[23]

In a similar fashion, Col. Francis Maceroni, a popular author in the Ashton and Stalybridge area in 1839, explicitly made this point in his pamphlet, *A New System of Defensive Instructions for the People*: 'Let each lover of his country—each lover of his wife, his children, and of himself—speedily procure a set of weap-ons, or a weapon, with which he may, when need be, prove himself *not* a sup-plicating, helpless, powerless slave, but A MAN, determined to have justice, and capable of commanding it!'[24]

In late 1838, about the time of these defiant assertions of the people's right to bear arms, the Ashton and Stalybridge Chartists passed beyond violent rhetoric and began to exercise this right. By December the first reports of widespread arming in the Ashton area appeared, and in March the *Manchester Guardian* charged that the making and selling of pikes and arms took place 'in the most open and barefaced manner'. In Hyde and Stalybridge shops and market stalls openly exposed for sale cutlasses, pike heads, and guns.[25] In Ashton Edward Hobson and John Williamson sold copies of Colonel Maceroni's pamphlet on guerrilla warfare in their shops for 4p.[26] At about this time, late March and April, Chartists had begun to drill in secluded spots, like Well Stiles, near the village of Waterhouses, an area where, as one young Chartist put it, 'they had been in the habit of amusing themselves for years.'[27] In terms of numbers, the true extent of rank-and-file support for the mass arming strategy was never really established; it was and remains difficult to sort through the combination of secrecy and bravura that surrounded the issue. One local militant bragged that 'the only means of admission to their rooms was a steel certificate (a pike)'. Two of the more sober-minded estimates suggested, however, that the physical-force party in Ashton probably amounted to as few as four hundred or as many as nine hundred.[28]

What was clear, however, was that the local leadership was deeply involved. In late April John Broadbent sold pikes at his workshop in Old Street, and by the early summer, George Thompson, a Birmingham gunsmith, had opened a shop in Bentinck Street, where he sold 'any description of defensive weapon', and had appointed Timothy Higgins as his local agent.[29] James Duke, whose Bush Inn was an important meeting place for the Chartists, visited Joseph Westwood, a Birmingham gun manufacturer, in May; McDouall also visited Westwood's shop that month and served with Duke as one of Higgins' sureties on arm sales.[30] Even William Aitken, who apparently avoided this kind of direct involvement, urged 'the people' to use 'a little of their hard earnings' to buy weapons. 'If they had had them many years ago,' he added, 'they would not have been reduced to the condition in which many thousands of them now were.'[31]

Determined to re-gain control of the situation, Ashton's magistrates took action to put an end to this and other threats to the peace and good order of their town. With the arrests of Stephens and then in May of members of a Well Stiles drilling party, the movement's leaders and activists sensed that a shift in momentum had taken place. Deeply disturbed by this local turn of events, they also viewed with growing concern (and impatience) events in London. In early 1839, when the convention first met, members of local Chartist associations looked to the people's parliament with high hopes and closely followed its proceedings and debates over the next few months. But, by the early summer, the convention still had not resolved the critical strategic question of ulterior measures; the leaders discussed at length the national holiday, the most popular measure in the May manifesto, but took no action until mid-July.[32] Meanwhile, in the cotton district, anger and concern over the always present threat of arrest continued to mount. 'They are exceedingly indignant,' wrote John Deegan about the Hyde Chartists, 'at the numerous arrests that are daily taking place in this neighbourhood.'[33] At a delegate meeting in late June, when thirty odd delegates and a few men from the convention gathered at Rochdale, the impatience of the militants was clear. 'To push the convention forward,' Timothy Higgins claimed, was the object of the meeting. 'The convention had sat six or seven months,' he went on to declare, 'and he thought that quite time enough. If they remained until the assizes came on, all the best men would go to prison.'[34] On the subject of a national holiday, or general strike, Higgins claimed that the Ashton Chartists were ready; they had unanimously adopted a resolution to that effect.[35]

At this point, sensational allegations about the personal life (and misconduct) of Rev. J.R. Stephens led to a far-ranging dispute within the ranks of Ashton and Stalybridge Chartism. This 'thunder storm in a tea pot', as Aitken euphemistically described it, drew its power from the ways in which gender and politics intertwined in sexual scandal. In late June 1839, despite the efforts of Aitken and others to keep the matter quiet, Peter McDouall publicly accused Stephens, champion of family values and the sanctity of the working man's cottage, of making improper advances to a young lady. McDouall went on to imply that Stephens had a hand in McDouall's near arrest a few weeks earlier. Several hours after this meeting Abel Williamson, a local leader and surety for both Stephens and McDouall, turned McDouall over to the Ashton police.[36] These two episodes touched off an internecine quarrel among the Chartists throughout Ashton, Stalybridge, and Hyde. This infighting over sexual impropriety, personalities, and the 'unEnglish conduct' of Williamson re-enforced and intensified growing divisions over strategy.[37] McDouall wholeheartedly supported the national holiday, but Stephens actively opposed 'the delusion of a National Holiday' and bitterly attacked the leaders who supported it. 'A National Holiday,' he declared in his farewell sermon of 3 August, 'means universal anarchy and confusion, and the insurrection of one portion of the nation, the weakest, the most divided, against other portions of the nation that are as one body, guided and directed by one head. Can you fight against that odds?'[38] This clash over the national holiday was all the more serious because it reflected divisions among the rank and file. Timothy Higgins noted that by early May the Ashton Chartists had already split over the question of arming and drilling: 'The people of Ashton had two Radical Associations, compromising upwards of a thousand people. In consequence of some of the parties offerring to learn the junior members to drill, the older members objected to it, and they also expelled the individuals so offending.'[39]

With the exceptions of Bolton, Bury, and Middleton, the three-day national holiday had only limited support in southeast Lancashire.[40] Divisions within Chartist ranks over the general strike, together with the determined response of local authorities and a wave of arrests, meant that Ashton and Stalybridge failed to cut, in the words of the *Manchester Guardian*, 'a very conspicious figure in the national holiday'.[41] In Stalybridge, where all the mills remained open, the Chartists decided, by a large majority, against observing the national holiday. Even the fiery John Deegan urged 'the people' not to leave work on Monday, August 12th; he admitted that he had originally voted for the 'the sacred month' at the convention in obedience to the wishes of his constituents, the

Hyde Chartists, but against his own opinions.[42] On Monday and Tuesday, the Chartists held public meetings in Ashton and organized on Monday mass processions of several thousand to visit Hyde and other neighbouring towns and villages, a popular tactic of the Ashton and Stalybridge spinners during their violent 1830-31 strike. 'The object of the Chartists from Ashton, etc. in marching into Hyde,' the *Stockport Advertiser* shrilly exclaimed, 'was the signal for all the hands in the factories to quit work and join them in parading the streets, by an augmeutation of their force, probably an attempt might have been made to overpower the military.'[43] And yet, despite all this activity, there was only a partial strike at Ashton, where the mill owners fired and blacklisted most of the spinners who turned out. In the days following the national holiday, a string of street clashes between the police and the Chartists took place. In Charlestown a crowd surprised several constables who were searching a house for arms and severely thrashed one of them.[44] On 16 August, the anniversary of Peterloo, the magistrates tried to prevent the people from holding their annual commemoration of the massacre at St. Peter's Field. A year later a local Chartist described what happened:

> The magistrates ordered fifteen policemen and one troop of the 6th Dragoons, stationed at Ashton, to go to Charlestown and seize the black flag and the cap of liberty, and the man that hung them out, and bring them to the Bench that was then sitting, but the Female Radicals fought the police and defeated them, and kept the cap of liberty.[45]

One thing that had become increasingly clear to most Chartists by this point was that there were some problems with, as Matthew Fletcher put it, their 'mode' of attaining the Six Points. Of central importance to the mass platform strategy and to their political identity was the myth of 'a united people'.[46] For all the financial, legal, and military resources at its disposal, the government, Aitken believed, could not 'put down the united voices and determination of the people'.[47] Right up until the Chartist confrontation with local and national authorities during the national holiday, this confidence held. 'The Charter must and will be the law of the land,' declared the Ashton Chartists in late July, 'if a united people desire it.'[48] But then, in mid-August 1839, this myth came into direct contact with reality. In the end, the first and most hopeful of the mass campaigns for the People's Charter ultimately worked to undermine this confidence in the invincible (and united) will of 'the people' and instead pointed to divisions within the movement over measures and men and the dangers of 'partial' or 'premature' uprisings; the Chartists never really recovered this sense of élan and confidence.[49]

The events of the summer of 1839 also undermined the confidence of many Chartist loyalists in the idea of a people's parliament as a potential alternative government and in the mass arming strategy. In the wake of the abortive national holiday, there were very few Chartists who were willing to defend, with any real enthusiasm, the convention or its handling of the crucial question of ulterior measures. Its members, Lowery later claimed, were urged 'into premature action by the impatience of some districts that had been long organised, while it ought to have been allowed to wait until the other parts of the country were up to the same mark of intelligence and determination. Many parts were urgent for the strike, but many others were averse to the measure.'[50] The Chartists in one such 'long organised' district, the Ashton and Stalybridge area, were left with an acute awareness of how differing levels of commitment and preparation from one area to another and divisions over ulterior measures left militant towns isolated and vulnerable. Their anger and despair came through clearly at a Chartist meeting that was held in the Hyde Working Men's Institute in early August 1839. This meeting of three thousand factory men and women instructed their delegate, John Deegan, to recall his vote at the convention for the fixing of a day for the national holiday to begin. 'For, although we in Hyde are fully prepared,' the meeting declared, 'yet we believe the whole country is not—and in consequence we had better put off than have a failure.'[51]

II

Just as Chartism emerged in the late 1830s out of overlapping crises in the economy, the work place, and the political world, the 1842 general strike for a fair day's wage and the Charter unfolded against a similar backdrop of economic and political crises. In the early 1840s the cotton industry was deeply mired in the worst and most prolonged depression in over twenty years. In 1841 and 1842, for the only time during the period between the end of the Napoleonic wars and the 'cotton famine' of the 1860s, the consumption of raw cotton, a reliable indicator of the volume of production, declined for two consecutive years, and the drop in profit margins ultimately led to a wave of bankruptcies in the cotton industry and intensified the efforts of mill owners to slash the costs of production.[52] Referring to the 'general depression of trade' in 1842, Charles Hindley told the Earl of Derby, 'It can scarcely be believed that the capitalist would go on, month after month, year after year, carrying on trade to an immense loss, but such has been the fact'. In March Hindley had in fact met with Sir Robert Peel to acquaint him with the desperate state of the cotton industry—'the large stocks they had, the sacrifices they were forced to make in sales, and the consequent reductions of wages which would inevitably follow'.[53]

In the Ashton and Stalybridge area, wage cuts and the high unemployment of these years coincided with a period of intense technological change in the cotton industry, especially in mule spinning, where labour was most expensive. The factory inspector Leonard Horner noted in 1841 that the drive to produce the 'manufactured article' at a 'diminished cost' had contributed to the spread of the self-actor and the practice of double decking mules and had also led to a greater reliance on cheap female and juvenile labour.[54] The extent and implications of these changes alarmed a broad range of contemporary observers from the Chartist leaders Peter McDouall and James Leach to the manufacturer and inventor W. Kenworthy and Lieutenant-General Sir Thomas Arbuthnot, the military commander of the Northern District.[55] One of the *Northern Star's* readers pointed out in the spring of 1842 that the introduction of 'long' mules and the spread of the self-actor had reduced the number of Manchester spinners from 2400 to 700 over the past dozen years; improvements in machinery, he emphasized, were taking place not only in other branches of the cotton industry but also in hundreds of trades throughout Britain.[56] The ex-handloom weaver Richard Pilling, 'the father' of the 1842 strike, charged that adult males were almost entirely excluded from the fast growing occupation of powerloom weaving; at Stockport, Orrell's factory, he pointed out, employed seven hundred women whose husbands stayed at home and attended to 'domestic' matters.[57] Well aware of these concerns about the effect of machinery on 'industrious operatives', *The Oddfellow* emphasized that 'one end' of the Six Points was to change this state of things:

> Machinery, in the present state of society, is ruining thousands of industrious operatives, as it is worked for the benefit of the few instead of the many, and as it performs more and better work in one hour than legions of manual workers can in ten. One end, of which then the People's Charter is the means, should be:— a state of society in which machinery should act for the benefit of all.[58]

This state of things, however, did not change; in May 1842, the House of Commons rejected the Chartist national petition. This was a source of bitterness and ill will (if not of surprise) in Ashton and environs, an area that boasted six NCA localities; Ashton alone contributed almost 15,000 signatures, an impressive show of support.[59] In early July five thousand gathered at a plot of waste ground near Thacker's foundry in Ashton to protest the rejection of 'the People's Petition' by the House of Commons. William Aitken rose to move the remonstrance and in his speech bitterly attacked the unrepresentative House of Commons and the '*soi disant* philosophers' of the middle classes; he also explicitly pointed to the relationship between the present 'condition of the industri-ous classes' and their lack of political power:

> So long as the supreme control over the laws was invested in the hands of a few, and that few the most worthless in society, the condition of the industrious classes can never be any better than it is. Mr. Aitken also alluded to the affected sympathy of our *soi disant* philosophers who ordain ministers to be sent across the Atlantic, to the interior of Asia and Africa, but will do nothing to mend the state of the sons of toil at home.[60]

After speeches and resolutions by James Taylor, Alexander Challenger, and Richard Pilling, the well-known Manchester Chartist James Leach, the future author of *Stubborn Facts from the Factories*, described in detail 'the evils of ma-chinery, as at present used', and the distress of the working classes and then urged the people to join the NCA.

By this point, feelings were also running high among supporters of the Anti-Corn Law League; in fact, rumours were afloat in Ashton and Stalybridge about League plans for creating 'a state of desperation' among the working classes 'to frighten the Tory government to a repeal of the corn laws'. A local Chartist later claimed: 'It had been for sometime previous to the present strike, gener-ally known by the working men of Ashton and the surrounding towns, that it was the intention of the League mill owners either to shut up their mills or re-duce the wages of the hands in their employ to that starvation point...by which means they hoped to drive the working people to a state of desperation, and that consequently anarchy and confusion would become the order of the day, during which time they hoped to frighten the Tory government to a repeal of the Corn Laws.'[61] These rumours were in part the product of the increasingly violent, threatening tone of Anti-Corn Law League rhetoric and propaganda in the summer of 1842 and in part the consequence of actions by the Ashton and Stalybridge mill owners. In early summer, at a large League conference in Lon-don, various leaders bitterly condemned the Peel government, and some mem-bers of the organization advocated the witholding of taxes and even revived talk of closing down their mills.[62] Several League publications, like the *Anti-Bread Tax Circular*, also backed the use of aggressive tactics; out in the provinces, Anti-Corn Law League lecturers, like John Finnigan and Timothy Falvey, who were both active in Lancashire during July, echoed these threats and clearly tried, as O'Connor later charged, 'to excite the masses'.[63] At about this time, around mid-July, John Gregory visited the Chartist shopkeeper James Wilcox and told him: 'How the Anti-Corn Law League had been treated in London and that it was impossible to get the Corn Laws repealed without the people...and that was the reason for the abatements.' The object of the reductions, Gregory claimed, was 'to throw the hands into such a state that they would be obliged to join the Anti-Corn Law League'. He also added that at the League reading room the masters had discussed plans for three more abatements before Christmas.[64] What gave these revelations an air of verisimilitude was that they came at about the same time as the announcement of a reduction by Alfred Reyner, one of Ashton's largest mill owners and an active supporter of the League.[65]

In the summer of 1842, against this background of an almost nationwide depression, wage reductions, technology-driven unemployment, and heated political rhetoric, a strike wave swept through the industrial North and the Midlands, from Lancashire and Yorkshire to Warwickshire and Leicester, and reached as far north as the Scottish Lowlands; before the summer was over, strikes had affected around fifteen counties in England and Wales and eight in Scotland.[66] In the weeks leading up to the beginning of the strike in early August, a steady round of meetings took place in Ashton, Stalybridge, Hyde, and Dukinfield to protest the proposed reductions, and at these meetings, the Chartists soon emerged as leaders and organizers of the strike. On 26 July, at a great open air meeting near Thacker's foundry, where the principal speakers were the Chartists William Aitken, Richard Pilling, Thomas Storer, Alexander Challenger, and George Johnson, the meeting came out in favour of 'a general strike for a fair day's wages and the Charter' and carried amid 'vociferous cheers' a memorial which condemned attempts by the League to disrupt the 'public tranquility'. After speaking to the crowd at length on the Charter, Aitken warned 'the cotton lords, particularly the Messrs. Reyners, to keep within the precincts of their own palaces, as dark nights were coming on, and the reckoning day was at hand'.[67] Several days later, Reyner withdrew, at least for the moment, the proposed reduction, but the Stalybridge firm of Messrs. Bayleys then announced its intention to introduce a reduction. Over the next week or so, throughout the Ashton and Stalybridge area, mass meetings again passed resolutions in favour of a general strike for a fair day's wages and the Charter.[68]

For the thousands who attended these meetings, the round of wage cuts was only one of many issues. In the summer of 1842, the spinners' grievances ranged from the importance of the Ten Hour day and a uniform list of prices and familiar complaints about fine systems and the growing reliance on female and juvenile labour to criticism of the use and abuse of 'improvements in machinery' and 'class legislation'.[69] The call for 'a fair day's wages for a fair day's work', a phrase which was imbued with a sense of the customary and moral rights of labour, also revealed that the general strike went beyond dissatisfaction over low wages. A fair day's wage, William Dixon declared, 'could not be calculated by pounds, shillings, and pence standard'; instead, it meant meat on the table, decent clothing, and the leisure to cultivate his mind 'in order that he might be enabled to fulfil his duties to society as a citizen, a freeman, and a human being'.[70] For Dixon and other Chartists, their insistence on a fair day's wage also sometimes referred to the working man's right to a wage that allowed him to support his family by his own labour, without recourse to charity or employment outside the home by his wife or children.[71] One Chartist lecturer explicitly expressed in 1842 his hope that the passage of the People's Charter would make possible this ideal:

> I think I hear some one ask, what would you do with us poor women if the Charter became the law of the land? Now I will tell you: degraded as you are, you are not so bad as the men; you have a spirit of independence left. I would decline answering a man—but if the Charter became a legislative enactment to-morrow, I would not [give] thank[s] for it, unless men were returned to Parliament who would make laws to restrict all females from working in factories; old or young, gay or grave, in no occupation whatever. Her place is at home, to provide a clean and comfortable meal for her husband, and to mend his linen; not as is now—she has no time to perform those domestic offices now.[72]

That summer striking trades and the Chartists usually stopped short, however, of this kind of explicit reference to the male breadwinner ideal. In their address Ashton operatives spoke in terms of 'a just and equitable remuneration for our labour' and called on manufacturers to support their demands for a uniform list of prices, the Ten Hour day, and a thoroughgoing reform of the fine system in weaving and spinning; they also advocated the exclusion of women from the spinning room as a way of raising the morals and respectability of 'both sexes'. Although they framed these demands as 'honest and manly inquiries' and defended 'our character as men', they never called for, however, an exclusion of all women from factory work and avoided any specific endorsement of the male breadwinner ideal. 'We wish and expect, when we commence work again,' they stated, 'to receive in return for our labour the means of procuring the necessaries of life with a portion of its luxuries— as we the operatives, collectively produce them all—we wish to enjoy the fruits of our industry in peace, leaving time for recreation, and to be treated by all like men. You never associate with us— hence you cannot know our wants, and desires, or opinions—our children want education—ourselves and our wives want repose from wasting, harassing fears of want.'[73]

'If the strike was universal and all the operatives would cease labour,' argued Alexander 'Sandy' Challenger, then there was hope; Challenger's point was a familiar one to the men and women who had gathered at Thacker's ground on that day.[74] 'The working men here,' an Ashton delegate recalled, 'knew well, that isolated and alone they could accomplish nothing; they therefore felt a desire to extend the strike.'[75] The day after the strike had begun, on 9 August, an Ashton meeting of striking factory workers appointed six men—all well-known Chartists—to go out in pairs to Bolton, Preston, and West Riding and to get the working classes of the other towns to turn out.[76] Just as the spinners had tried to use processions and marches in 1830-31 as a means of spreading the strike, factory workers in early August also turned to direct action to expand the strike. On the first day, Monday, 8 August, roving crowds turned out mills throughout Stalybridge, Dukinfield, Ashton, Hyde, and surrounding towns and villages. In the ensuing days, when crowds closed down factories, mines, and workshops throughout the cotton district, from Glossop and Stockport to Todmorden and Preston, the Ashton and Stalybridge area remained an important driving force behind the strike wave and continued to serve as a centre for organizing marches and sending out delegates. An intercepted letter from Ashton vividly expressed the heady atmosphere of the first week: 'Now's the time for Liberty. We want the wages paid 1840 if they won't give it us Revolution is the consequence. We have stopt every trade—tailors, cobblers, brushmakers, sweeps, tinkers, carters, masons, builders, colliers, etc and every other trade—not a cart is allowed to go through the streets.'[77]

That summer the striking trades also drew upon a familiar stock of radical and trade union tactics; these measures ranged from advocacy of a 'run on gold' and attempts to create 'a more general union' among the trades to the calling of a national holiday, or general strike. For the *Manchester Guardian*, the call for a general strike for the Charter evoked memories of 1839 and the prospect of a revolutionary confrontation between the 'the people' and the authorities:

> Those who look upon this outbreak as a mere turn-out for wages, an attempt to resist a reduction of a half penny per piece in weaving calico….—fall into a mistake, which is not only great, but exceedingly dangerous. What is now taking place has not come upon us by surprise. We know that it has been agitated for several months past; that it has formed the subject of discussion at the Chartist Sunday meetings which have been held in many parts of the district; and that it is, in fact, the carrying-out of…the "sacred week", and the "national holiday".[78]

What heightened these memories of 1839 was the meeting of around sixty delegates in Manchester in mid-August for a NCA conference. Originally convened to discuss organizational problems and to unveil a monument to 'Orator' Henry Hunt, the conference quickly brought the strike to the forefront of the agenda; it opened its proceedings with delegate reports on the state of their districts.[79] 'It was evident,' Thomas Cooper recalled, 'they were, each and all, filled with the desire of keeping the people from returning to their labour. They believed the time had come for trying, successfully, to paralyse the Government.'[80] Although some of the national leaders, like the editor of the *Northern Star*, William Hill, dismissed the strike as 'a great folly and mistake', the delegates approved, by a large majority, McDouall's resolution in favour of extending and continuing the strike for the People's Charter. This resolution, together with two addresses that were drawn up, officially committed the movement to the strike for a fair day's wage and the Charter.[81] 'Let union and peace,' urged the more moderate of the two addresses, 'be the Chartist watchword. We council you against waging warfare against recognized authority, while we believe the moral strength of an united people to be sufficiently powerful, when well directed, to overcome all the physical force that tyranny can summon to its aid.'[82] Soon after the publication of the addresses, the conference broke up; the authorities swiftly responded to this new challenge. 'The publication of the address, with the names of the Executive appended to it,' noted Cooper, 'caused the police to look after them very sharply. Campbell got off to London, McDouall got away into Yorkshire, and only Leach was left at his own home in Manchester, where the police soon found him. Bairstow, I took back with me to Leicester.'[83]

On Monday 15 August, at about the same time as the Chartist conference in Manchester, over a hundred delegates gathered in Manchester for what the *Guardian* called 'a sort of general convention of the operatives'; this meeting of trades delegates grew out of the increasingly close relationship between the trades and Chartists in 1842 and also drew upon the various experiments in general unionism over the past twenty-five years.[84] At the close of its second day, the trades conference came out overwhelmingly in favour of the Charter; this act marked the high point of the efforts to join together the call for a fair day's wages and the People's Charter.[85] But, by this point, the second full week of the strike, the issue of linking together the wage question and the Charter had already emerged as a matter of dispute even in Ashton and Stalybridge, where the strike took its most highly politicized form. The ensuing debate over this issue revealed the divisions within the movement over the relevance of the Six Points to the struggle for a fair day's wage. On Monday morning, at an Ashton meeting, the spinner 'General' Lee argued that their goal of a fair day's wages was impossible without the Charter, but William Aitken stressed that the dispute over whether the strike should turn on wages or the Charter must be left to the delegates; the meeting's decision to appoint the Chartist leader Albert Wolfenden and the Ten Hours veteran Thomas Pitt, who appeared to have no ties to the Chartists, perhaps symbolized the growing divisions over this question.[86] At the trades conference, the delegates' reports on the state of mind in the Ashton area also reflected these differences in opinion. In its summary of the delegates' statements, the *Northern Star* reported that in the area where the strike had begun, the working classes regarded the turn out as a matter of wages: 'Those [delegates] principally from Stalybridge and the other localities in which the strike began were instructed that their constituents regarded it merely as a trades' strike, a question of wages, and trades' rights.' Ashton and Hyde delegates emphasized, however, in their accounts that the working classes strongly supported the call for the Charter.[87] 'It had been put to the vote,' reported the Ashton delegate, 'at the most numerous meeting he ever witnessed in that town, and the voice of the people was the Charter and no surrender.'[88] On Tuesday evening, when rumours about the conference's decision on the question of wages and the Charter were the talk of the town, crowds filled the streets of Ashton, eagerly awaiting word of its resolutions. The next day, thousands gathered at Thacker's ground to hear the delegates' reports on the proceedings at the Hall of Science.[89]

The high drama of the third week of August marked the climax of the move that summer to join together political and wage demands. Over the next few weeks, as the prospects of gaining the Charter through a general strike rapidly faded amid a wave of arrests and continued confusion over the strike's objectives, the always controversial demand for the Charter receded into the background, and a fair day's wages, itself an ambitious goal in the depression year of 1842, became the central demand of the turn outs. The mass of special constables, troops and police who surrounded the Hall of Science on Tuesday the 16th signalled the beginning of this crucial shift in momentum and demonstrated the determination of the authorities to reassert control. By the end of the week, the conference had disbanded, and its leading figures, chairman Alexander Hutchinson and secretary Charles Stuart, were under arrest.[90]

In the surrounding towns and villages, like Ashton, where the civil power consisted of a handful of constables, the magistrates and police faced a far greater challenge than their Manchester counterparts. During the first two weeks of the turn out, Ashton's local bench was simply overwhelmed by the rapid turn of events. The magistrates, a local silk manufacturer complained on 17 August, were in a state of paralysis and had done nothing to restore order or to put an end to the strike.[91] By this point, near the end of the climactic second week of the strike, Ashton's magistracy had begun, however, to reassert its authority. At about this time, the strikers' daily meetings abruptly ended, and in the ensuing days the magistracy regularly called out the military to break up pickets and meetings and processions.[92] Over the next few weeks, the constables also arrested more than twenty men, and several leaders, like William Aitken, who eventually left the country, went into hiding. By the time of Pilling's arrest in mid-September, the strike had begun to fall apart.[93] 'The town is now under military law,' reported the *Northern Star*, 'the magistrates have issued large placards, cautioning the people not to assemble in large numbers, or to attend public meetings, or to form processions.'[94] Several days later, on 21 September, the *Guardian* noted with evident satisfaction that most of the mills in Ashton and Stalybridge had returned to work.[95]

III

In addition to causing Charles Hindley and a number of the leaders of the Anti-Corn Law League some embarrassment, the 1842 general strike intensified concern among the middle classes and the authorities about what Sir James Graham, the Home Secretary, called 'a state of social disorder'.[96] In July, during the debates on the distress of the country, Richard Cobden also raised the spectre of 'social dissolution' in a speech in the Commons and warned the government about the potential dangers of the present 'extraordinary crisis':

> I do not mean to threaten outbreaks—that the starving masses will come and pull down your mansions; but I say that you are drifting on to confusion without rudder or compass. It is my firm belief that within six months we shall have populous districts in the north in a state of social dissolution. You make talk of repressing the people by the military, but what military force would be equal to such an emergency?[97]

These kinds of concerns about the state and future 'progress of society' recurred in the annual reports of the Manchester Ministry to the Poor during the early 1840s. Unemployment and poverty, low wages, and the always simmering resentment over 'improvements in machinery' intensified the 'ignorance, misery, and recklessness' of the working classes and deepened what George Buckland called 'too wide a separation between employers and the employed'.[98] In May 1842 John Layhe also chose to highlight this theme and candidly discussed his concerns about 'the feeling of alienation which takes place between the different classes of society'. Among the operatives in Manchester's poor neighbourhoods, there was, he reported, a widespread belief that 'their legislators, their magistrates, their employers, and even the ministers of religion, are, in general, their oppressors and enemies'.[99]

It was, Layhe believed, this sense of alienation and desperation that helped to create mass support for the 'acts of insubordination and disorder' in August and September. The turmoil and strife of that summer, together with the collapse of authority in so many towns and villages, sent a shock of 'unreflecting alarm' through the middle classes and fed their fears about the imminent

destruction of all 'the institutions of society' in the manufacturing districts.[100]
On 13 August, Absalom Watkin wrote in his diary about 'the explosion' that
threatened to turn Manchester upside down:

> Many of the workers appear to think that a revolution accompanied by the putting
> down of the rich would not be at all an evil. The man who delivered our coal today
> told Elizabeth that they should bring no more, and that they would now have the
> Charter, that the soldiers dare not fire and we should see what they would do at
> Manchester next Tuesday, August 16th, as they meant to attack it from all quar-
> ters.[101]

From Watkin's perspective, the situation was at once immensely infuriating
and deeply disturbing. 'I really believe,' he added, 'the fools think that they are
now undisputed masters, and this belief may lead to great excesses.'[102]

Looking back to those troubled years, Charles Hindley could no doubt summon up similar memories. 'Who would not shudder to see,' he asked a meeting
of factory workers, 'the return of another period like '42. There was wisdom to
be learned from the lessons of the past; and he entreated both masters and men
to profit by it.'[103] For John Fielden, Hindley's fellow mill owner and Ten Hours
advocate, one such lesson of 1842 was that the government must listen to and
address the grievances of 'the people' and must pledge itself 'to the most strenuous efforts to remove the evils which afflict the great mass of the community';
the alternative was violence and insurrection.[104] In a rather more condescend-
ing and offhanded way, W. Cooke Taylor drew the same conclusion from the
1842 strike. 'These and similar cries from a population,' he advised, 'should
be regarded by their rulers as similar to the cries of children—indications of
sufferings from those who feel pain without any precise knowledge of its cause
or cure. They are a summons for the state-doctor to interfere lest the patient
should apply to quacks.'[105] John Layhe moved beyond the responsibility of the
state to attend to its patients; instead, he chose to emphasize the importance of
religious instruction and guidance and regarded compassion and personal contact 'on easy and friendly terms' as the key means of bridging the social divide
between rich and poor. 'Those in prosperous circumstances,' he argued, 'should
shew on all occasions, they recognize the brotherhood and just claims of the
poor, and are anxiously desirous to remedy their distress.'[106]

For the Chartists too, the 1842 general strike was a cause for reflection and a
source of political 'lessons'; above all, the events of that summer drove home
'the lessons' of the past four years of struggle and forced the leaders and activists
of the movement to think critically about and to re-evaluate many of the basic
beliefs and practices that underlay Chartist political identity. First and foremost,

their experiences in 1839 and 1842 dramatically underscored the strengths and weaknesses of one of the cornerstones of their democratic political identity: popular constitutionalism. On the one hand, the Chartist version of the constitutional past clearly had its political uses. In the minds of many, especially those of a conservative or loyalist cast, democracy was seen as foreign and alien and was closely associated with the violence and anarchy of the French Revolution and mob rule in the young American republic. By tracing the historical origins of their movement and its programme through 1688 to the Magna Carta and the Anglo-Saxon past, the Chartists countered these negative associations and were able to claim constitutional sanction for their democratic vision and the right of resistance and the mass arming strategy.[107] On the other hand, the Chartist approach to history and the constitution clearly ruled out certain political alternatives. It was difficult, as Thompson and Epstein have pointed out, to make historically-based arguments for women's rights, republicanism, or the redistribution of wealth.[108] (And, for the most part, the Chartists avoided these very issues in 1839 and 1842.) Precisely because their people's history never really broke with the constitutionalist outlook of elite politics and continued to emphasize the roles of Whig aristocrats and 'patriots' of all classes, the Chartists' version of the past, and ultimately their political identity as well, were open to re-interpretation and expropriation.

Although the general strike for a fair day's wage and the Charter represented the high point of the Chartists' success in integrating political and trade demands, its failure led many Chartists to question the emphasis on democratic reform as 'the only measure that can secure the people from ruin' and highlighted the problematic relationship between the locality and centre in Chartist democracy.[109] In July and August, the adoption of the Six Points as one of the objectives of the strike had been in fact a subject of debate even in the Ashton and Stalybridge area. As the strike began to wind down, a very real sense of disillusionment was apparent. 'The Chartists,' the *Northern Star* reported about the situation in nearby Oldham, 'have been much disappointed by the results of the late movement; and many of the spinners are confident that if the purpose of the strike had been confined to a demand for an advance of wages, the operatives would have been substantially benefitted.'[110] In the columns of the Chartist press, complaints also cropped up about the failure of the *Northern Star* and the national leadership to give direction and a sense of unity to the strike wave. 'The men of this place,' the Trowbridge Chartists complained, 'are ready to strike, but they are in want of information as to whether those on strike intended to hold out, and whether others intend to strike.'[111] There were even accusations that O'Connor and the NCA Executive had deserted 'the people' in their hour of need.[112] By the end of the strike, Chartists and striking workers in militant towns, like Ashton and Stalybridge, were left, once again, with an acute awareness of their isolated and vulnerable position both within the country at large and the movement itself.

Perhaps the most sobering of all the 'lessons' of the 1842 general strike was what it revealed about Chartism's dilemma as a mass movement. On the one hand, the Chartists' identification of the movement with the working classes and labour set them apart from Whigs, Tories, and 'Sham Radicals' and gave leaders and ordinary men and women a sense of élan and destiny. For all of its liabilities, this aspect of Chartist self-definition also served as a rallying standard for the movement, like the Six Points themselves, and as a way of transcending divisions along the lines of craft, ethnicity, religion, gender, and ideology. The events of the summer of 1842 demonstrated the potential power of a united and determined people and marked the high point of Chartist optimism about the capacity of the working classes for what James Leach called 'a oneness of action'.[113] On the other hand, this sense of 'oneness' was fleeting and elusive; as the events of 1839 and 1842 also demonstrated, 'an united people' stood little chance of overcoming the wealth, power, and 'the physical force that tyranny can summon to its aid'.[114] Even McDouall conceded this point and in fact warned in August 1842 that the time had not yet arrived for a confrontation with the authorities and the military. 'Revolution was not ripe,' he admitted, 'as it was in France. The middle class oppose us still, and the trades are not wholly with us. Either or both are necessary to the success of a revolution.'[115]

One way out of this dilemma was a union with the 'honest' middle classes, a possibility that McDouall and other Chartist militants had never ruled out.[116] After all, despite their very real differences over trade unionism, 'class legislation', and the question of universal suffrage, the Chartists and the middle-class radicals generally agreed upon the need for suffrage extension, the ballot, and a redistribution of seats and shared a common hostility toward aristocratic privilege, the Established Church, and the centralization of political power as well as a common interest in humanitarian and libertarian issues.[117] On the subject of family and gender relations, there was also common ground. The decision of the Chartists to avoid socialist or secularist critiques of the family and organized religion, together with their emphasis on universal male suffrage and their tentative embrace of the male breadwinner ideal, meant that the movement also shared at least some of the values and outlook of the middle-class ideology of separate spheres for men and women.[118]

Just as the 1839 campaign had revealed the serious limitations of the strategy of mass arming and the calling of a convention, the 1842 campaign re-emphasized the problems inherent in the mass platform and the Chartist vision of 'a united people' against the tyrannical state and the middle and landed classes.

In the midst of the strike, the *Manchester and Salford Advertiser* enumerated in an editorial 'the errors which seem to prevail among the working classes as to the nature of their power which they possess'. Of these the most dangerous was the belief in physical force. 'In a political point of view,' observed the editorial, 'and for any purposes of overawing the Government, they are literally nothing.... Numbers of ill-armed and undisciplined people are of no avail against troops.'[119] The former Chartist R.J. Richardson also chose to emphasize the illusions of the physical-force strategy and the relative weakness and isolation of the Chartists in his assessment of the events of that summer. 'Every one must be aware,' he observed, 'from the formidable opposition of the middle class during the late movement, that much remains to be done before the people have the slightest chance of gaining the Charter either by moral or physical means. The physical force of the middle classes in the disturbed districts was tremendous; every town swarmed with horse and foot patrols of the middle classes.'[120] In the end, the unity and resources of the Chartists' opponents and local and national authorities simply overwhelmed the impressive (if less than unanimous) show of mass support by 'the people' for a fair day's wage and the Charter. 'The present unjust laws of England,' concluded the South Lancashire delegate meeting, were kept in operation by 'the enormous physical force powers of the ruling few and the disunion of the working classes.'[121]

Chapter IV

A United People?
Leaders and Followers in a Chartist Locality, 1838-1848

'The Charter must and will be the law of the land, if a united people desire it.'
(Address of the Chartists of Ashton-under-Lyne, to their Brethren in Scotland,
Northern Star, 27 July 1839)

On a wet afternoon in August 1840, an 'immense crowd' of Ashton's working men and women marched in procession, with flags waving and the Woodhouses band blaring, through the streets of the town in honour of a visit by the
recently liberated Peter McDouall, their delegate to the 1839 convention. This
public display of the movement's organized strength and mass support also
bore witness to the success of Chartism in arraying a wide range of causes and
identities under the standard of 'UNIVERSAL SUFFRAGE AND NO SURREN-
DER'. Headed by the marshals John Deegan and Bernard Treanor, two Irish
Catholics, on horseback, the procession included the local Chartist association,
the trades of Ashton and surrounding towns, the female Chartist society, and
factory boys and girls bearing a banner with the inscription 'Look at us, look
at us; do we not need the Ten Hours' Bill?'[1] This was the public image that
Chartists tried to present to the outside world. 'The souls of all being in accord,'
men and women, Irish and English, factory workers and artisans, were all 'one
in feeling and desire'; 'the sympathy of mutual feeling and mutual indignation'
linked together, in an almost mystical bond, speaker and listener, leader and
follower, to create 'a united people'.[2]

Under the best of circumstances, this sense of unity was fragile and fleeting.
Within the movement, there was always the centrifugal pull of localism, gender
and ethnicity, and trade sectionalism; over the years, historians have studied
these problems in some detail.[3] With a few exceptions, they have not examined,
however, potential divisions between leaders and followers. Although historians
have devoted a fair amount of time and energy to the study of the complex relationship between 'the people' and national leaders, like Feargus O'Connor, they
have not really explored the stresses and strains that shaped the relationship
between leaders and followers out in the localities; more specifically, historians

have not examined how the varying levels of literacy, intellectual and cultural sophistication, and radical commitment affected this crucial relationship.[4]

Over the last twenty years, studies of Chartist leadership on the local level have typically displayed one of two tendencies. One has been to assume that Chartist leaders and activists out in the localities were solidly anchored, socially and politically, in the collectivity, 'the people', that they claimed to represent; they were, to use Antonio Gramsci's concept, 'organic intellectuals'.[5] In depicting the organizers and activists of the movement in this way, historians have generally accepted the Chartists' emphasis on the oneness of leaders and followers and their portrayal of local leaders as 'the *elite*' or 'the *cream* of the working classes'; the most significant qualification has been to acknowledge the leadership role of shopkeepers and small tradesmen and professionals.[6] A second tendency has drawn on the work of the philosopher and historian Jacques Rancière for inspiration. In his study of the French worker-poets and intellectuals of the 1830s, Rancière has argued that the main motivation behind the politics of this marginalized group of workers was to escape the drudgery and degradation of their labouring lives; they ultimately turned to republican and utopian politics as a way of 'seeking intellectual growth, an escape from the worker's world'.[7] This way of conceptualizing the plebeian intellectual and activist also existed, in a somewhat different (and cruder) form, in the nineteenth century; contemporary critics often portrayed Chartist leaders as idle or disaffected workers who turned to politics as an easy alternative to earning a living by honest labour.[8]

This study of the activists and plebeian intellectuals in Ashton suggests a different way of conceptualizing the relationship between leaders and followers, a third way between the two extremes of the heroic 'organic intellectual' and the alienated worker-intellectual. To borrow Samuel Bamford's characterization of his relationship to 'the people', they were at once 'one of them, and still apart,— having thoughts, and ways, and views of [their] own'.[9] The overwhelming majority of the leaders and activists in Ashton came from the manual working classes and chose to identify themselves with their 'fellow operatives' and their rights and wrongs; in this sense, they were certainly one with 'the people'.[10] The 'views' and 'ways' of thinking of this highly politicized group of plebeian intellectuals and activists always threatened, however, to set them apart from the working men and women of their locality. Within the movement, the relationship between 'these true Chartists' and 'the multitudes' turned on the issues of radical commitment and intellectual and cultural difference; this complicated and at times uneasy relationship profoundly influenced the political fortunes and final fate of Chartism there and elsewhere.[11]

I

Although the movement in Ashton relied heavily on and defined itself through its identification with the working classes, Chartism was made up of individuals who came from diverse social backgrounds and brought to the movement different life experiences and differing levels of commitment to the Six Points. At the heart of the movement was a small but determined band of plebeian intellectuals and activists who organized and led the movement and linked it up to national leaders and organizations. Despite all the problems in reconstructing even this, the most well-known, group of Chartists, it is possible to identify for the first five years of the movement (1838-1842) about sixty-five activists and leaders who resided in the Ashton area. Their names and information about their Chartist careers have been culled from the columns of the Chartist and local newspaper press and the various files of the Home Office and Treasury Solicitor's papers as well as records of the Palatinate of Lancaster. To fill in details about family and marital status and missing information on occupation, I turned to the census enumerators' books for 1841 and 1851 and local directories.[12]

The sixty-five Chartists who made up this small but crucial group were speakers and lecturers, nominees to the NCA General Council, propagandists and writers, traveling delegates, and neighbourhood organizers. They sold Chartist newspapers and publications, drew up addresses and broadsides, chaired or spoke at mass meetings, and served as delegates, Chartist missionaries, and lecturers. Along with carrying out the mundane committee work and correspondence of the locality, these leaders and activists raised money for Chartist and labour causes and performed the necessary, but often boring and time-consuming, work of organizing and publicizing meetings, lectures, tea parties, and dinners. 'A Mr. Joshua Hobson,' recalled Richard Carlile about one of his visits to Ashton, 'did the business, engaged the suitable room, prepared the convenient accommodation, announced our intentions, distributed our circulars, assembled our friends, and walked to and fro between Stockport, Manchester, and Ashton, as if it were nothing.'[13] Through these varied activities and the web of relationships, personal and political, that they had built up over years of radical and labour activism, William Aitken and the other members of the local leadership were able to foster a sense of unity and mission among 'the people' of their community and to forge connections between their locality and the greater Chartist world. Known to and trusted by both national leaders, like O'Connor, and the local rank and file, they were the crucial figures, the political and cultural go-betweens, in the bond of 'democratic friendship' that linked the national movement to the hopes and dreams of ordinary men and women.[14]

Twenty-five of these leaders and activists briefly appeared on the Chartist scene and then disappeared, leaving behind only a name and a passing reference to their role in the movement. For forty of these individuals, however, their occupations, and sometimes something more about their lives and careers, have been established; out of this impressionistic collection of biographical details, certain distinctive features of the Ashton leadership emerge. All forty were men, mainly English.[15] The only Scot was William Aitken, who was born in a barrack room near Dunbar; there were four Irishmen, a group that included John Deegan and Timothy Higgins, two of the most well-known and capable of the local leaders.[16] In its broad outlines, this ethnic profile of the leadership closely matched the findings of the Manchester Statistical Society in its survey of the native 'country' of members of the Ashton working classes.[17] The religious opinions of leaders and followers also appeared to coincide; apart from a handful of ardent followers of the Rev. J.R. Stephens, there were within the ranks of the local leadership apparently quite a few of what Horace Mann called 'unconscious Secularists'. This lack of contact with organized religion was in line with the findings of the 1851 religious census on Ashton's working classes. On 30 March, only about 25 per cent of the inhabitants of the town and environs attended a worship service; the majority of those who neglected to go to church or chapel on that Sunday were working men and women.[18] The mean age of the group (35.4) obscured the extent to which this leadership cadre spanned the generations, from the teenage cotton piecer Samuel Sigley to John Hilton, a handloom weaver in his mid-fifties. For the most part, this was also a group of family men, husbands and fathers, typically with several children.[19]

The occupational profile of the forty Chartist leaders and activists varied in some significant ways from the statistical portrait of Ashton's industrial society as it appeared in the 1841 census (see Tables 5 and 7). One of the most striking (but not entirely surprising) differences was the absence from the ranks of the Ashton leadership of even a single member of the wealthy industrial and professional middle classes. Unlike the situation in neighbouring mill towns, like Bolton, this small but powerful elite chose to avoid all contact with the Chartists.[20] In the late 1830s, the mass arming campaign in the Ashton and Stalybridge area and the violence of the rhetorical attacks on the 'over-grown and all-devouring capitalists' had sent a collective shiver of fear through the ranks of 'the owners of property' and had thoroughly alienated them from the movement.[21] Bound to the working classes by common economic interest and often by ties of kinship and the shared experience of factory work, the shopkeepers, master artisans, and small-time professionals of the lower middle classes represented, however, a proportionally high number (40 per cent) of the leaders of Ashton Chartism.[22] In terms of wealth and status, they ranged from Abel Williamson, a prosperous shopkeeper who was supposedly worth three to four thousand pounds, to the 'highly respectable' schoolmaster William Aitken and the tea dealer John Wilde, who was 'dependent upon the working classes' for his livelihood.[23] But, overall, the majority of leaders came from the manual working classes; at the time of their involvement in the movement, twenty-four of the forty Chartist leaders (60 per cent) were members of the manual working classes.[24]

One way (perhaps the only way) of putting together this kind of socio-economic profile of the Chartist 'masses' in Ashton is to turn to the Board of Trade list of Land Company subscribers. In the late 1840s, O'Connor and the directors of the company tried unsuccessfully to register the organization under the Joint Stock Companies Act; their efforts did lead to the collection of a national (though incomplete) list of subscribers.[25] Dorothy Thompson and others have pointed to some potential problems with using this source to reconstruct the social composition of the movement's mass following. In the cotton district, the rolls of the Land Company included at least some subscribers who had no previous connection to Chartism. 'Although the name of the society is the Chartist Co-operative Land Society,' remarked James Leach, 'yet its members were not confined to the Chartist body; a large portion of its members are not, and never were Chartists.'[26] Even in the case of Ashton, obvious gaps exist in the Board of Trade list. At the high point of enthusiasm for the land question, the *Northern Star* published two lists of officers and Committee members for the Land Company locality in Ashton; only about two-thirds of these individuals appeared in the national list of subscribers.[27]

And yet, despite these problems, the fact that these men and women were willing to entrust their subscriptions to the Land Company suggested that they had some sympathy for the goals of Chartism and a substantial degree of confidence in its leaders. In the end, the Board of Trade list represents, as Alan Little has argued, 'the largest sample of ordinary Chartist sympathisers we are ever likely to have'.[28] From this rich but very disorganized source, Jamie Bronstein has abstracted lists of subscribers for eleven mill towns in the cotton district; in the case of Ashton, the number of subscribers came to about 940 men and women.[29] The occupational profile of Land Company subscribers (see Table 6) underscored the similarities between the social backgrounds of leaders and followers. In this sense, there was no dramatic differences between the leadership cadre and the Chartist 'masses' in Ashton; the critical fault line in their relationship was not social or class difference.

One thing that did distinguish this cadre of leaders and activists from the rank and file was their occasional earnings from the 'trade of agitation'. Although very few were able to make, for any length of time, a full-time living as Chartist professionals, at least eighteen of the group of forty earned, from time to time, a few shillings (or a few pounds) through the sale of Chartist newspapers and products or through their services on behalf of the movement. The fact that Edward Hobson was able to sell 1330 copies of the *Northern Star* suggests the extent of the potential market for Chartist publications and goods; at about the same time, another big seller in Ashton and Stalybridge was a line of 'pots and mugs and other articles of crockeryware' that were 'embellished with the portrait of Mr. Stephens'.[30] More mundane, but just as crucial to the 'informal economy' of the movement was the Chartist lecture. In many ways, lecturing to 'the people' was, however, a labour of love. Uncertain and erratic at best, compensation often took the form of hospitality during the visit or a collection at the meeting. 'Although occasionally offered payment,' William Lindsay recalled, 'I never accepted a penny beyond railway or coach fares and hotel expenses, and very frequently not even that.'[31] From time to time, nevertheless, members of the Ashton leadership delivered lectures on the local circuit; on occasion, they also took to the open road, like William Aitken 'to revolutionise the empire, with 25s. in his pocket', as Chartist delegates and missionaries.[32]

Unfortunately, though necessary and indeed crucial to the Chartist attempt to create 'a united people', these kinds of activities fit uneasily with the Chartist vision of democracy, one that emphasized volunteerism and participation and sought to break down the distinction between leaders and followers.[33] The practice of paying delegates and lecturers struck Bamford and others as 'a beggarly [way] of ... supporting a great Cause' and fed rank-and-file suspicions about the 'jobbing politician' and the 'paid political advocate'.[34] In Bradford, there were, Peter Bussey proudly pointed out, 'no paid missionaries' to agitate 'the people'; 'the organization of that place,' he added, 'was solely owing to the spirited exertions of a few individuals who felt that ardent love of liberty which carried them through everything.'[35] This negative stereotype of the radical or labour activist as an unscrupulous agitator with a keen interest in 'the people's pennies' was a fact of public life that Ashton's leaders knew firsthand and understood. 'It was quite natural,' Timothy Higgins conceded, 'they [the people] should keep a watchful eye over those who were entrusted with the care of their interests.'[36] At times, though, these suspicions on the part of 'the people' led to hard feelings and bitterness. 'They are,' claimed a Manchester man about the working classes, 'the worst masters alive. Anybody almost who works for them must work for nothing or lose their confidence .... No wonder we have so few reformers, since the way of the reformer is so hard.'[37]

A second experience that set apart many of the local leadership from the Chartist 'masses' was that of arrest and prison; between 1839 and 1843, fifteen were arrested at least once.[38] Imprisonment affected individuals differently; overall, however, the prison experience highlighted several issues for these leaders and activists. The isolation and hardship of prison life, together with the emotional and financial toll on prisoners' families, underscored the cost of activism and created tensions between the imprisoned 'patriot' and 'the people'. The leaders of the movement, McDouall claimed in December 1839, 'have generously sacrificed themselves to poverty, to neglect, and to a dungeon, and many, most likely, to the scaffold, that they might thereby save a people who had promised much, but never intended to fulfil anything.'[39] Worn down by worry about his family and by his own 'bodily sufferings', Higgins described with tears in his eyes the poverty of his wife and four children and bitterly criticized O'Connor for his failure to set 'a bold and magnanimous example' at his trial and in prison. 'A very trifling encouragement,' concluded W.J. Williams, 'would induce him to emigrate to the U.S.'; apparently, the interviewer's impression was not far off the mark.[40] On his release from Chester Castle, Higgins was saddened to discover the apathy and divisions of 'the people'; he soon dropped out of Chartist politics.[41] Even though he left Kirkdale with his Chartist principles intact, William Aitken knew only too well the 'ingratitude' of 'the people' and the high cost of 'boldly advocating' the democratic cause. Shortly before his trial, he wrote a letter to the *Northern Star* in which he criticized 'the great bulk of the Radicals in this neighbourhood' for their neglect of the imprisoned McDouall and Higgins.[42] His own memories of the 'solitude and gloom' of the prison cell also served to remind him that the reward of the 'high-souled patriot' was too often 'penury and insult, and all the woes that human flesh is heir to'.[43]

II

Although Aitken and his fellow leaders out in the localities were well aware of these difficult questions about the 'paid political advocate' and the 'ingratitude' and apathy of 'the people', they typically chose to emphasize instead an optimistic set of beliefs about democracy and to depict themselves simply as the 'instrument' or 'mouthpiece' of the people's will.[44] In some ways, this self-portrait was a realistic one. Closely tied to the working classes by family, friendship, and the shared experience of factory work, Aitken and his fellow activists and leaders identified themselves and the movement itself with the cause of labour and tried to relate democratic reform to the everyday problems of working men and women. Their self-conscious identification with 'the people' served to mask, however, the cultural and political differences that stretched between leaders and followers in their own locality and in the movement as a whole. Throughout this period, there was, as James Epstein has argued, a 'constant tension' between the rationalism and far-reaching intellectual and political interests of the plebeian intellectual and radical activist and the 'rougher' and less literate world of the 'larger working-class public'.[45]

At one end of the political and cultural spectrum was the autodidact and 'true' Chartist William Aitken. 'The rudiments of knowledge,' recounted his biography in the *Oddfellows' Magazine*, 'were by him labouriously acquired in the jenny room, amidst the whirl of machinery, and in his solitary chamber after the day's prolonged toil.'[46] Driven by 'an extreme desire to acquire knowledge', Aitken urged all to 'gather knowledge each passing hour' and to expand their intellectual horizons through the study of literature, history, science, and morality.[47] 'How essential,' he argued, 'it is to make good use of our spare moments; and, instead of spending them in light frivolities let us be gathering the rich conceptions of men of science and literature from their books and periodicals.'[48] This kind of passionate pursuit of learning, often until late in the night, 'when the world around me was lost in the torpidity of sleep', was a transforming experience, one that opened up a whole new way of thinking and of perceiving the world.[49] 'Every principle that ennobles,' Aitken concluded, 'is brought from the human mind by education'; reading itself was 'a habit as necessary to an educated man's comfort as warmth and clothing'.[50]

Well-read in literature, history, and science, Aitken embodied this 'spirit of inquiry' and the high intellectual standards of the autodidact tradition.[51] Over the course of the 1840s, he lectured on current events, scientific and political topics, ancient and modern governments, 'The Progression of Man' from his savage state to the present, and 'The Life, Times, and Doings of Socrates'; he also published *A Journey Up the Mississippi* as well as popular science articles on hydrostatics and Archimedes and poetry.[52] 'He was extensively acquainted,' noted the *Ashton News* in its obituary notice, 'with the writings of our best poets, with many of the best passages of which he was accustomed to adorn his speeches.'[53] Among Aitken's favourites were William Shakespeare, Lord Byron, William Cowper, John Milton, Robert Burns, and Alexander Pope.[54] For Aitken, the pursuit of 'useful knowledge', scientific and literary alike, opened one's eyes to truth and freed the individual from the chains 'of sophistry, and the bewilderments of superstition'; he firmly believed in the power of reason and science to liberate the human mind and dismissed 'superstitions' and 'visions and signs' as 'relics of a barbarous by-gone age':

> Science will remove the unhallowed influence which a venal and hypocritical priesthood, have for thousands of years held over the whole human family, it will shed a ray of light over all your musings, wanderings, and private conversations, and will eventually (to use the emphatic words of the great Lord Byron,) "Conduct the world at last to Freedom." The improvements which are now making in the scientific world, will remain, as so many land-marks in the flood of time, to show the wish of the philosopher, to mend the social condition of mankind, and will also show the perfidy of the government who allowed a nation's best and most

useful prop – the people – to fall amidst so many great and beneficial improvements.[55]

Although Aitken scattered references and allusions to authors and books
throughout his speeches and writings, he left behind no narrative account of his
nights of study and reading; however, two of his fellow poets and radical autodidacts, Samuel Bamford and Benjamin Brierley, devoted considerable space in
their autobiographies to their entry into the world of books and ideas. In both
cases, learning to read was one of the great formative experiences of their lives.
'When I first plunged, as it were,' recalled Bamford, 'into the blessed habit of
reading, faculties which had hitherto given but small intimation of existence,
suddenly sprung into vigourous action. My mind was ever desiring more of the
silent but exciting conversation with books.'[56] From the very beginning, their
choice of reading material was a highly eclectic mixture of famous works from
the canon of English literature, popular tales and romances, and Enlightenment
and radical writings. The young Brierley started his life as a reader with the Bible; he then moved on to 'Cleave's Gazette', the *Pickwick Papers*, and the *Northern Star* and read with equal enthusiasm penny copies of 'Gulliver's Travels' and
'Tom Thumb' as well as Burns, Byron, Shakespeare, and Shelley.[57] The list of
titles in the small personal library of Samuel Collins of Hollinwood highlighted
the far-ranging, restless curiosity of the plebeian intellectual; on the blank pages
at the end of his copy of Paine's *Age of Reason*, he proudly jotted down a cata-
logue of his library. Classical works, like the *Iliad* and the *Aeneid*, rested side
by side with poetry in the Lancashire dialect, Shakespeare, Milton, Byron, and
other classics of English literature; there were also books on grammar, geography, arithmetic as well as Hume's history of England, a biography of Oliver
Cromwell, and Volney's *Ruins of Empires*.[58]

Of course, not all Chartist leaders and activists shared this passion for reading
and knowledge; however, there was a strong autodidact tradition in Ashton and
neighbouring localities. This came through clearly in the 1840-41 prison interviews with twenty-five of the leaders from the cotton district.[59] Of these individuals, twenty-one were able to read and write with some degree of fluency, and
almost half of the group (eleven in all) devoted serious time and energy to study
and self improvement.[60] 'In prison,' Timothy Higgins noted, 'I have been writing poetry and have improved myself greatly in arithmetic. We are permitted
to have Scotts' novels and common Historical works but they were so common
out of doors, where I read everthing I could find.' James Duke likewise pursued
an ambitious programme of self improvement and 'assisted in the instruction
of others'.[61] All in all, a fair number of these Chartist autodidacts regarded this
aspect of their time in prison in a positive way. 'I have improved myself much,'

claimed Christopher Doyle, 'I would not take £50 for what I have learnt. I have lately been reading, Watt's Logic and Improvement of the Mind, also Locke and Bacons essays.'[62]

At the other end of the cultural and political spectrum were the Chartist 'masses', ordinary men and women who seemed to inhabit an altogether different mental universe. A telling sign of this difference was the fact that in the early 1840s only around 40 to 50 per cent of the grooms in Ashton and other mill towns of the cotton district were able to sign the marriage register; for this same period, the percentage of bridal marks ran at a considerably higher level.[63] 'If writing, therefore, is to be considered a criterion of the education of a people,' Coulthart gloomily concluded about the situation in Ashton, 'verily the inhabitants of this town are in a pitiable condition.'[64] The emphasis that Sunday Schools and dame schools placed on reading, at the expense of writing and other skills, meant that in the cotton district these figures on the ability to sign clearly underestimated, however, the size of the reading public.[65] A house-by-house survey of the state of education in a working-class neighbourhood in Salford underscored some of the problems with the practice of relying on signature rates as the basic test of literacy. 'About half of those who can read,' the report concluded, 'can write also, but not quite one-third can ciper.'[66] In the mid-1830s, another survey by the Manchester Statistical Society suggested that among the working classes in Ashton, the number of persons 'who can read only' (4334) almost equalled the number of persons 'who can read and write' (4723).[67]

And yet, even if the majority of working men and women had access to the world of print, they often read at a very basic level and lacked what Samuel Smiles called the 'means and opportunities' to develop or even to practice their reading skills.[68] 'When I was a little boy,' Aitken recalled about the 1820s, 'such a thing as a child reading was almost unknown, and boys who could work the rule-of-three were considered wonders'; with little free time or spare money for even the cheapest of publications, the young Samuel Fielden kept in practice by reading 'all the advertisements that I could see on the dead walls and in the shop windows' of Todmorden.[69] Things did not improve dramatically once one reached adulthood. There were only a limited number of places that offered working men the 'means and opportunities' to read newspapers or books; in the 1840s, these 'reading sites' in Ashton and environs included: 'conservative' and 'reform' newsrooms, the mechanics' institution, the Dukinfield Village Library, the Chartist Association's room, various circulating libraries, and friendly society lodges.[70] For all but 'the better-paid mechanics or artisans', the relative expense of books and newspapers or a subscription to a circulating library or mechanics' institution (10s. p.a. for the latter in Ashton) placed serious limitations on the reading habits of most working men and women; in fact, many members of the working classes, Smiles and others claimed, eventually lost 'the art of reading in their adult years'.[71]

For many of those who did not completely fall out of the habit, reading was often a difficult and labourious task, more work than pleasure. 'There are,' observed James Heywood about a working-class neighbourhood in Miles Platting, 'very few of the heads of families, included within this enquiry, who have formed the habit of reading, or are capable of understanding or enjoying a book.'[72] In the mid-1840s the prison chaplain Rev. John Clay described the limitations of the 'mechanical' style of reading that he encountered among inmates at Preston:

> Very often have I found boys and young men able to read fluently the printed characters in the New Testament, though quite unable to comprehend the sense of what they read …. To one of these young men I expressed my surprise that, though he could *read* so well, he should be so ignorant of what he read. He replied, in a tone of indignation,— whether at what he considered injustice or imposition, I know not,— "Why! they never learned me the *understanding* of the words!"[73]

This same young man was able, however, to unlock the meaning of other texts and 'easily comprehended, assisted by coarse but intelligible engravings, the exciting stories of "The Newgate Calendar *Improved*", and of Dick Turpin and his black mare!'[74]

Among the working classes of the 1840s, 'studious' readers, with a taste for Hume and Smollett or the writings of Paine and Cobbett, were, Thomas Frost claimed, 'as they still are, the minority among readers, and the majority wanted only to be amused'.[75] The relatively well-to-do shopkeepers, artisans, clerks, and factory workers who used the library of the Ashton and Dukinfield Mechanics' Institution preferred the novels of Dickens and Marryat and other forms of light reading; 'abstruse and learned works, requiring close application', the library committee noted, 'lie upon the shelves quite neglected—the members have neither time nor taste to read them.'[76] The favourite reading matter of 'the poorer reading classes' typically did not run to 'works of a high scientific character' or even to *Oliver Twist*, but rather to penny copies, often 'adorned with woodcuts', of 'The Brigand', the dubious 'Memoirs of Lady Hamilton', 'Jack the Giant Killer', or the dialect classic 'Tummus and Meary'.[77] For many of the readers of these tales, the line between fact and fiction blurred or sometimes disappeared altogether. As a young boy Samuel Bamford spent every farthing that came his way on 'Saint George and the Dragon', 'Account of the Lancashire Witches', and other romances and 'implicitly believed them all'.[78]

Unlike Aitken and other like-minded opponents of the supernatural and magic, many of Ashton's working people turned, not to science, but to cunning men and women, astrologers, and fortune tellers and all sorts of 'weird legends and superstitions' to explain the mysterious workings of society and the physical universe. 'Dreams,' noted the *Ashton Reporter*, 'are still read, charms and spells are occasionally resorted to, and signs and omens yet prognosticate lucky and unlucky events to follow.'[79] Belief in 'fairies and boggarts' lived on in the 'vales and nooks' and isolated hamlets of the cotton district. 'Many an old wood,' Edwin Waugh claimed, 'many a retired clough and running stream, many a lonely well and ancient building is still the reputed haunt of some old local sprite or boggart.'[80] People continued to consult 'cunning men and wise women' about lost property (and persons), money matters, and love affairs and to believe, in some cases, 'in the power of certain persons to do ill through peculiar connection with the evil one'.[81] There was also a tendency among many working men and women 'to attribute a wonderful, a sort of super-human influence' and 'sovereign authority' to the role of luck, good and bad, in human affairs.[82]

For all his rationalism and passion for science, Aitken understood the power of these beliefs and admitted that 'giants and ghosts' had haunted his imagination as a child; however, he had little sympathy for those who continued to believe in 'superstition' and divination. 'In these days of literature and of science,' he argued, 'the man who believes it is deceived with his eyes open—is the dupes of knaves, and is to be pitied for his credulity.'[83] For Aitken and other politically committed autodidacts, dispelling the mists of superstition and the irrational was central to their struggle for freedom and democratic reform; 'searching into the depths and mysteries of science', Aitken argued, was an invaluable means of training the mind 'to trace out cause and effect' and exposing political and religious error.[84] 'Science, with its eagle eye,' Aitken confidently asserted, 'is irradiating the world. The errors and superstitions of other days are vanishing before the influence of cause and effect; and mankind generally can never again be led away by the bewilderments of superstition or of priestcraft.'[85] Students of science, like all seekers of 'useful knowledge', were thus participants in the struggle to overturn religious and political oppression and corruption and to bring about social and political change.

At the same time, though, the pursuit of 'useful knowledge' also set apart the plebeian intellectual and radical activist and threatened to strengthen the divisions between the highly politicized and 'studious' autodidact and ordinary men and women.[86] There was, as Robert Roberts noted, a persistent strain of anti-intellectualism in working-class life: '"Put that book down!" a mother would command her child, even in his free time, "and do something useful."' Among many working men, moreover, 'any interest in music, books or the arts' was seen as unmanly and suspect.[87] The depth and extent of this kind of intel-lectual and cultural difference came through clearly during a chance encounter between an 'old man from Yorkshire' and Aitken during his American travels. The one thing that the fellow countrymen had in common was a hearty, mu-tual dislike. 'A more illiterate and vulgar fellow,' Aitken, the proud autodidact, noted, 'it would be impossible to meet. His greatest enjoyment being eating, emptying a whiskey bottle, and talking the essence of vulgarity and brutality.' Between bouts of drinking and fishing, he devoted his spare time to mocking and annoying the high-minded Aitken and his friends and dismissed 'with a grunt of dissatisfaction' their earnest conversations about politics, science, and literature: *'youn to mich sense for me, yo han'*. The old man, Aitken fumed, 'had as much contempt for an intelligent man as an intelligent man had for him, and on that score he was level'.[88]

To a dedicated Chartist, like Aitken, the politics of the Chartist 'multitude' in Ashton and elsewhere in the cotton district also fell short of the ideal of 'a free and enlightened people'; in fact, their political opinions probably bore an un-comfortable resemblance to the vague, pro-Chartist notions that Henry May-hew discovered among London's costermongers in the late 1840s. As a body, these 'street-folk' regarded with deep-seated mistrust the police and 'an aris-tocracy of birth or wealth' and were, in terms of political sympathies, *'nearly all'* Chartists. And yet, although the costermongers regularly attending meet-ings and thought Feargus O'Connor 'a trump', they looked to 'one or two of the[ir] body, more intelligent than the others' for guidance on political matters and lacked a sophisticated grasp of the movement's ideas and goals. 'A Chartist costermonger told me,' Mayhew recalled, 'that he knew numbers of costers who were keen Chartists without understanding anything about the six points.'[89] The illiterate 'T.H.', who wound up in prison in Preston for selling ale without a license, viewed politics from a similar perspective. In a prison interview, he dismissed Whigs and Tories alike as 'gentlemen' and enemies of 'the poor' but spoke favourably of the Chartists: 'men as stands up for their rights, and for sending who they like for parliament-men'.[90] Even worse was the apathy and indifference of many to politics. One mule spinner dismissed with contempt the passion of his work mates for radical reform. 'It had never cost him,' he muttered, 'from first to last, a single thought— for his part he was content, for he thought it would do us no good in the world.'[91]

Once the Chartists left London and the towns and cities of the manufactur-ing districts and ventured into the dark corners of the land, they encountered the ever present problem of 'ignorance' on a much more extensive and daunt-ing scale. The travels of the Chartist missionaries Robert Lowery and Abram Duncan through Cornwall, one of 'the unawakened districts' in 1839, opened their eyes to the true state of things and undermined their belief that the whole country was 'up to the mark'.[92] The working classes there, reported Lowery, 'have never heard of the agitation, and know nothing of Political principles'. Surprised and disturbed by this discovery, his partner dryly observed that the convention 'might have just as well sent missionaries to the South Sea islands, to instruct the natives there in the principles of a free government, as to Cornwall'. There was also, Lowery and Duncan believed, a direct link between 'the ignorance of the people upon general politics' and widespread belief in magic and 'ghosts and apparitions'.[93] Ten years later, Harney believed that very little progress had been made. The truth is, he claimed, with a certain amount of exaggeration, 'that a vast portion of the working men are politically ignorant, or indifferent'. This was the case not merely of agricultural labourers, who had indeed remained for the most part outside of the movement, but also of 'a considerable portion of the town population'. In the end, the two great impediments to the triumph of the democratic cause, Harney concluded, were 'the want of knowledge, and the want of perseverance'.[94]

Even in militant localities, like Ashton and Stalybridge, leaders and activists were well aware that these problems were not unique to 'the unawakened districts'; they too had concerns about the 'ignorance' and apathy of 'the people' and about the presence of many like 'T.H.' in the movement. 'He considered,' declared James Taylor, 'the education of the people a question of great and paramount importance, for if ever the people were instructed as he could wish them to be, they would not suffer oppression and insult as they had done.'[95] Worried about this very issue, John Deegan brought forward at the 1839 convention a motion about appointing missionaries to instruct 'the people'; he argued that the 'ignorance' of thousands of 'the multitude' in effect debarred them from full participation in the Chartist struggle:

> By acceding to his present resolution, the Convention would assist to dispel the vast masses of ignorance which floated over the minds of the multitude, with regard to the means in their hands of obtaining liberty and happiness. (Hear, hear.) Thousands upon thousands of them were not in the knowledge of what their rights consisted in; they knew nothing of the objects of the Chartist principles, and by consequence were debarred from taking any part in the struggle going on to vindicate the rights of labour against the monopoly and aggression of the oppressors of the people. (Hear, hear.) It was their duty to prepare the people by proper instruction for the great change which must soon take place in the institutions of the country.[96]

The drunken violence and destruction that marred the 1841 parliamentary election in Ashton underscored these concerns of Deegan and raised awkward questions about the political progress and Chartist commitment of 'the people'. Setting aside their earlier attachment to the Six Points, hundreds of working men took to the streets in early July in support of either Jonah Harrop, local coal owner and Conservative candidate, or the well-known Liberal and mill owner Charles Hindley. Over the course of two days, the town slipped into chaos, as partisan crowds brawled in the streets, threatened shopkeepers and publicans, and smashed windows. Although Aitken ultimately blamed the election riots on the failure of 'our perfidious government' to provide the working classes with the means of expanding 'their intellectual faculties', he was deeply disturbed about what the riots appeared to reveal about 'the people'. 'Lowering themselves to the condition of brutes,' the drunken railway navvies and factory workers who rioted under Tory or Whig banners committed, to his mind, the worst of all political sins—they helped to prop up the political ascendency of the corrupt 'factions who have brought our nation to bankruptcy and disgrace, and are literally starving to death the industrious classes'.[97]

III

And yet, despite these doubts and misgivings, Aitken and his fellow activists and plebeian intellectuals do not closely resemble the alienated workers of Rancière's account; they never really formed an estranged group of outsiders 'at the frontier of encounters with the bourgeoisie'.[98] The attitude of Aitken and the other leaders toward Ashton's middle classes was at times hostile and antagonistic and at best cool and distant for much of the late 1830s and 1840s. Once, in the early 1840s, there had been an attempt by the Anti-Corn Law League to enlist Chartist support; but, as one anti-corn law activist put it, their leaders 'could make nothing of' the Chartists.[99] Nor did the mill town of Ashton offer leaders and activists many opportunities to make a living either from the 'trade of agitation' or from the republic of letters. Over the course of his public life, Aitken supplemented the income from his day school with odd jobs as an accountant, delegate and lecturer, and writer for local newspapers and friendly society publications; however, he was apparently unable to support his family on these occasional earnings from politics or journalism.[100]

For the most part, then, members of the Ashton leadership did not find Chartist politics a ready means of entry into the world of middle-class culture and politics; nor did they show any real inclination to pursue this possibility. In this way, they also differed from the alienated worker-intellectuals who figure so prominently in Rancière's work. Most of the local leaders and activists came from and maintained close social and economic ties to 'the people' and chose to identify themselves with 'their fellow working men'; this was true even of those who had no direct connection to the world of manual labour.[101] Well-liked among people from all walks of life for his outgoing and 'free and generous nature', Aitken avoided, however, the social and political circles of Ashton's middle classes and 'Mr. Hindley's friends'.[102] Among his friends and associates, were old work mates from his days as a spinner, neighbours and former students, fellow labour and radical activists, and friendly society members. The students at his flourishing day school came almost entirely from the 'operative' classes; in the early 1840s, he lived in a working-class section of town, with an Irish pig dealer and a family of card room hands as his next-door neighbours.[103]

Many members of Ashton's 'shopocracy' relied almost exclusively, like Aitken, on the working classes for their livelihoods and felt almost immediately the ill effects of any reverse in the cotton trade. In his study of the family economy of the working classes in Manchester and Dukinfield, William Neild noted the close connection between the small tradesman and his working-class customers:

> It is a very common, if not the general, practice for the working classes of this district to select a particular shopkeeper with whom they deal for all their provisions, and to whom they are generally in debt, and when a time of suffering comes, arising from reduced wages, want of employment, dear food, or the combination of all three, as is the case at present, they become more and more involved with the shopkeeper. This class of persons (the shopkeepers) are generally the first to feel reverses in manufacturing districts; and in all instances of considerable depression in trade numbers of them are ruined.[104]

There were also personal and family ties to the factories among many of the lower middle-class members of the Ashton leadership. Forced to leave the spinning room, because of either the blacklist or old age, a number of ex-mule spinners became publicans, street sellers, small tradesmen, or grocers and tea dealers; one well-known member of this group was James Duke, who ran the Bush Inn, an important meeting place for the Chartists in the late 1830s. In Ashton and environs, it was also a common practice for the sons and daughters of small masters and shopkeepers to work in the spinning mill or weaving shed.[105]

Although this cadre of radical activists and plebeian intellectuals typically lived and laboured side by side with 'the people', they were at the same time very different as well. The irony of their situation was that the very qualities that made them ideal leaders of a working-class movement, like Chartism, also set them apart from the majority of working men and women; their fluency as speakers and writers, together with a studious (or even artistic) turn of mind and boundless energy and enthusiasm, were at once marks of distinction and signs of difference (and even of strangeness and peculiarity).[106] To portray them simply as 'organic intellectuals' is to overlook the ways in which these kinds of intellectual and cultural differences complicated the relationship between leaders and followers; they had, as Bamford put it, 'thoughts, and ways, and views of [their] own' and were often of two minds about 'the people'.[107] An 1842 address of the South Lancashire delegate meeting voiced these ambivalent feelings in an unusually straightforward manner. On the one hand, this group of leaders and activists looked, with hope, to 'a united people' to vanquish the enemies of liberty and to overturn 'class-constituted tyranny'; on the other hand, they knew only too well 'the disunion of the working classes' and acknowledged that many of 'the people' were apathetic and 'ignorant of true politics'.[108] This perspective came through, in an indirect way, in 'The Captive's Dream', a poem that Aitken wrote in prison.[109] Under the influence of 'bright reason', 'working-men' joined together 'throughout the earth's extensive ball' to debate their rights and to take action against injustice. United and determined, they 'slew the monster tyranny' and ushered in a new age; the poem concluded:

> Equality her banner wav'd,
> And from destruction Britain sav'd;
> Despotic laws were known no more,
> And freedom rang from shore to shore.
>
> And rich and poor in union join'd,
> And all their energies combin'd,
> That freedom's star might brightly beam,—
> I 'woke, alas! 'twas but a dream.

But what was the dream? Was it the union of the rich and the poor, or was it a united and rational working class?

At the heart of Chartist attempts to create a seperate and distinct political identity was this ambivalence on the part of leaders and activists; however, they did not have a monopoly on these sentiments. Just as leaders and activists viewed 'the multitude' with hope as well as concern, so 'the people' were of two minds about the leadership. The Chartist rank and file certainly acknowledged and appreciated the sacrifices and contributions of national and local leaders, but they never regarded themselves simply as passive followers and had no intention of turning control over the movement to a professional leadership of 'paid missionaries' or 'jobbing' politicians.[110] These tensions came through clearly in the distinctive reform programme of the movement and in one of its founding texts, the Crown and Anchor petition. Presented to a meeting of 'four thousand democrats, at least' in early 1837, this petition called on parliament to bring about 'a thorough reform' by enacting 'A Law for Equally Representing the People of Great Britain and Ireland'; the proposed reform programme consisted of six points. Its emphasis on universal suffrage for 'every person' of twenty-one years of age asserted the civic and political equality of all people, certainly of adult males (and perhaps of women as well). After stressing this 'universal political right of every human being', the Crown and Anchor petitioners took the argument to the next step; they went on to demand payment for members as a way of breaking the monopoly of the landed and middle classes and opening up parliament to working men of proven ability and talent. The insistence on annual parliaments was, however, an attempt to limit the autonomy and independence of all MPs and to make them more responsive to the wishes and concerns of their constituents.[111] The nature and practice of Chartist democracy, with its emphasis on popular participation and strict accountability for all leaders, embodied these tensions and sought to prevent, above all, the rise of 'dictators' and over-powerful leaders. 'We have,' boasted a group of Manchester Chartists, 'no rich men leading or driving us but, in the true democratic spirit manage our own affairs. We will have no such dictators holding over us the threat of disunion if we rebel against their particular crotchets and mandates.'[112]

The stresses and strains in the relationship between leaders and followers also shaped another crucial part of Chartist political identity; this was the identification of the movement with the working classes and the cause of labour. Deeply suspicious of the middle classes and the 'over-grown and all-devouring capitalists', the leadership in Ashton and other militant localities were at the same time torn between their belief in the potential of 'a united people' and their concerns about the apathy and 'the disunion of the working classes'.[113] What tempered their criticism of working men and women was their awareness of how the daily vicissitudes of working-class life contributed to and intensified these problems. For all but a fortunate few among the working classes, life was always difficult and uncertain; living on the edge of poverty, the labouring poor, Thomas Frost recalled, tended to focus on the immediate problems of the here and now—'how to get the next meal, to replace some worn-out garment, or to pay the rent'.[114] The hard and precarious nature of their daily lives drained away the time and energy available for politics and discouraged any easy optimism about the ability of the Six Points (or any other plan of reform) to bring about a real improvement in their situation. Perhaps a pint of ale or a cup of tea, mused one lecturer, 'would do them more good than any amount' of Chartist speeches.[115] In the end, though, the harsh realities of everyday life in mill towns, like Ashton and Stalybridge, fostered not so much an acceptance of the status quo as a recognition of the difficulty of changing things. On a wet evening in Rochdale in the early 1840s, George Holyoake experienced himself the 'damp' and depressing weight of life in a 'manufacturing town'. That night he was to deliver a lecture on cooperation in a 'small Dutch-looking meeting-house':

> It was one of those damp, drizzling days … when a manufacturing town looks like a penal settlement. I sat watching the drizzling rain and hurried mists in the fields as the audience assembled—which was a small one. They came in one by one from the mills, looking as damp and disconsolate as their prospects. I see their dull hopeless-looking faces now. There were a few with a bustling sort of confidence, as if it would dissolve if they sat still—who moved from bench to bench to say something which did not seem very inspiring to those who heard it.[116]

Right before he began, as he looked out on his audience, Holyoake too was overcome, for a moment, by a sense of weariness and the hopelessness of it all.

Over the years, the experience of defeat, together with the melting away of the Chartist 'masses', re-enforced these longstanding concerns among the plebeian intellectuals and activists of the movement and undermined their faith in the mass platform. 'I cannot count,' claimed one Chartist true believer, 'the thousands, or say millions, who made noises at monster meetings. Indeed they were never counted. Why should they have been? They were no part of our party. This is what we *were*.'[117] Discouraged by the collapse of the 1848 campaign, the veteran Chartist James Taylor shared this growing sense of disillusionment with the mass politics of the platform. Looking back over the history of 'the democratic cause' during his lifetime, he singled out the 'indiscriminate admission of members' as one of the most serious problems for the movement:

> They were in times of excitement too eager to admit members regardless of their character or condition; this was the cause why Ashton had brought disgrace on the cause; one of the men who was to give evidence against the Chartists in the Lancashire trials, was the very man who was the most anxious to force them into a physical outbreak. He had watched the democratic cause from the Blanketeering movement, the Peterloo massacre, and Reform agitation, until the present time, and was certain that this indiscriminate admission of members was a primary cause of their previous and present misfortunes.[118]

In many ways, this concern about the policy of admitting 'members regardless of their character or condition' was nothing new. From the 1790s on, there had been a constant tension in democratic politics between an optimistic belief in the mass politics of 'members unlimited' and deep-seated suspicions about the dangers of relying on the 'superficial strength' of 'numbers only'.[119]

Chapter V

Liberalization versus Radicalization:
Some Causes and Consequences of the Decline of Chartism,
1848-1860

> TIM. Why every fool knows what chartism means. Ask the very idiot that is pass-
> ing down the street, and even he will tell you that chartism means doing away with
> government, and bringing about a general scramble for property. A very pretty
> state of things we should have then: let me rather remain as I am.
> TRUE. You are perfectly right in attributing such notions to fools and idiots, for I
> imagine that men with a moderate share of wisdom know better. Pray, Mr. Tim-
> orous, did the classes you have named supply you with your stock of political
> knowledge?
> TIM. You are an impudent fellow! Is this the way in which you treat respectable
> people?[1]

In this piece of Chartist propaganda from the 1850s, the anonymous author used a dialogue between 'impudent' John Trueman (working man) and 're-spectable' Samuel Timorous (shopkeeper) to revisit some familiar issues and to introduce some new ones. Over the course of their conversation, Trueman tried to answer honestly Timorous's concerns about the 'un-English' nature of some of the Six Points and to correct his misconceptions about the movement. At times, though, the warm and aggrieved tone of Trueman's replies suggested that his opponent had touched on a sensitive subject. On several occasions, he vig-ourously disagreed with Timorous' characterization of 'the people' as immoral and ignorant. The time and space that Trueman devoted to a discussion of the Chartist programme suggested, however, that many members of 'the people' still viewed the movement with indifference or at least were unfamiliar with its most basic principles; in fact, over half of his conversation with Timorous took the form of a detailed explanation of the Six Points.[2]

Determined to avoid any 'half measures of reform', Truemen concluded his discussion of Chartist democracy with a firm and unequivocal rejection of any thought of compromise:

You cannot take away from it a single point out of the six, without depriving it of one of its fair and necessary proportions. Take away universal suffrage, you destroy its groundwork; clip it of the ballot, you leave the voter unprotected; leave out equal electoral districts, you fail to secure the just balance of power between constituencies; retain the property qualification, and although by giving the vote you have given the people the power of choosing, you compel them to choose from the ranks of their oppressors; neglect to pay members for their services, and you make it almost impossible for any but the rich to be members; and without annual parliaments, you weaken the member's responsibility.[3]

In making this strongly-worded defence of the policy of 'the whole charter, and nothing less than the charter', Trueman alluded to one of the ongoing controveries of the movement—the divisive question of a cross class reform alliance and the strategy of securing democratic reform in 'instalments'; the different social backgrounds of the two disputants, and their sometimes acrimonious exchanges, were also indirect references to this long-running debate.[4] A little later, Trueman boldly engaged a second and more recent controversy; this was the question of 'the people's social rights'. Of these, 'the first great measure', he argued, was 'the nationalization of lands, mines, and fisheries.' On this crucial subject, 'social rights', the Chartist consensus about the core beliefs of the movement, a consensus that had survived for almost a decade and a half, finally collapsed. 'There are,' Trueman admitted, 'differences of opinion, and I can, therefore, only state the views which appear to me to be the most correct.'[5]

After 1848 the steady growth of these 'differences of opinion' about principles and strategy led to the decline and breakup of the movement. 'He felt certain,' James Leach sadly noted about Chartism, 'that the democratic principle was steadily progressing, although they, as a party, were all but extinct.'[6] In the years that followed, Chartists and their critics engaged in a series of debates over the causes of this extinction; later generations of historians have attributed the breakup of the movement to a variety of causes ranging from the onset of economic prosperity and the creation of a labour aristocracy to the ideological weaknesses of the movement to the process of liberalization.[7] While the mid-Victorian boom, technological change, and shifts and changes in the attitude of the propertied classes and the state toward the movement all made a contribution to Chartism's decline, the true significance of these developments stemmed from the ways in which they interacted with one another. Just as the coming together of Chartism in the late 1830s grew out of a convergence of crises in the economy, the labour process, and the political world, the decline of the movement grew out of the easing of these crises and the ways in which these changes contributed to and intensified divisions within the movement over strategy, ideology, and goals.

From the mid-1840s onward, the easing of these overlapping crises progressively undermined the very foundations of Chartist political identity. Just as they had collectively re-enforced the intertwining of social, economic and political grievances in the late 1830s, the passing of these crises presented a very real challenge to the Chartist emphasis on democratic reform as the only way of dealing with 'class legislation' and of improving the social and economic condition of 'the people'. In the late 1830s, trade depression and struggles on the factory floor between labour and capital over technological change and the organization of work converged with the 'class legislation' of the Whig governments to produce an insurgent mass movement for the democratic reform of the state and society. The expansion of the cotton industry, together with a very modest increase in wages between 1848 and 1860 and the failure of the self-actor and the powerloom to fulfill the dire prophecies of the late 1830s and early 1840s, eased class tensions and broadened the scope for negotiation and bargaining between the mill owners and their workers. Over the course of the 1840s, the governments of Sir Robert Peel and Lord John Russell in turn retreated from the controversial legislative initiatives of the previous decade and even passed the Mines Act of 1842 and the Ten Hours Act in 1847. This circumspect (and even accommodative) tone of the Tory and Whig governments forced leaders and the rank and file to question their assumptions about the 'tyrannical' state and its alliance with 'the manufacturing and commercial interests' against the working classes.[8]

After 1842 the passing of this unique set of circumstances, together with the experience of defeat, deepened doubts within the movement about some of the defining features of Chartist political identity. The 1839 and 1842 campaigns underscored, above all, Chartism's dilemma as a class movement. With few allies or supporters outside of the working classes, 'the people' stood alone against a daunting set of obstacles. 'There is no example,' Thomas Clark pointedly observed, 'of the political constitution of a country having been reformed by the efforts of a section of one class, against the inclinations of two more powerful and influential classes.'[9] By evoking memories of 1839 and 1842, the failure of the third and final campaign also contributed to the Chartists' growing disenchantment with the mass platform and democratic reform as the only solution to 'class legislation'. Over the last ten years, the Chartists, Leach observed with an obvious sense of weariness, 'had expended money in forming processions, painting flags with "The Charter, and no surrender, and more pigs and less parsons!" They had collected money to defend their leaders, and all to no purpose, and he now wished them to stay agitation and do something for their own practical good.'[10] In the early 1850s, the move of George Julian Harney and Ernest Jones toward the adoption of a social democratic programme, 'The Charter and Something More', sought to revive the mass politics of the platform and to reassert the class nature of Chartism. They also tried to save democratic reform from, as John Belchem has put it, 'the weary and disheartened drift to liberalism'; but instead, their advocacy of 'The Charter and Something More' only generated further divisions over the nature of Chartist political identity.[11] There was, *pace* Margot Finn, no *démoc-soc* consensus within the post-1848 movement; as John Trueman noted, 'differences of opinion' were deep-rooted and often bitter and antagonistic.[12] Discouraged by these divisions over ideology and strategy and by infighting among the national leadership, plebeian intellectuals and activists in Ashton and other localities turned away from the mass platform and the physical-force strategy; instead, they organized democratic dinners and lectures and schools and libraries and took up a wide range of radical and labour causes as a way of putting their democratic beliefs into action and improving the social and political prospects of 'the people'.

Just as the defeats of 1839 and 1842 forced the plebeian intellectuals and activists of the movement to re-examine and re-evaluate the foundations of Chartist political identity, the insurrectionary spirit of the working-class challenge during these years raised fears about 'social dissolution' and led the state and the landed and middle classes to adopt a more accommodative stance toward the working classes. 'The progress of Chartism,' claimed John Stuart Mill in 1842, 'is … creating an impression that rulers are bound both in duty & in prudence to take more charge, than they have lately been wont to do, of the interests both temporal and spiritual of the poor.'[13] The events of August 1842 also left Disraeli with a sense of foreboding and unease about the future. 'No stirring news,' Disraeli reported, 'from the disturbed districts. They say things are lulling, wh: eventually of course they must, but what has happen'd is a lesson & a warning of what may come or what we must avert.'[14]

Although the attempts of the state and the local elites to meet some of the demands of the working-class challenge never amounted to the thoroughgoing (and unified) counteroffensive of John Foster's account, these efforts of government and the propertied classes after 1842 nevertheless represented a crucial shift in the tone and nature of class relations and politics.[15] Historians have noted the effects of liberalization on working men and women, but, with a few recent exceptions, they have too often said little about the impact of Chartism and 'the democratic principle' on middle-class politics and attitudes.[16] In towns like Ashton-under-Lyne, where the movement had exerted a powerful influence on the hearts and minds of working men and women, Chartism left, however, an indelible imprint on the two-party system and in fact redefined and radicalized the political culture in which the mass parties of the age of Gladstone and Disraeli grew and matured. Pointing to the latent strength of the movement, the *Reporter*, the official voice of Ashton Liberalism, emphasized in 1856 the importance of providing 'skillful guidance' and trying to meet the legitimate grievances of the Chartist 'party':

> They may sing foolish songs abounding in bad rhymes, and make foolish speeches abounding in bad grammar, —they may do very unwise things, and show lit-tle tact in the managment of their party; but the inert strength of that party is prodigious, and under skillful guidance would be terrible; and it would be more patriotic, as well as more manly, to remove the alarm by liberal concessions than to conceal it under an affected grin of derision.[17]

By demonstrating their willingness to make 'liberal concessions' to working-class demands, Ashton's middle classes after 1848 increased the centrifugal pull of divisions within the movement and further re-enforced the breakup and de-mise of Chartism as a coherent political identity.

I

Speaking before a mass meeting in the Ashton marketplace in early 1842, the mill owner Hugh Mason called on his fellow middle-class reformers to assist 'the working classes to obtain the People's Charter' and assured the crowd of working men and women: 'Our interests are identical. We all sail in the same boat; and we must sink or swim together.'[18] Although the sincerity of Mason's attachment to the Six Points was somewhat suspect, he clearly had high hopes about the possibility of winning over the Chartists to the cause of Corn Law repeal. What ultimately doomed such attempts to bridge the class divide in the late 1830s and early 1840s was the political and social context in which these overtures took place. The militant, independent working-class politics of Chart-ism grew out of a convergence of crises in the late 1830s in politics, the economy, and the work place. The intertwining of political, social, and economic griev-ances against the backdrop of these overlapping crises shaped Chartist political identity and re-enforced the logic of its analysis of the situation of 'the people'. The easing of these crises in turn undermined the movement's sense of identity and mission and its ability to mobilize mass support for democratic reform.

  At the centre of the crises was the 'tyrannical' state of the 1830s. Focusing on the relationship between Chartist ideology and the changing character of the state between 1832 and 1848, Stedman Jones has seen the disintegration of Chartism as 'a coherent political language and a believable political vision' as the key to the movement's decline during the years after 1842. By passing the

Mines Act and the Ten Hours Act and by repealing the Corn Laws, the administrations of Peel and Russell dealt a fatal blow to the Chartist analysis of the connection between the monopoly on political power and 'class legislation' and undermined, in Stedman Jones' words, 'the conviction and self-certainty of the language of Chartism'. Above all, the factory acts, Anna Clark has argued, 'took the wind out Chartist sails'.[19] Relations between the state and the Chartists in the 1840s were more far complex, however, than these two accounts suggest. Although the Tory and Whig governments passed several acts which sought to accommodate working-class grievances, they continued to sponsor unpopular pieces of 'class legislation', like the 1844 Master and Servant Bill, and even managed to undermine the Ten Hours Act, one of the few genuine reforms of the decade. Well into the 1850s, the Ten Hour day remained an elusive goal, especially in the Ashton and Stalybridge area, where from the very beginning almost all of the mill owners, even Charles Hindley's firm, used a system of shifts and relays to evade the restrictions on hours. During the late 1840s and early 1850s, the Ashton and Stalybridge spinners and weavers organized a series of strikes and walk outs over the issue of the relay system but met with few successes.[20] Deeply disillusioned by the working of the Ten Hours Act, the veteran Chartist and trade unionist Richard Marsden claimed that the 1847 Act was nothing more than 'an act under which the millowners would force them to work any number of hours they liked'.[21]

And yet, despite these continued problems, the political crisis of the late 1830s had clearly eased. Looking back over the reforms of the past twenty years, James Kay Shuttleworth emphasized in 1854 that parliament and the middle classes had learned their duties to the working classes and had tried to remove 'every legitimate cause of discontent':

> Our legislation has of late taught the great mass of our countrymen to rely with confidence on the *parliament* of this country. We have rendered the electoral and municipal franchise more accessible. We have freed trade from its shackles; cheapened almost all the necessaries of life; .... Above all we have protected the operative in the factory and the mine against excessive labour, and the neglect of sanitary precautions. We have given considerable impulse to sanitary reform, and we have laid the foundations of a system of national education. We have reaped the fruits of wisdom in the defeat of *chartism*.[22]

Although he regarded 'the defeat of *chartism*' as a crucial development, Kay Shuttleworth knew, however, that the conflicts and bitter class animosities of the 1830s and early 1840s had not suddenly disappeared. When he delivered this speech in January 1854, during the third month of the great 'ten per cent and no surrender' strike at Preston, he used the occasion in fact to warn his audience about the dangers of 'socialism' and the 'tyranny' of trade unions. While he harbored no illusions about the continued strains and tensions within the first industrial society, Kay Shuttleworth clearly overestimated the very limited nature of the concessions by the state and the middle classes. On the crucial question of the suffrage, he spoke in terms of a 'more accessible' franchise and carefully avoided any mention of the Six Points or democracy. And yet, even though the list of reforms which Kay Shuttleworth proudly pointed to were not fully realized in 1854, his roll call of the reforms of the 1840s and early 1850s gave an indication of the agenda of the middle-class reformers and demonstrated how the worst case scenario of the late 1830s had failed to materialize. The alliance between the state and capital against the working classes had not taken place; nor did the actions of the middle classes in the 1840s fulfill the worst expectations of the Chartists.

In a similar fashion, the onset of the mid-Victorian boom in the economy did eventually improve the situation of working classes but did not translate into dramatic gains for working men and women. While the expansion of the cotton industry, especially the weaving sector, certainly demonstrated the restabilization of the economy after the crisis years of 1839-42 and perhaps helped to create a sense of optimism and hope about the future, the immediate effect of the mid-Victorian boom on wages and living standards was negligible. Between the mid-1840s and the early 1860s, the production of yarn and cotton goods almost doubled, and over the course of the 1850s, the productive capacity of the spinning and weaving sector of the industry grew respectively around 31 per cent and 38 per cent (see Tables 8 and 9). This expansion of production and the productive capacity of the industry, however, was not accompanied by a like increase in earnings. The situation in Ashton was similar to that of many of the mill towns of the 1850s. Although weekly wages in the cotton industry rose on average around 10 to 15 per cent between 1849 and 1859, these very modest increases mainly occurred during the boom years of the late 1850s, and in some cases, like that of the hand mule spinners, merely raised weekly earnings to their 1839 level (see Table 10). At the 1857 court leet dinner John Ross Coulthart emphasized this point in his report on the state of the cotton industry in Ashton. Over the past twelve months, the parish had been the site of a wave of factory and warehouse building; mill workers found full-time work with ease but received only, as Coulthart put it, the 'ordinary rate of renumeration'.[23] This was, as Kirk and Gray have pointed out, the key to the very limited improvement in the standard of living during most of the 1850s—more secure and regular employment, not a dramatic increase in wages.[24]

In the late 1840s and 1850s, the easing of tensions between labour and capital in the work place was also shot through with contradictions and ambiguities. Even though the introduction of new technologies increased divisions within the working classes along the lines of skill and gender, the slow, gradual introduction of the self-acting mule and powerloom had not fulfilled by the 1850s the dire predictions of the 1830s and early 1840s. Because of the continued importance of skill on both the hand and self-acting mules, the adult male spinner and the spinner/piecer system survived the introduction of the self-actor and double decking. Over the course of the 1840s, the age, gender, and ethnic composition of Ashton's spinners in fact changed very little, although their wages stagnated or declined; however, the introduction of new technology clearly drove a wedge between Ashton's spinners and minders and led to the creation of separate trade societies for hand mule spinners and self-acting minders.[25] The limited impact of these technologies, together with the gradual establishment of local wage lists, began during the 1850s to reduce the intensity (and desperation) of the work place struggles in the spinning room. The creation of the standard lists contributed to this development by institutionalizing the principle of dividing between masters and men 'all advantages arising from improved machinery'.[26]

Even in the weaving sheds, where a cluster of technical innovations in the 1840s supposedly rendered the powerloom almost 'perfectly automatic', the worst fears about the effects of technological change on wages, skill, and the gender division of labour had failed to materialize by the 1850s. By decreasing the amount of downtime for repairs and adjustments and by improving the quality of the cloth, the technical innovations of the 1840s allowed the weaver to manage as many as four to six looms and at the same time increased earnings. Because the almost 'perfectly automatic' loom still had not eliminated all of its technical problems or the need for 'skill and diligence', the four loom weaver earned in the late 1850s an average weekly wage of 18s, or only a few shillings less than the hand mule spinners.[27] Although women and adolescents made up the bulk of the workforce in the weaving shed, adult males were still able to find work as powerloom weavers and monopolized the high paying jobs of dresser and overlooker. From the 1840s onward, the increasingly important position of the adult male overlookers as supervisors and recruiters of labour also helped to ease concerns about the relative scarcity of married men in the weaving shed.[28]

In the late 1840s and 1850s, the technologies of the spinning room and the weaving shed were thus in a state of flux. The decision of John Mayall to install both kinds of mules, sometimes in the same spinning rooms, in his new coarse spinning mill at Mossley symbolized this state of flux and demonstrated the slow, gradual nature of the industry's transition from the hand mule to the self-actor; the struggles over the introduction of new technology and the organization of work were ongoing struggles in the 1850s, not settled issues.[29] At the same time, the spinners and their employers also began to work out informally the ways in which new technologies would effect piece rates and the organization of work. By demonstrating the possibility of negotiating the differences between masters and men and thus the importance of strengthening the organization of the trade, these first halting steps toward the creation of a formal system for bargaining and negotiation contributed to the withdrawal of the spinners and powerloom weavers from the political struggle; democratic reform was no longer, as the powerloom weavers put it in 1842, 'imperatively necessary for the protection of wages'.[30] By the mid-1840s Richard Pilling directed attention away from the People's Charter and instead urged Ashton's spinners and weavers to concentrate on trade unionism, 'the only means' of ensuring a respectable wage, and the weapon of the strike.[31] From this point on, the call to do 1842 again came up only rarely during strikes in the Ashton and Stalybridge area. In the minds of many working men and women, the main lesson of 1842 was the 'complete folly' of the events of that summer.[32]

II

In the late 1840s, there was, however, a momentary reversal of these long-term trends in the work place and politics. A downturn in the economy and political developments on the national and international scenes temporarily recreated, in a somewhat different and milder form, the crisis situation of the earlier period and led to the intertwining of 'bread-and-cheese' questions with the demand for democratic reform.[33] By late 1847, the cotton industry had slipped into a slump that was almost as serious as the depression of the early 1840s. Unemployment and short-time were on the increase; output was down. Only in the second half of 1848 did this situation begin to improve. 'Hungry in a land of plenty,' Bezer recalled, 'I began seriously for the first time in my life to enquire WHY, WHY— a dangerous question.'[34] The onset of this slump in the economy triggered these sort of thoughts among unemployed artisans, like Bezer, and factory workers; it also converged with a general election in Britain and renewed attempts to create a 'CHARTIST BENCH' in the House of Commons.[35] Soon after the mass meeting at Newton to congratulate Feargus O'Connor on his victory at Nottingham, Ashton and Stalybridge delegates joined with the representatives from other mill towns to raise the call for another national petition and a London convention to coincide with the opening of the new parliament.[36] From February 1848 on, the dramatic (if short-lived) victories on the continent of 'the brave French' and others intersected and re-enforced this renewal of interest in democratic reform and stirred up memories of 1789 and the emergence of 'the people' as a new and potent force in politics. If an armed and determined 'people' stood together 'as one man' and were to rise up as 'in France, Prussia, and Italy', then the triumph of Chartist principles, it seemed, was inevitable.[37]

What also contributed to the revival of Chartism in 1848 was the tolerant attitude (and sometimes the open support) of the local authorities. In the recently incorporated towns of the manufacturing districts, like Halifax and Bradford, where the middle-class Liberals who dominated the new municipal governments were eager to preserve and to build upon the emerging rapprochement between middle-class radicalism and Chartism, the Liberal elites gave their support to the demand for the Six Points and even tacitly permitted the selling of pikes and drilling.[38] In early 1848 Ashton's middle-class reformers also took a tolerant view of the revival of the mass platform and in fact encouraged and even supported the movement. A legacy of their alliance with the leaders of Ashton Chartism during the incorporation struggle in the mid-1840s, the middle-class reformers' support for the Six Points, of course, was highly qualified and disappeared as soon as the movement began to discuss ulterior measures and the use of physical force. Although their sympathetic stance toward the Chartists quickly changed, their initial support contributed to the revival of the campaign for the People's Charter in Ashton and raised, once again, the fleeting possibility of an alliance between the middle-class Liberals and the Chartists. During March and early April, the local authorities allowed the Chartists to hold several meetings at Town Hall; on one such occasion, when the Chartists organized a meeting of the 'middle class and the shopkeepers', the town councillor John Grundy took the chair.[39] Along with many of the town's shopkeepers and small tradesmen, a number of the aldermen and town councillors signed the petition, and Robert Wild, Ashton's delegate to the convention, went so far as to claim, 'Only one middle class man had refused to sign the petition when asked'.[40]

Although an alliance with the middle-class reformers, once again, failed to materialize, the Ashton and Stalybridge Chartists succeeded in forging a union with the Irish Confederates in early 1848. Most members of the local leadership sympathized with the plight of the suffering Irish and the cause of Irish nationalism; over the course of the last two years, they had closely followed events in famine-stricken Ireland and had repeatedly called on the government and the people of England to help relieve the suffering of the Irish.[41] The 'fraternisation' of the Irish and the Chartists at the mass meetings at Free Trade Hall on St. Patrick's day and at Oldham Edge informally 'sanctified', as Treanor put it, the 'marriage' between the two causes.[42] At Oldham Edge the men and women who attended the demonstration pledged themselves to support their Irish brethren in repealing the act of union, and Michael Doheny, one of the deputation, in turn endorsed the Six Points:

This present time, when thrones were crumbling and despots were being flung away, was the time for Irish freedom and English Chartism.—(Applause.) He was accredited to say, on behalf of the Irish people, "The Charter, the whole Charter, and nothing but the Charter"; and he asked them in return for "Ireland, all Ireland, and nothing but Ireland, for the Irish."[43]

By this point, the mass platform agitation was already underway in the cotton district. While the Ashton and Stalybridge Chartists concentrated on the collection of signatures for the national petition and the mobilization of mass support through public meetings and debates, they also broached during the weeks leading up to Kennington Common the always dangerous questions of ulterior measures and the people's right to arm. It was, William Aitken told a meeting at Town Hall, 'high time to overturn the present system, and all ought to rise in arms against it'.[44] Speaking before the convention on the state of mind in the Ashton area, Robert Wild reported that the people thought it was too early for a 'collision with the authorities'; but, he added: 'They were tired of petitioning, and resolved that if London did its duty, Lancashire would not be behind.'[45]

As the day of the Kennington Common demonstration approached, the Ashton Chartists, like their counterparts throughout the towns and villages of Lancashire and Cheshire, looked to London with great anticipation. 'There appears to be,' the mayor of Manchester worriedly observed, 'an undefined expectation that some general disturbance is to take place early next week after the presentation of the Petition for the People's Charter.'[46] On Monday 10 April, amid rumours in Ashton about a general strike for the Charter, an Oldham crowd set out for Manchester. Years later William Chadwick recalled what had awaited the crowd in Manchester that morning:

> Thousands of miners were expected to come in the morning to Manchester. When I rose in the morning I found cannon planted all about, and the military parading with drawn swords. I knew that these thousands of men were marching in from Oldham, Royton, and Shaw, and I at once ran "for my life" by Oldham-road, and reached a place called Droylsden Lane. Here I met thousands of men marching in, armed with pikes and other implements of warfare.[47]

Forewarned by Chadwick about the situation in Manchester, the crowd turned back and returned home. Over the course of the day, a group of about thirty or forty trade delegates who had recently passed resolutions in favour of the Six Points and repeal reconvened at the Railway Inn, Deansgate, and mass meetings took place at Ashton, Hyde, Bolton, Bury, Rochdale, and Manchester; however, April 10 passed without further incident.[48]

In the cotton district and West Riding, the Chartists quickly overcame their initial disappointment over the setback at Kennington Common and the hostile reception of the national petition at parliament and increasingly turned their attention to the question of ulterior measures. Deeply concerned about divisions within the national leadership over strategy and about the always present threat of government repression, leaders and activists discussed the possibility of what Pilling called 'a general cessation from labour' and raised the issue of defensive arming. Pointing to the revolutionary events in France, they emphasized the limitations of relying upon 'moral force' alone and reminded the people of their right to bear arms.[49] At Middleton the Droylsden man Isaac Dawson angered several of the other speakers by his blunt words on the necessity of arming:

> It was quite necessary for the people to possess themselves of arms, because government kept them down by force; it was necessary to possess themselves of arms to gain their liberties. France would never have had a republic had she not had a military people …. The aristocracy was kept up by an armed force, and therefore the people also must arm for the defence of their lives and properties. As soon as the millowner proposed a reduction of wages, certain of the workmen, more degraded than the rest, were willing to work at lower prices, and when these were attempted to be turned out, an armed force was called out to put down those who would make the others turn out; if the people were armed, would that be done?—(Three or four voices cried "No.")[50]

On the same day, the south Lancashire delegates also met at Middleton and urged all Chartists to organize themselves into National Guards; but, unlike Dawson, they portrayed this move as a defensive measure and justified it by stressing 'the present state of insecurity in the country'.[51] Well before the delegates issued this call, by early May in fact, the Ashton Chartists, like the Chartists of Aberdeen and Nottingham, had already begun to enroll members into what they referred to at first as a 'Protection of Life and Property Society' and later as the National Guard.[52] 'We have,' reported an Ashton constable, 'what is called a National Guard formed in this town, numbering from 300 to 400 persons, all of whom are very young men—they meet about three times a week in the Chartist room in Bentinck St, they are arming themselves with pikes, pistols, and some few with rifle pieces.'[53]

On 23 July, just as Russell's government was in the process of rushing a bill for the suspension of habeas corpus in Ireland through the houses of parliament, William Smith O'Brien, who was then on a speaking tour of the southern counties of Ireland, yielded to the urging of his fellow Confederates and agreed to make an attempt to raise the countryside; about a week later, the abortive insurrection came to an ignominious end in Widow McCormack's cabbage patch.[54] Although the imminent suspension of habeas corpus precipitated the Irish rising, it was not a spontaneous act of defiance. Shortly after the trial and conviction of John Mitchel in late May, a secret committee of the leaders of the Irish Confederates started to make plans for a rising sometime after the harvest. Apart from seeking arms and money from aboard, the leaders of the conspiracy also encouraged club members to take part in training and drilling and tried to enlist the Confederate clubs in England as a fifth column.[55] Meanwhile, by mid-July, an Ulterior Committee of Chartists and Confederates had begun to meet several times a week in London to organize and coordinate plans for an insurrection and to maintain communications with fellow conspirators in Manchester, Liverpool, and the Midlands. On 5 August, in response to a request from Manchester, the committee dispatched William Lacey to visit the cotton district, where he was to act as the committee's representative.[56] Over the course of about a week, from around 9 to 14 August, delegates from Manchester and surrounding towns, London, Liverpool, Birmingham, and other places attended a series of secret meetings in Manchester and discussed plans for a general rising. On 12 August William Lacey reported to the Ulterior Committee that the Manchester area was to rise on Monday next, 14 August. 'The object was,' John Latimer later claimed, 'to be a general strike & to get the Charter by rising.'[57]

On Monday afternoon, 14 August, soon after the close of the delegate meeting at Manchester, James Milligan hurried back to Ashton and told the leaders of the National Guard that tonight was the night for 'the outbreak' to take place.[58] Armed with pikes and a few firearms, the men of the National Guard assembled around midnight at the appointed places and then headed off to secure the town and to prepare for the march on Manchester. While passing through Ashton, members of one of the companies caught sight of constable James Bright and broke ranks to chase him down. In the ensuing uproar, a shot rang out, and Bright fell to the ground. Still determined to meet the Stalybridge men at the rendezvous point, the men resumed their march toward Whitelands; when they arrived there and saw no sign of the Stalybridge men, the company broke up, and the men started to hurry home or, in some cases, to look for a safe hiding place. Thrown into a state of confusion by the shooting of Bright and the swift response of the local bench to the rising, the other companies of the National Guard soon followed suit.[59] Meanwhile, several miles south-east of Ashton, a small crowd from Hyde marched from mill to mill, letting off the water in the boilers and pulling the plugs. Filled with a sense of grim defiance, the leader of the Hyde turn outs told one of the constables: 'They are out now over England, Ireland, and Scotland; and before this time to-morrow, will either make it better or worse, for we may as well turn out and be killed, as stop at home and be starved to death.'[60] Across the Pennines a small band of men from Bagley, at the urging of an Ashton delegate, set out that night for Hurst Brook; at Bradford hundreds of Chartists with pikes in their hands anxiously awaited news of the insurrection at Manchester.[61] But, with the exceptions of Ashton, Hyde, and Oldham, none of the mill towns of the cotton district heeded the call for a general rising. That night the Manchester Chartists and Confederates gathered 'in much greater numbers than usual at their respective clubs' in anticipation of the arrival of crowds from the outlying towns and held a vigil in their rooms until about 4 a.m., when they lost heart and quietly dispersed.[62]

Just as the collapse of the insurrectionary side of the movement in August evoked memories of similar failures in 1839 and 1842, the final campaign for the People's Charter also focused attention on the limitations of the constitutional side of the mass platform agitation. In the end, despite the endless round of mass meetings and the collection of over two million signatures, the 1848 campaign collapsed amid controversy over the national petition and the 'fiasco' at Kennington Common and charges in the middle-class press about how the Chartists were mere tools of 'the Irish conspiracy'.[63] This 'Irish-phobia' was particularly fierce in the Manchester area; there newspapers rarely missed an opportunity to highlight the association between Chartism and those 'apostles of sedition' and mischievous and destructive 'monkeys'— the Irish.[64] The *Manchester Examiner* repeatedly gave sensational and at times hysterical warnings about the Irish danger: 'The MOONEYS, and ROONEYS, and the LOONEYS, who start up here and there, now as Chartists, and now as Confederates, are blackening the faces of their countrymen, and endeavouring to sink them in the scale of humanity.'[65] By drawing parallels between the Chartists and Thuggery, the Parisian clubs, and the 'blackness' of 'Tailor Cuffay and Co.', the *Examiner* and like-minded papers provided the finishing touch to their portrait of Chartism as something alien, foreign, and definitely unEnglish.[66]

Although the Chartists vigourously disagreed with this caricature of the 1848 campaign and their alliance with the Confederates, many of its leaders and activists viewed the strategy and some of the core beliefs of the movement with a growing sense of disenchantment. 'No repetition, nor modification, of the old methods of Chartist agitation, or action,' charged the *English Republic,* 'can avail us anything. They may be tried for thirty generations, and they will not change the Government or regenerate the People.'[67] After 1848 Chartist true believers also took an increasingly sceptical view of the ability of 'the people' to bring about immediate social and political change. The recent uprising in Ashton, James Taylor argued, was a direct consequence of the policy of admitting 'members regardless of their character or condition'; in fact, Taylor and other veteran members of the Ashton leadership rarely joined the National Guard and generally were careful to avoid any direct involvement in the insurrectionary plotting of that summer. The majority of those who joined the National Guard were new converts to the democratic cause, for the most part, young men in their teens and twenties.[68] The events of August 1848 also made a lasting impression on the youthful members of the Ashton Mutual Improvement Society. The commitment of this small group of autodidacts and plebeian intellectuals to radical politics and cooperation never wavered, but they came to see the 1848 campaign as one more example of 'the folly and uselessness' of the physical-force strategy and Chartist reliance on numbers alone. These lessons of 1848, J.K. claimed, 'lingered in the minds of the working classes of Ashton'.[69] In an editorial, the *Ashton Chronicle* also underscored the dangers of 'misreckoned and ill-directed risings' and called on men of all classes to work together to effect 'an honourable reconciliation' of their differences. 'Until a reconiliation be effected,' the paper warned, 'there will be strife and deadly warfare. If reconcilation be not effected, there will be universal ruin.'[70]

While these criticisms of the movement and its strategy were present in 1839 and 1842, they grew in frequency and intensity after the third and final campaign for the People's Charter. This loss of faith in the policy of 'members unlimited' shaped Chartist politics after 1848 and pointed to a crucial shift of emphasis, one that set in motion the breakup of Chartist political identity.[71] Too often, Christopher Shackleton charged, the thousands who attended Chartist meetings typically gave 'no assistance beyond shouting at the said gatherings'. The optimistic belief in the power of 'the people', he added, underestimated 'the anti-democratic habits, prejudices, and indifference of a vast number of the population'; any plan of Chartist organization required, above all, an effective system for 'the better dissemination of our principles'.[72] From this point on, plebeian intellectuals and activists in Ashton and other localities chose to distance themselves from the class confrontation and insurrectionary spirit of the platform; in doing so, they in effect stripped the movement of two of its defining features, the mass platform and its identification with the working classes, and opened up the possibility of a middle-class alliance. The retirement of O'Connor from politics, together with the collapse of the Land Company, deprived the movement of two crucial sources of unity and continuity with the radical past. In the early 1850s, Jones and Harney made a valiant effort to overcome these problems and to halt the slow ideological slide toward Liberalism; however, their attempt to attach a social democratic programme to the Six Points failed to revive the movement and in fact accelerated the breakup of Chartism. Discouraged by these setbacks and by the fading of hopes of winning political power, some of the Ashton leadership emigrated or dropped out of public life; others turned their attention to alternative means of ameliorating the social and economic condition of the working classes, such as cooperation and friendly societies, and retreated from the platform into the quietist world of lectures, education, and self-help.

Over the course of the 1840s, the vigorous leadership of O'Connor and the popularity of the Land Plan had helped to preserve the unity of the movement and to hold in check these concerns about the platform and its vision of 'a united people'. But, after 1848, O'Connor's growing incapacity and the collapse of the Land Company deprived Chartism of these sources of unity and hastened the breakup of the movement. Worn down by the long years of agitation and bad health, O'Connor withdrew from an active role in movement in August 1851 and soon afterwards sold the *Northern Star*. Within a year, his erratic public behaviour, his 'repeated signs of derangement', as Gammage put it, led to his commitment to Dr. Harrington Tuke's asylum at Chiswick, where he remained until his death in August 1855.[73] And yet, despite the signs of his decline and the controversy over his role in the failure of the Land Company, the Ashton Chartists stood by O'Connor in the early 1850s. 'However some of you may have differed from the policy he has sometimes pursued,' the Chartists and Land members of Ashton declared, 'all must admit that his untiring zeal, his indomitable perseverance, and almost Herculean labours, are such as few men either can or would go through, to carry out the principles of government best suited to ... the social advancement of the working classes of this great country.'[74] William Aitken, like many Chartists, blamed O'Connor's decline on the hostility of the middle-class press and the government toward the Company and fervently defended his 'noble aim' of resettling the people upon the land; in the summer of 1850, the members of the Ashton branch reluctantly came to realize, however, that O'Connor's vision was doomed. Discouraged by the legal and financial problems of the Company and the 'disorganised state' of many of it branches, they called on O'Connor and the directors to decide upon 'the best course to be pursued with regard to the winding up of the Company'. By this point, even after the endless legal setbacks and disappointments, the Ashton branch still had two hundred paid up members.[75]

Just as the loss of national leaders, like O'Connor, contributed to Chartism's decline, the steady thinning out of leaders and activists on the town and village level also weakened the movement over the course of the 1840s and 1850s. The wear and tear of years of activism, together with the cumulative effects of these setbacks and disappointments, eventually took their toll and caused many leaders to drop out of Chartist politics or to leave the country, sometimes one step ahead of the authorities. In the aftermath of the 1842 general strike, Alexander 'Sandy' Challenger fled to the United States and eventually settled in Fall River, Massachusetts, a mill town with a substantial community of Ashton immigrants.[76] Apart from the seven Ashton Chartists who were transported for their participation in the August uprising, Richard Pilling, Bernard Treanor, and Samuel Sigley also left the country in 1848, probably because of their involvement in (or knowledge of) the insurrectionary plotting of that summer.[77] George Johnson and John Wilde, two of William Aitken's old friends and fellow activists, emigrated sometime after 1848 and settled in the United States.[78] The decision of these leaders to leave the movement represented a serious loss of human capital for their locality and weakened the personal and political ties of 'democratic friendship' that joined the locality to the national movement.[79] While Harney, who later spent sixteen years in America, lamented the loss of 'the best and bravest of the working men', he understood the sense of despair that led many veteran Chartists to seek a new life in the United States or Australia. 'At times,' he sadly noted, 'we lose heart in our struggle, though we never lose faith in our principles, nor in their ultimate triumph, only it may be so long first; meanwhile, Hope has grown grey by the watch-fire, and wearies of her long watching. And what wonder that we at times lose heart and are driven to echo the cry "Let's Emigrate".'[80]

By placing an ambitious social democratic programme, 'The Charter and Something More', at the centre of the ongoing debate over strategy and goals, Jones and Harney tried to counter this sense of weariness and disillusionment and to redefine Chartist political identity; their efforts to redirect the movement toward socialism, however, encountered serious opposition within the movement and ultimately contributed to the decline and fragmentation of Chartism.[81] O'Connor vigourously opposed any attempt to mix up the Six Points with 'Communism or Socialism' and warned that those who styled themselves as 'Chartists and SOMETHING MORE' threatened to stir up dissension within the movement and only created new enemies for the Chartists.[82] Many of the rank and file shared O'Connor's misgivings, and this was true even in Manchester and environs, the industrial heartland of Chartism. It was a mistake, James Williams argued, to attach other causes, even worthy and proper ones, to the Charter; democratic reform was the necessary first step.[83] 'The movement in Manchester,' added George Mantle in 1851, 'was not a Red Republican movement. Social economics were a subject of great debate.'[84] Displaying a nationalistic disdain for 'the Parisian school of philosophers' and a very real concern about the centralizing impulse of the social democratic programme, several of the leaders of Manchester Chartism criticized efforts to attach 'Social Rights' to the People's Charter:

> Attempts have recently been made to attach a kind of mongrel Socialism to Chartism; this notion has been borrowed from the Parisian school of philosophers; in England we are content that government should mind its own business; what we

desire is, that we should be allowed to mind ours, interrupted as little as possible by the officiousness of centralised power.[85]

In their view, the introduction of 'the great stumbling block, "Communism"' into Chartist politics represented a direct break with the past policies of de-centralizing political power and drawing a clear distinction between Chartism and socialism; they also tended, like many Chartists, to associate an active and interventionist central government with the Whig 'tyranny' and 'class legisla-tion' of the 1830s.[86]

What heightened the controversy over 'The Charter and Something More' was the way in which it converged with the renewed debate over an alliance with the middle-class reformers. With the launching of the 'Little Charter' move-ment and the Parliamentary and Financial Reform Association in the late 1840s, middle-class radicals once again made a bid for Chartist support. Keenly aware of the continued strength of the landed interest and the narrow social base for their reform programme, Sir Joshua Walmsley, John Bright, Edward Miall, and other advanced middle-class radicals increasingly thought in terms of a cross class reform alliance and saw the working classes, as Walmsley put it, as 'their best auxiliaries in obtaining just and impartial laws, and in carrying and maintaining those measures upon which the lasting prosperity of both would depend'.[87] Although he remained hostile to an alliance with 'the money-lord employers' and continued to think in terms of an alliance between the working classes and the 'shopocracy', O'Connor overcame his initial suspicions about the Parliamentary and Financial Reform Association and gave the organization his support in 1849 and 1850; impressed by the sincerity of its leaders, whom he described as men who held 'veritable democratic and Chartist principles', he advocated, in the columns of the *Northern Star* and from the hustings, a union with the middle classes on the basis of the People's Charter. But, concerned by their unwillingness to adopt the entire Six Points and by evidence that their true object 'was to extinguish Chartism altogether', O'Connor eventually broke with the Parliamentary and Financial reformers in late 1850 and warned that the goal of the organization was to make the Chartists 'puppets in the hands of the middle classes'.[88]

Unlike O'Connor, the leaders of the social democratic wing of the move-ment, especially Harney and Jones, steadfastly opposed in the late 1840s and early 1850s both 'the moderate sham-reform movement' and any compromise on the Six Points and criticized Chartists who favoured a cross class reform alli-ance as 'decoy ducks of the middle classes'.[89] These divisions within the national leadership reflected, in many ways, the bitterness and vigour of the debates on this question among the leaders and activists of the localities, and nowhere was the debate more fierce than in Manchester. Edward Hooson and others roundly condemned attempts in Manchester to ally the Chartists with 'the humbug promulgated by a certain class of politicians', but other well-known leaders, like James Leach, were willing to agitate for 'lesser measures of reform' and to work with the Parliamentary and Financial reformers. Convinced that working men by themselves lacked the means to win the Charter, these leaders of Manchester Chartism regarded the working-class character of the movement as a weakness and looked to the middle classes as their allies:

> The hostility which has been excited between the Chartists and the middle classes has tended most materially to damage our interests as a party; because the middle classes are the persons, along with ourselves, most interested in just and equitable government, and because without the liberal and direct aid of a large section of that body, it is utterly hopeless to effect any extension of political power.[90]

Discouraged by the bitter infighting over 'The Charter and Something More' and the question of an alliance with middle-class reformers, plebeian intellectuals and activists in Ashton and other localities chose to distance themselves from the national movement and the mass politics of the platform; instead, they channelled their time and efforts into lecture series, discussion classes, libraries, and democratic dinners. They in effect abandoned the mass politics of the platform for the commemorative toast and the schoolroom. During the 1850s, 'a few choice spirits' continued to organize democratic dinners to celebrate the people's history and to keep alive radical values and memories. Important moments in their commemorative calendar were the birthdays of Paine and Hunt and the Peterloo massacre. On these occasions, friends of 'the people' reminded their audiences of the sacrifices and accomplishments of local heroes, like the dialect poet and radical Robert Walker, and 'all the illustrous dead of every nation, who by their acts or deeds, have contributed to the cause of liberty'.[91] They told stories about the persecution of local 'Jacobins' at the hands of 'church and king' loyalists and participated in dramatic readings of selections from Paine's *Age of Reason* and Emmet's speech; participants at these 'democratic dinners' also sang songs, like Bamford's Peterloo hymn and 'Ye wealth producers', and offered toasts to O'Connor and the People's Charter and to 'the people, the only true source of power'.[92] In the Ashton and Stalybridge area, two of the last Chartist public meetings were essentially commemorative events. Their purpose was to recognize and honour the lives and sacrifices of two prominent champions of 'the people': the recently departed Feargus O'Connor and the recently returned John Frost.[93] On the day of the public oration to honour O'Connor, the organizers clearly used the decorations at the Foresters' Hall, Stalybridge to position him within the history of 'the people'; the reporter for the *People's Paper* vividly described their handiwork:

All along the front of the gallery, was stretched a piece of deep mourning, in the centre of which was inscribed, "Do justice to his memory". On the right side, on entering the hall, the full-length portraits of the "Welch victims," Frost, Williams, and Jones; on the left, the full-length portrait of our departed friend; while over the rostrum was stretched another piece of deep mourning, with the words inscribed in the centre, "He lived and died for us". And from the dome of the hall, was hung an oil-painting, describing the horrid butchery of Peterloo, in 1819.[94]

'Devoted as ever to the cause of Chartism', many of the faithful in Ashton and Stalybridge also looked to education as a way of keeping alive the memories and principles of the movement. By the early 1850s, though, educating 'the people' was no longer primarily a complement to the mass platform; lectures, discussion classes, and book funds increasingly replaced the platform as the primary (and indeed the only) form of Chartist activity. In the opinion of many leaders and activists, education came to represent 'the best way to advance the cause of democracy'.[95] Of the educational initiatives of the 1850s, the most important (and long-lived) was the Chartist Institute in Stalybridge. Its goals were, according to William Hill, to provide Chartists there with a sense of purpose and engagement and to educate the next generation of democratic leaders and activists.[96] By the standards of the day, the Chartist Institute was a modest success story for the local movement. In Stalybridge, unlike the situation in neighbouring mill towns, the locality continued to hold quarterly elections and had dues-paying members, mainly 'steadfast, highly principled workingmen', throughout most of the decade; the situation of the Institute also improved steadily.[97] In the mid-1850s it sponsored Chartist discussion classes and tea parties and boasted a school of 'forty and upwards' that met on Tuesday and Thursday evenings and on Sunday; its library had acquired a stock of several hundred titles for the education of young democrats. 'Works which libraries established by the upper and middle classes of society,' Hill proudly claimed, 'would scorn to have enclosed in their cased doors.'[98]

By this point, many of the leaders and activists of the movement had begun to channel their energies into an ever-growing number of democratic and labour causes and campaigns; in doing so they tried at once to put into action Chartist values and aspirations and to link self improvement to the mental (as well as to the social and political) emancipation of 'the people'. In the 1850s and early 1860s, several members of the Chartist leadership, like Thomas Storer and John Williamson, were active in founding and leading the Ashton Secularist

Society.[99] Led by 'radicals of a very extreme kind', this organization drew its support mainly from 'intelligent' working men; it sought to free 'the people' from priestcraft and superstition and to 'promote all principles calculated to improve the physical, moral, and social condition of mankind, and likewise to aid in obtaining all useful and beneficial reforms'.[100] Some secularists, like Stalybridge's J. Bilcliffe, viewed with approval the emergence in the late 1850s of cooperative societies in the Ashton and Stalybridge area and embraced cooperation as a way of redeeming and emancipating the working classes.[101] By 1860 the almost 500 members of the Stalybridge society supported a drapery, butcher's shop and a store that stocked all of 'those articles of consumption which are daily required in the home of the working man'; it also intended to open in the near future a free library and reading room.[102] In terms of governance and organization, these new societies were thoroughly democratic and placed 'all men on the same level in respect to controul over management, eligibility for office, and equally-divided profits'.[103] For William Patten and other true believers, cooperation was not simply 'a pounds, shillings, and pence question'. Cooperation, he argued, had the potential to secure 'greater social reforms' and ultimately 'to procure those political reforms which were so much wanted amongst the working classes'.[104] Much less enthusiastic about the potential of cooperation, Aitken worked in the early 1850s with the trades in their campaign against evasions of the Ten Hours Act; he also devoted himself to promoting friendly societies and to creating the Odd Fellows Hall. For Aitken, friendly societies were the embodiment of Chartist ideas about democratic participation and volunteerism. In their lodges, he noted about the Odd Fellows, 'all were upon an equal footing, breathing the air of freedom, and standing upon the rock of equality'.[105]

Drawing on these ideas and the long-standing Chartist emphasis on the importance of pursuing 'local power', leaders and activists also poured considerable time and energy into Ashton politics. 'Chartists,' Richard Pilling argued in 1844, 'would do well to take part in all local affairs, and prove their power by putting their friends in office.'[106] During the incorporation campaign of 1846-47, Pilling and his fellow Chartists allied themselves with Ashton's middle-class reformers and tried to turn these words into actions. Apart from providing the Chartists with an opportunity to 'prove their power', the incorporation campaign gave them a chance to put their democratic beliefs to work in the political world of their own community and to reform the town's 'wretched government'. By incorporating their town, they hoped to block the introduction of the rural police, a long-standing goal, and to create what Aitken optimistically described as a responsible, honest form of government, 'chosen by a free and enlightened people'.[107] Afterwards, on all public occasions, during election campaigns and at ward meetings, Thomas Storer and Richard Pilling quizzed elected officials and candidates about vote by the ballot and the abolition of property qualifications and urged the necessity of frequent meetings between the representative and 'the people'; above all, they never lost an opportunity to criticize 'the shady side of the town hall' and to press for a more democratic system, one that included the working man 'who got his living by the sweat of his brow'.[108]

In pursuing these worthy (and impeccably radical) goals, Pilling and his fellow Chartists unfortunately realized the worst fears of O'Connor and Jones about diverting Chartist energies into 'endless separate-movements' and contributed to the decline of Chartism as a coherent political identity.[109] From the mid-1840s on, their pursuit of self improvement and education, together with their support for trade unionism and the Land Company, undermined belief in democratic reform and the mass platform as the only means of improving the condition of 'the people'. In a similar fashion, cooperation also challenged this core belief. 'He wished to impress upon them,' one cooperator told an Ashton meeting, 'that if they wished to advance their social condition they must do it themselves. They must not rest upon any government to improve their social condition; they must neither believe in Whigs, Tories, nor Radicals.'[110] This determination to exclude politics, Peter Gurney has argued, was the 'truly innovative' aspect of cooperation after 1844 in Rochdale and the other mill towns of the cotton district.[111] Cooperation, like secularism, appealed, moreover, in the 1850s primarily to socialist-leaning and freethinking minorities within the working classes and carried with them many negative associations—communism, republicanism, and atheism. As O'Connor had always warned, these associations created a host of enemies and stirred up antagonisms toward the democratic cause.[112] In a more subtle way, the involvement of Pilling and others in local politics also posed certain problems for Chartist political identity. The pursuit of 'local power' encouraged after 1848 the withdrawal into their 'own domestic circles' at the expense of national organizations and campaigns.[113] It also led them back into the world of middle-class politics.

III

Although the breakup and demise of Chartism as a coherent political identity ultimately grew out of its own internal problems, middle-class attempts to bridge the gulf between classes and to accommodate some of the demands of the Chartists contributed to and hastened the fragmentation of the movement. Liberalization was not, however, simply a response to the working-class challenge; it was also an extension of ongoing stuggles over 'political and religious differences' within the middle classes.[114] In the 1840s, cotton spinners and manufacturers together formed the most significant and cohesive group within the ranks of Ashton's wealthy middle classes; however, their religious loyalties were split between the Established Church and Dissent. These religious differenc-es in turn translated into political differences and ultimately divided Ashton's 'steamocracy' into two roughly defined rival groups—'Liberal' Dissenters and Tory Anglicans; in fact, in the hard fought 1841 election, the mill owners split their vote almost evenly between Jonah Harrop and Charles Hindley.[115] After 1848 these 'political and religious differences' gave a partisan edge to the liberal-izing impulse there and in other towns of the cotton district. Over the course of the next ten years, members of the Ashton middle classes clashed on occasion with one another in their efforts to bring church and chapel into the lives of working men and women and to promote education and rational leisure. Along with these religious and educational initiatives, a group of wealthy Ashton mill owners took the first steps toward the creation of a social and cultural system of employer paternalism. Middle-class politicians, Liberal and Tory alike, in turn competed with one another to address working-class grievances and to integrate members of the Chartist leadership in Ashton into the emerging party system.

And yet, despite the existence of these 'political and religious differences', liberalization in the cotton district nevertheless reflected common fears of the middle classes about 'social dissolution' and the mill owners' acute sense of their isolated position in Victorian society and politics.[116] Memories of the 1840s stayed with W.E. Forster and others of his generation and convinced them of the necessity of addressing the just and 'reasonable' demands of the working classes. 'Unless some political concessions be made to these masses,' he warned, 'and unless all classes strive earnestly to keep them better fed, first or last there will be a convulsion; but I believe the best political method of preventing it is by the middle-class sympathizing with the operatives, and giving themselves power to oppose their unjust claims by helping them in those which are reasonable.'[117] At the same time, these concerns of Forster and other mill owners also drew upon their awareness of the continued strength of the landed classes and their own inability, in the words of Thomas Thomasson, 'to rescue the government out of the hands of a band of titled aristocrats'. In its present state, parliament was, he added, 'little better than "an organized conspiracy" for the benefit of the few against the rights, the interests, the prosperity, and the comforts of the great masses of this industrious community'.[118] In full agreement with this view of things, John Bright went a step further and emphasized the need to find allies to weaken the power of the 'privileged class' at Westminster. 'At this moment,' he told a sympathetic audience at Free Trade Hall, 'parliament is so balanced, that it can neither get backward nor forward. (Laughter.) We are numerous enough to prevent anything very bad from being done; but the other party are numerous enough to prevent anything very good from being done.'[119]

In Ashton and other militant Chartist towns, liberalization also represented an attempt by the Tories and Liberals to come to terms with the growing electoral strength of the working classes. In Ashton working men and women made up over 75 per cent of the population, and the bitter class tone and insurrectionary spirit of Chartism had vividly demonstrated the potential dangers of an independent working-class movement, especially in towns like Ashton, 'the worst policed town within fifty miles of Manchester'.[120] During the 1840s and 1850s, the Ashton working classes had also emerged as an influential force in parliamentary and municipal politics. Between the 1832 Reform Act and the advent of the American Civil War, the number of parliamentary electors who belonged to the working classes grew from around 7 to about 50 per cent of the electorate.[121] By the early 1850s, after the adoption of the Small Tenements Rating Act increased the number of burgesses from around eighteen hundred to about twenty-six hundred, working-class voters probably made up the majority (or at least a near majority) of those who were listed on the burgess roll. The ability of working men and women to sway the vote of the shopkeepers, another large voting bloc, through exclusive dealing further enhanced the political position of the working classes.[122] Because of this growing electoral power of the working classes and the depth and extent of their 'feeling in favour of universal suffrage', the integration of the working-class challenge into the framework of politics and society in Ashton and other mill towns was not a simple case of the embourgeoisement or incorporation of working-class leaders, but rather it was a two-way process, one which transformed and radicalized party politics.[123]

Deeply concerned about the widening cultural and social gulf between 'the two great classes of society', the Ashton middle classes made a determined effort from the mid-1840s onward to bridge this gulf and attempted to do so through a series of religious and cultural initiatives which sought to bring the working classes into the world of the chapel and church and to promote 'sound' education and rational leisure.[124] Of central importance to these efforts was their related concern about the apathy of the working classes toward organized religion. 'If people of this description go to church or chapel,' John Layhe observed about working men and women in Manchester, 'it is rather from a regard to outward appearances and traditional rules, than a sense of spiritual wants. For the most part, however, they are not in the habit of frequenting the house of prayer, but reserve themselves for such events as the baptism of a child, the marriage of a friend, or the death of a relative.'[125] The situation in Ashton was much the same. In the mid-1830s, one-third of the heads of working-class families in Ashton claimed that they belonged to no religious denomination; in Stalybridge and Dukinfield, 35 and 40 per cent respectively of the heads of families made the same claim.[126] Fifteen years later the religious census revealed that on 30 March

1851 only about 25 per cent of Ashton's population attended a worship service, and the majority of those who stayed away were working men and women (see Table 12). Disturbed by this lack of interest on the part of 'the working population' of cities and large towns, Horace Mann came to the unsettling conclusion that most labourers and small shopkeepers were by nature '*unconscious Secularists*'.[127] The presence of so many '*unconscious Secularists*' (as well as a fair number of ardent freethinkers) among the working classes took on an air of menace during these troubled years. 'All this is sorrowful,' noted a prominent Independent minister in 1848. 'It is, moreover, dangerous. It must work to disastrous issues, if not soon remedied. The continent of Europe multiples on us its examples and warnings.'[128]

Determined to counter this tendency, the Independents in Ashton had always taken a keen interest in reaching out to working men and women. Although the first generation of leaders at the chapel included a number of mill owners and small employers, mule spinners, weavers, and journeymen artisans made up the bulk of Ashton's Independents during the 1820s and 1830s (see Table 13). In the 1850s and 1860s, this was still the case at Albion chapel. 'The Church was composed,' noted its minister, 'mainly of working people, but there was a considerable element of their employers, and a still larger infusion of what may be regarded as the middle class.'[129] During these decades, the Albion congregation established Sunday schools and preaching places throughout the neighbouring villages and hamlets and opened in 1849 a new chapel in Ryecroft, on the west end of town, near where the Buckleys and Masons had established communities for their workers. With the arrival of Rev. James Guinness Rogers in 1851 as the new pastor, the Independents redoubled their efforts to reach out to the working classes through lectures and adult education classes and carefully included working men in 'the councils' of the church.[130] 'While there were two or three magistrates of the highest standing amongst the deacons,' Rogers claimed, 'no one secured more attention in our delibrations than those who were working men, and who were treated by all their colleagues as Christian gentlemen.'[131]

Over the course of the 1840s, the Established Church, strengthened and reinvigorated by recent reforms, launched an ambitious wave of church building in Ashton parish and took on an aggressively populist tone. During that decade, new places of worship opened at Bardsley, Audenshaw, Ashton, and Hurst; between 1841 and 1857, the Anglicans in turn increased the number of their Sunday School scholars from 2400 to 3100 and opened several day schools and a Church Institute for the instruction of young men.[132] The new generation of Evangelical clergymen, like Rev. Williams and Rev. Eager, made a very real attempt to portray the Church of England as 'the labouring man's temple' and even on occasion self-consciously adopted the symbolic wooden clogs and unrolled sleeves; they also championed what one of their number called 'the pure, Protestant, evangelical character of the Church, against the unfaithful representations of some few teachers within her pale, who were disturbing her peace by Romish innovations'.[133] By the time of the 1851 religious census, the Church of England had re-emerged as a powerful force in the religious life of the parish (see Table 12). Although Dissenters as a whole still outnumbered Anglicans, the Church represented by far the largest single faith in Ashton, and in addition to a growing number of working-class followers, the Established Church had the support of the local Anglican elite, a wealthy, influential group that included mill owners, coal magnates, and the lord of the manor.[134]

Just as the presence of so many 'unconscious Secularists' troubled Ashton's middle classes, the high illiteracy rate among working men and women and the almost complete absence of any elementary education facilities were likewise sources of concern; the lack of 'sound education', Leonard Horner pointed out, left working men highly susceptible to the 'specious reasoning' of demagogues who skillfully appealed to 'their passions and prejudices'.[135] In a similar fashion, Rev. Aspland saw education as a valuable means of 'civilizing' the inhabitants of mill towns, like Ashton, and of dealing with crime and social disorder.[136] While the chapels and churches of the parish tried to address this danger and in fact helped to sponsor several public day schools during the mid-1840s, Ashton's Dissenters and Anglicans repeatedly clashed over the issue of non-sectarian education and consequently concentrated the bulk of their energies and talents toward expanding and improving their Sunday Schools. These efforts clearly met with some successes; by the late 1850s almost 80 per cent of all English children in the town attended some Sunday School, where they received basic instruction in reading and writing.[137] The first step in innoculating children of the working classes against dangerous ideas and in inculcating 'honesty and sobriety', Sunday Schools were also seen as an invaluable way of bringing the different classes into social contact. In the Manchester area, these schools, more than any other institution, Angus Reach argued, 'tend to bind different classes of society together. Men in the middle ranks of life very commonly act as teachers, or at all events take a practical interest in the proceedings'. This was certainly the case of Albion chapel, in Ashton; to a considerable extent, the Sunday School teachers there, Rogers observed with pride, came from 'the families of high social standing in the congregation'.[138]

Along with these efforts to bring working men and women into the chapel and church and to provide their children with a 'sound', if meager, education, Ashton's middle classes, especially the mill owners, displayed a decided hostility toward several of the old rural sports which had retained a largely working-class following, like cock fighting and the Stalybridge races; they also tried to domesticate the rowdy Ashton and Stalybridge wakes and to denude the popular custom of Riding the Black Lad of its overt class tone.[139] Of these popular forms of leisure, they singled out for special attention the Easter Monday festivities. On that day, a group of low and 'disorderly' men placed an effigy of the Black Knight, or Black Lad, on a horse or 'sorry nag'; then, they paraded through the streets of Ashton, with frequent stops at public houses, where his thirsty attendants extorted drink from the publicans. 'When the journey is finished,' recounted one contemporary observer about the peregrinations of the Black Knight, 'it is tied to the market cross, and the shooting is continued till it is set on fire, and falls to the ground. The populace then commence tearing the effigy in pieces, trampling it in mud and water, and throwing it in every direction.'[140] The *Ashton Reporter* recalled in 1866 how in past decades men of 'the very lowest order' had used this centuries-old custom to hold the town 'in undisputed possession':

> From morning till night on Easter Mondays, the most disorderly rabble that could be raked together from any place out of perdition held the town in undisputed possession .... Dirty rags, dragged through the gutters and dipped in every conceivable abomination, were flung in all directions. Broad cloth and rich satins were especially attractive of these filthy rags. Drunkness, riot, and lawlessness were characteristic on Easter Mondays.[141]

From the mid-1840s onward, 'a party of gentlemen' tried to restrain this kind of 'disgraceful' excess and to remake the Easter Monday procession as a 'respectable local attraction'. After some false starts, they managed to put an end to the practice of shooting and then burning the effigy of the Black Lad at journey's end; initially, they were less successful in limiting the heavy drinking of his retainers.[142] By the 1860s, the Easter Monday festivities had clearly undergone, however, a fairly dramatic change. Much more respectable and commercial in nature, Riding the Black Lad was now a holiday for all to enjoy. 'All classes,' observed the antiquarian W.E.A. Axon, 'are so well represented, and such is the conglomeration of individuals, that we should hardly have been surprised to see a bishop, in shovel hat and gaiters, rubbing shoulders with the vendor of Chelsea buns.'[143]

Along with their participation in these religious and cultural initiatives, several of the wealthy mill owning families of Ashton and Stalybridge also tried to bridge the class divide through the development of a system of factory paternalism. Although isolated examples of employer paternalism occurred during the 1830s and 1840s, examples grew more and more common during the next decade, especially during the boom years of the late 1850s. Dinners and 'treats' for overlookers and skilled workers, free excursions to the seashore and to the country estate of the master, philanthropic support for infirmaries and Sunday Schools, and even the public observance of the rites of passage in the life cycle of the employer's family began to become standard practices in the large firms of Ashton and Stalybridge during the 1850s.[144] By this point, the Buckleys, the Kershaws, and the Masons had already erected their model factory communities on the edge of town, where Reach discovered 'every mill surrounded with neat streets of perfectly uniform dwellings, clean and cheerful in appearance, and occupied by "the hands"'.[145] Impressed by the sound construction and comfort of the cottages in these model factory communities, he noted that the building of these communities also enabled the mill owner to exert control over the lives of the workpeople outside of the factory gate:

> The first of these snug little colonies to which we went was that attached to the mills of Messrs. Buckley. Here are ranged in rows and squares, some of them with gardens attached, a little town of dwellings, regularly planned…. The Messrs. Buckley, I am informed, live among their people, and are in the habit of familiar intercourse with them—facts which operate as very great checks upon drunkenness, and all sorts of disorderly behaviour.[146]

These first steps toward the creation of what Patrick Joyce has called 'the new paternalism' allowed the Ashton spinners and manufacturers to soften the image of the 'haughty' and 'grinding' capitalist and gave meaning and substance to their often-repeated claims about the mutual interests of labour and capital.[147] To a certain extent, some of the workers accepted this claim. At a dinner for the operatives at the Buckley's Carr Hill mill, one of the speakers made this very point. 'Masters and men,' he declared, 'were in one boat, and the welfare of the one was identical with the other; and therefore if masters prospered, the workmen must prosper also.'[148] The Chartist and trade unionist John Teer likewise wrote a poem, 'Lines, To Commemorate the Convivial Party, Given by J. and G. Tysoe, Esqs., to Their Workpeople, at Victoria Mill, Salford, on Saturday, July 18th 1857', in honour of one such convivial occasion when the 'jealous line' of class distinctions was erased; Teer proclaimed in another poem, 'We Envy Not Our Master's Wealth', the unity of interests between masters and men.[149] Praising Robert Platt of Stalybridge for his generosity toward his workers, the *Ashton Reporter* also raised these points and went on to portray to Platt as an example of the new kind of employer, the employer who saw his wealth as 'a sacred trust':

> Maintaining as we do that the interests of employer and the employed are identical, and that on all points connected with their mutual relations the dictates of

pure benevolence and sound policy are perfectly harmonius, it is particularly grat-
ifying to find employers going beyond the hard relations of trade and approaching
their working hands with substantial tokens of good will and sympathy…. He is
one of that—we trust—increasing class which views wealth as a sacred trust and
influential position as chiefly valuable from its opportunities for doing good.[150]

One member of this 'increasing class' was John Whittaker, devout Methodist
and a wealthy mill owner at Hurst. He saw all men as 'one and the same' in the
family of Christ and emphasized his duties and responsibilities as a Christian
employer. 'He was,' Whittaker told members of the Mossley Mechanics' Institution, 'one of those who were of the opinion that those who possessed property,
either by their own labour or their predecessors, had certain duties to perform
towards the great mass of their fellow creatures, and he had no doubt that what
was now being done in recognition of this principle, would greatly contrast with
what was done 20 or 30 years ago'.[151]

At the heart of the symbolism and rhetoric surrounding the emerging system
of factory paternalism was a vision of gender relations that associated femininity
with the home and masculinity with the work place. What was significant about
this view of the working-class family was that a number of powerful and influential mill owners now openly accepted, in theory at least, the male breadwinner ideal. Turning away from the orthodox political economy of the 1830s, they
dropped their opposition to the Ten Hour day as well as their insistence on the
necessity of female and child labour in the cotton industry.[152] One prominent
local example of this trend was Hugh Mason, whose attitudes on these issues
underwent a fairly dramatic shift. As a boy he had worked long hours for his
father's cotton spinning firm. The young Mason consequently grew up a firm
believer in the gospel of work and had little sympathy for the short time movement or its efforts to make the domestic ideal a reality for working-class women
and children. But, by the early 1860s, his views on the matter had changed. At an
entertainment for his workers at the recently opened reading and lecture rooms,
Mason proudly reported that a survey of fifty cottages in his Oxford Mills community revealed only six cases of wives working in the factory. 'He believed,'
Mason told the gathering, 'that the place of the mother was at home among
her little ones—(hear, hear), and nothing pleased him more than working men
keeping their wives at home to attend to family duties.—(Cheers.)'[153]

And yet, despite these efforts to create the image of the mill owner as a be-
nevolent, public minded steward of wealth, many working men and women
remained sceptical. Although the *Reporter* praised John Whittaker as a model
employer who 'has honourably distinguished himself by the interest he evinces
in the social condition of his workpeople', some of his workpeople took a rather

different view of his record as a mill owner; they roundly condemned Whittaker for his routine violations of the factory acts and his elaborate system of fines and abatements and criticized his habit of linking employment to the renting of one of his cottages.[154] At certain heated moments, like the powerloom weavers' strike in 1861, the limited impact of factory paternalism came through even more clearly. The employers, Jonathan Bintcliffe told a cheering crowd, 'could have given all the operatives wanted, and have had a large profit; but they intended to grasp all the wealth of the country, and they had got so much out of the workpeople that they were in many cases wealthier than many of the aristocracy—(hear, hear)—nay, they (the cotton masters) had become so rich as to almost govern the country'.[155] In the bitter aftermath of the strike, there were also attempts in Ashton and Stalybridge to establish mills on a cooperative basis as a way of creating a new system 'by which they and future generations will be freed from the despotic hands of a few avaricious capitalists'.[156] Even those workers who stopped short of this kind of thoroughgoing critique frequently saw through the ritualistic demonstrations of good will and testimonials to the mutual interests of capital and labour. 'Our masters think to put us off with a plate of beef and a glass of beer,' declared one Ashton man, 'but he will find himself mistaken. What we want is more wages, and we will have it before we have done.'[157]

Just as their religious and cultural initiatives of 1850s and the 'treats' and excursions were attempts to heal the bitter class divisions which prevailed in their town, the Ashton middle classes also grappled with this problem in the political arena, where their efforts to defuse the Chartist challenge radicalized the tone and substance of party politics and had a particularly dramatic effect on Ashton Conservatism. Although William Aitken, Richard Pilling, Thomas Storer, Edward Hobson, and most of the other members of the Ashton leadership ultimately aligned themselves with the Liberal party, many of 'those whose names were enrolled on the books of the Chartist Association', Aitken sadly noted, turned to the Tories; for Aitken, the emergence of the Tory working man was not only a disturbing development but also a surprise. In the 1830s and early 1840s, even with the creation of Operative Conservative Associations, 'a wooden-shod Tory' was a uncommon figure in Ashton politics.[158] And yet, by playing upon growing ethnic animosities and by adopting a populist (even democratic) tone, the Ashton Conservatives dramatically increased their following among working men during the years after 1848. With the onset of depression and then the Great Famine in Ireland, a steady stream of immigrants doubled the number of Irish in Ashton and environs between 1836 and 1851, and this influx aggravated anti-Catholic prejudices and raised fears about the effect of cheap Irish labour on piece rates and jobs.[159] Apart from an increasing number of street rows and drinking brawls between the Irish and the English, two serious ethnic riots took place in Ashton during the 1850s, one in the Irish neighbourhood of Flag Alley in 1854 and one in 1858 between the men of the 100th Regiment of the Royal Dublin militia and the townspeople.[160]

Hoping to capitalize on this upsurge of ethnic tensions, the Ashton Conservatives combined the cry of 'no popery' with support for the Ten Hour day and universal suffrage in an attempt to broaden their party's base of support among the working classes. In an attempt to recruit the respectable working man and to protect him 'in the exercise of his vote', they formed Church and Conservative associations, with relatively inexpensive (1s p.a.) memberships, 'payable the first Monday in January, April, July, and October'.[161] Several of the Anglican clergymen in Ashton and Stalybridge likewise tried to depict the Established Church as the friend of the labouring man and preached a gospel that was at once fervently Protestant and evangelical but also socially compassionate. Only the Established Church, claimed Rev. Williams, devoted itself to educating the poor man's child and dared to venture into the slums and 'crowded courts and alleys in our large towns' to spread God's Word and to reach out to the working classes.[162] In Ashton this new brand of Conservatism came together in the politics of Booth Mason, the older brother of Hugh Mason. A violent Orange man, who damned Catholics as 'a beastly popish rabble' and compared them to bloodthirsty cannibals, Booth Mason stood in 1857 as the Conservative candidate for parliament and fought the election on a thoroughgoing radical programme. 'Universal suffrage, if it were now the law,' Mason proclaimed on nomination day, 'three-fourths of the constituents would vote in his favour—(cheers and laughter.) He was for both vote by the ballot and short parliaments …. He was for the altar, the throne, and the cottage; for the church, so long as it was protestant, and no longer; the throne, so long as it maintained the principles of the constitution; and for the cottage, its rights and liberties.'[163] Carefully cultivating a populist image, Mason went on to declare himself an advocate of the Ten Hour day and an opponent of legislation to close public houses on Sunday. Over the course of the 1850s and 1860s, Ashton Tories also made a virtue of what William Haslam Mills called their 'larger share of original and mundane humanity'. Reflecting on the Tories' successful efforts to portray themselves as the friends of factory reform and John Barleycorn, Mills observed:

> Not that the Conservative employers, who won elections out of this state of things, were any more in favour of Factory Acts than their Radical brethren. They had, however, a larger share of original and mundane humanity; they had redeeming vices, and their names slipped easily into the diminutives of Dick and Harry and Tom, Ashton-under-Lyne, for example, being represented for many years by a gen-

ial obscurantist whom all the mill and all the town knew gloriously as "Tommy Mellor". No one would ever have thought of abbreviating the name—even if any possible abbreviation had suggested itself—of Hugh Mason, and John Bright remained "John Bright" to the end, majestic, stark, and formidable.[164]

Although Charles Hindley and Hugh Mason perhaps lacked the 'mundane humanity' and 'redeeming vices' of the leaders of Ashton Conservatism, the party of Hindley and his friends appealed to many working men because these middle-class radicals, unlike the Tories, had a long-standing commitment to an advanced political programme and a cross class reform alliance. On several occasions, Hindley even described himself as a Chartist and tried to identify the Liberal cause with the movement. 'He would not attempt,' he admitted at a reform dinner, 'to deny that he was a Chartist, and he believed that they were all Chartists more or less; but he would deny that he was a physical force Chartist.'[165] This was one of the reasons why Liberalism attracted so many of the leaders of Ashton Chartism; most of them also disliked the virulent anti-popery rhetoric of Ashton Conservatives and viewed the Tories' sudden democratic conversion with a healthy cut of scepticism. By contrast, for all of his infamous propensity for compromise and waffling, Hindley had clearly earned the respect of many working-class leaders through his labours in the short time movement and through his sympathetic attitude toward the Six Points and his role in saving the young Chartist Joseph Radcliffe from the gallows. 'No individual,' proclaimed William Aitken, 'had done more to raise the humble and lowly, to promote education, to ameliorate and improve their condition, and to make the cottage homes of England what they ought to be than Mr. Hindley.'[166] Thomas Milner Gibson, Hindley's successor as Ashton's MP, continued this tradition of radical Liberalism. Although he was a landowner and a member of the Church of England, Milner Gibson was a strenuous advocate of free trade, civil and religious liberties, and an unfettered press and took an advanced stance on the question of parliamentary reform. Speaking before a packed meeting at Ashton Town Hall in 1857, he gave his support to the ballot, equal electoral districts, triennial parliaments, and the principle of universal suffrage.[167]

From the mid-1850s on, the *Ashton Reporter* likewise pushed an advanced reform programme and provided Ashton's working men with a forum for discussing and publicizing their trade grievances and political demands. Edward Hobson and his staff consistently upheld the 'fair claims of labour' and 'the rights of combination and co-operation'.[168] At the same time, however, Hobson's newpaper also took the lead in expropriating the Chartist version of the people's history and grafting it onto Liberalism. In its columns, the struggle for 'Liberal principles' came to include the brave stand of local Jacobins against loyalist persecution as well as the war of the unstamped and even Peterloo. 'Fifty years ago,' the *Reporter* claimed in its 'The New Liberals' article, 'the charge of being a liberal was sufficient to consign a man to legal persecution and social ruin. Nay, within forty years the yeomanry of Lancashire rode down and sabred at Peterloo a meeting held to advocate the principles now so popular. A suffrage which should comprehend the masses; a ballot scheme which should protect the voter; and a curtailment of office which should restrain the representative, were then the cries only of men branded as revolutionaries or as dreamers of a political Utopia. What a change since then!'[169]

What hastened this blurring of the line between radicalism and Liberalism was the decline of the harsh, Malthusian side of middle-class political economy, a source of much ill will during the early years of Chartism. By the late 1840s, Hindley, like many other middle-class reformers, had begun to back away from his earlier enthusiasm for unrestrained competition and the rules of the market:

> As to political economy, it was a very good thing in itself, but it might be carried too far. For himself, he had yet to learn that the object of a man's existence was to accumulate as much wealth as he could scrape together. A far nobler purpose was that of doing all the good one could to one's fellow creatures; and, more than all, they were commanded to love their neighbours as themselves. —(Cheers.) Man was not constituted of thinking materials only. God had given them hearts to sympathise with the sufferings of their fellow mortals.[170]

In recent years, experience and 'more human influences', argued the *Ashton Reporter*, had modified the hard, scientific laws of political economy. 'Capital is bound,' the editorial added, 'for its own sake, by natural as well as by moral obligations, to attend to the physical and moral condition of its servants.'[171] Though 'not indifferent to the teachings of political economy', even the flinty, austere Hugh Mason acknowledged the need to modify its 'rigid' and 'abstract' principles and to move beyond 'the cold band of the mere buyer and seller of labour'; instead, he emphasized his 'deep interest in the welfare of his workpeople' and chose to portray himself and his workers as 'brothers and sisters' who worked together 'for one common end, that end being the mutual welfare of the workpeople and the employer'.[172]

IV

In the 1850s, the effect of Chartism on the emerging two-party system went beyond ideology and programmes; the working-class challenge shaped and influenced not only the agenda of middle-class politics but also the style of campaigning and methods of mobilization. Commenting on the impact of the mass platform of the 1830s and 1840s on party politics, Henry Jephson emphasized how the platform campaigns of O'Connor and other leaders of the movement had transformed party politics: 'Everything that had been contemned and legislated against before—public meetings, great demonstrations, peripatetic orators, harangues—have become in the progress of years common occurrences; even the greatest statesmen descended from the lofty seclusion of Parliament to take part in the more robust and less constrained publicity of the Platform.'[173] From the late 1850s on, Bright and Gladstone certainly borrowed, with great success, the platform style and rhetoric of the gentleman radicals and used the platform to recreate themselves as champions of 'the people'; Conservatives likewise took the torchlight procession and other tactics of 'the old Radical party' and put them to use in local and parliamentary campaigns to advance the cause of 'Our Queen and Glorious Constitution'.[174]

In their own communities, the Chartists also transformed the art of the canvass and urban electioneering; they went far beyond in the 1830s and 1840s the usual means of getting out the vote. After dividing up their town or parish into districts, activists and neighbourhood organizers took to the streets and created from scratch a thorough and effective 'system of agitation'; they explained their objects to all interested parties, recruited new members, and canvassed homes, shops, and even mills for subscriptions and signatures to petitions.[175] For William Farish, the creation of a new system of organization, 'which is at present called the "caucus"', was the movement's most important contribution to electoral politics. 'The organization,' he recalled about his native Cumberland, 'was very complete, nearly every village had its committee, with proper officers and collectors.... Membership only involved the payment of a penny a week, and was open to anybody on that condition. The city was divided into districts, with representation in the council proportioned to the number of members.'[176] In their later years, Farish and other veterans clearly derived a sense of satisfaction from this belated (if indirect) vindication of Chartist democracy; the elderly William Chadwick, who styled himself as the last of the Manchester Chartists, proudly noted in the 1890s that 'both political parties' eventually came to recognize the value of the ideas and methods of the movement.[177]

In a similar fashion, Ashton's working classes proceeded to transform the new industrial society from within the system. 'For the workers, having failed to overthrow capitalist society,' E.P. Thompson has pointed out, 'proceeded to warren it from end to end. This ... is exactly the period in which the characteristic class institutions of the Labour Movement were built up—trade unions, trade councils, T.U.C., co-ops, and the rest—which have endured to this day.'[178] In doing so, plebeian intellectuals and radical activists in Ashton simultaneously made their peace with the new order of things and ensured the steady progress of 'the democratic principle' and its impact on industrial society. But, in the process, Chartism 'as a party' faded away.[179] By the late 1850s the defining features of Chartist political identity were blurred almost beyond recognition. Through the columns of the *Ashton Reporter*, Edward Hobson had successfully expropriated and re-interpreted several of the defining moments in the Chartist history of 'the people' and had turned Peterloo and the war of the unstamped into heroic episodes in the unfolding of progress and the triumph of 'Liberal principles'.[180] Although many of the Chartist leadership continued to believe in the Six Points, they abandoned the old strategy of 'Universal Suffrage and No Surrender' and took an increasingly flexible approach to the question of reform; they were willing to consider the reform initiatives of the 1850s with an open (but critical) mind. It was, Aitken remarked about one such proposal, worthy of support, because it bore a close resemblance to 'the Charter itself, in a modified form'.[181] In a similar fashion, Aitken opened up and modified the Chartist definition of 'the people' to include 'all men, who by the sweat of their brows, or their brain contributed to the happiness and improvement of society'. Those who laboured in the counting house or schoolroom, as well as coal miners and mule spinners, were all of 'the people'.[182] Over the course of the 1850s, William Hill and other Chartists likewise came to accept the idea (and indeed the inevitability) of some kind of union with middle-class reformers and acknowledged the 'mischievous and destructive' side of the Chartist 'mode' of mass politics.[183] Sitting side by side with 'a party of gentleman' at an 1861 reform dinner, Richard Pilling tacitly agreed with this criticism of the movement and tried to distance himself from Chartist attempts to create 'a row and revolutionise England'. He admitted to mistakes in the past, but asserted that he had 'more sense now' and now served 'a better cause'. The toast that he proposed underscored the changes that 'the father' of the 1842 general strike had undergone; he offered a toast to the Liberal inheritors of the mass platform, John Bright and William Gladstone, and to Richard Cobden.[184]

There were by this point various institutions that countered this tendency and kept alive an alternative set of radical memories and values—the Secularist Institute, cooperatives, friendly and trade societies, and the People's Educational Institute. Over the course of the 1850s, the plebeian intellectuals and activists of the movement had often taken the lead in creating these institutions of working-class life and thus had helped to shape their values and methods. In doing so, however, they turned away from the Chartist emphasis on the central importance of democratic reform; their retreat into their 'own domestic circles' also snapped one by one the personal and political links in the bond of 'democratic friendship' that joined the locality to national organizations and leaders.[185] As a separate and distinct political identity, Chartism 'pined away silently to the shadow of its former self' and then disappeared altogether.[186] With the fading away of Chartism, 'democratic friends' there and elsewhere found themselves in a situation that closely resembled the state of things in 1837. The democratic cause took the form, once again, of a scattered host of small radical communities, alone and isolated, 'without unity of aim and method'.[187]

Conclusion

Chartism Remembered:
William Aitken, Liberalism and the Politics of Memory

Early one Sunday morning, in August 1839, 'a very authoritative knock' on the door awoke the young Chartist William Aitken and his family. After a thorough search of his house for 'revolutionary and seditious documents', the chief constable and his men placed Aitken under arrest and marched him through the silent streets of Ashton-under-Lyne. Recalling his sense of distress and anguish some thirty years later, Aitken tried to find solace in the ultimate triumph of his principles, in his conviction that 'the cause of liberty is eternal, and that the principles of democracy, which are now becoming universal, must be right and must in the end prevail'.[1] This optimistic reaffirmation of his life's struggle for 'bread and liberty' appeared in the fifth installment of his autobiography in the *Ashton News*, a Liberal newspaper. Unfortunately, the tone of quiet confidence and hope that pervaded his autobiography apparently masked a growing sense of private despair and ever deepening bouts of depression. Some two weeks before the publication of this instalment, his wife, Mary, found Aitken lying on the bedroom floor, 'with a fearful gash in his throat'. At the inquest, the only real clues to his state of mind came from his wife and neighbours; they described how ill health had forced him to give up his school and had deepened his 'low desponding state'. Based on this formation, the jury unanimously returned a verdict of 'suicide whilst labouring under temporary insanity'. In doing so, the jury protected his family from legal penalties and ensured an honourable burial.[2]

On the day of his funeral, thousands of working men and women lined the streets as 'a token of respect to the memory of' his years of devoted and selfless service to the cause of 'the people'. The son of a Scottish cordwainer and later sergeant-major, Aitken had always considered himself a member of the working classes; his identification with 'the people' came through clearly in the title of his autobiography, 'Remembrances and Struggles of A Working Man for Bread and Liberty'.[3] And yet, for most of his adult life, Aitken was not a member of the manual working class. In many ways, his decision to describe himself as 'a working man' was a revealing one; it pointed to the intertwining of class and gender and, above all, to the role of imagination and empathy in the creation of his sense of self. This form of self-portrayal certainly did not fit, in any straightforward way, the social and economic realities of his life over the previous three decades. Blacklisted for his role in the Ten Hours movement during the early 1830s, he left mule spinning for a new and 'useful calling'; at the advice of friends, he decided 'to commence a school, having devoted a deal of spare time to the acquisition of useful knowledge'. From time to time, he also supplemented the family income through work as an accountant and the 'trade of agitation' and turned his hand to versifying and writing fiction and essays for newspapers and friendly society magazines.[4]

In 1869 there was no consensus in Ashton about the meaning of either his melancholy death or his life of struggle for 'bread and liberty'. On the one hand, James Hindle, poet and radical freethinker, looked to the young Aitken, the Chartist militant, as a source of inspiration for the future generations that would carry on his 'unfinished' work. On the other hand, Hugh Mason chose to remember the Aitken of later years, as someone who had 'rendered essential Service to Free Trade and to Liberal Politics'.[5] The fact that Aitken's autobiography appeared in the columns of the Liberal *Ashton News* lends apparent support not only to Mason's assessment of Aitken's legacy but also to the 'currents of radicalism' interpretation of Chartism and Liberalism. Building on the accepted wisdom of the Victorians (especially those of the Gladstonian Liberal persuasion) as well as the work of later scholars, Eugenio Biagini and Alastair Reid have raised important questions about the currents of continuity, in terms of ideology and outlook, between Chartism and popular Liberalism; moreover, they have rejected the emphasis on a sharp discontinuity in popular politics around 1850 and have moved away from the idea of class as a basis for Victorian politics. Biagini and Reid have also pointed to biographical studies of mid-Victorian radicals, like Robert Lowery and George Howell, as examples of 'the personal continuities from early nineteenth-century radicalism, through Chartism, and into the Liberal party'.[6]

Although approaching the question from a very different theoretical position, Gareth Stedman Jones and Patrick Joyce have put forward a similar line of argument about Chartism and class. Placing the movement for the Six Points within a long tradition of radical opposition that stretched back to the 1770s, Stedman Jones has emphasized that radicalism was, above all, 'a vocabulary of political exclusion whatever the social character of those excluded'.[7] Joyce has likewise criticized the 'fixation' on class as an analytical category and has described how Aitken's career and style of leadership 'spanned both radicalism and Liberalism, cementing their shared vision of the world'. Joyce has gone on to argue that Aitken's autobiography was a classic expression of this shared vision. 'It is clear,' Joyce noted, 'from his autobiography that he saw no fissure between the two: Liberalism was completing the business of Chartism, and both were yet one more step in the history of liberty.'[8]

This very literal reading of his autobiography overlooks the often subtle ways in which he struggled to construct a coherent sense of self through the careful selection and presentation of his 'remembrances' about his public life.[9] Even then, despite his efforts to reconcile somehow his Chartist past with his Liberal present, he was acutely aware of the problems that this involved. Throughout his narrative, there was a tension between his stated goal of telling the truth about his public career as a radical working man and his desire to create what Jerome Buckley has called 'a continuity of self'.[10] To strike this delicate balance, Aitken took a highly selective approach to his memories of the 1830s, especially in the case of his portrayal of the movement for the People's Charter, 'that much abused and misrepresented embodiment of the people's political rights'.[11] While remaining silent about his own connection to and defence of the insurrectionary side of the Chartist movement in 1839, he frankly acknowledged, however, the existence of mass support for the physical force strategy and the general strike. By placing his emphasis on the hostility of 'the higher and middle classes' to democratic reform, he also chose to give the term 'the people', in the case of his account of the 1839 campaign, distinct class overtones.[12]

My re-reading of Aitken's autobiography thus points to some of the difficulties inherent in any attempt to place Chartism and Liberalism within a shared radical tradition. Just as Aitken downplayed or omitted altogether many of the inconvenient aspects of his own Chartist past, so the proponents of the 'currents of radicalism' approach have tended to accentuate the similarities between the two traditions and to minimize the very real differences. This is not to say that their perspective does not provide some valuable insights into reform politics of the mid-nineteenth century. After all, radicalism, and later Chartism, intersected Liberalism at a number of points; many Chartists and advanced Liberals shared a commitment to a progressive reform programme and a common hostility to the Established Church and aristocratic privilege.[13] What gave Chartism a separate and distinct political identity in the late 1830s and 1840s was the way that its activists and leaders chose to define their reform programme and their strategy for winning political power. Along with their emphasis on the Six Points, and especially universal (male) suffrage as the solution to 'class legislation', the Chartists defined their movement through their use of the mass platform, with its myth of the invincible will of 'the people', and through their identification with the cause of labour and the working classes. For the Whiggish historian and politician Thomas Macaulay, one of the movement's many critics, all this meant that Chartist democracy was synonymous with 'rebellion', 'the destruction of all property', and 'ignorant labouring men'.[14]

The process of carefully selecting and interpreting memories of the past was central to Aitken's creation of a sense of self through all 'the battles of a chequered life'.[15] The writing of his autobiography was never a simple case of retrieving timeless, unchanging memories of his individual past and fitting them into a narrative form. Memory involves forgetting as well as remembering; with the passage of time, details of long ago conversations and events fade and change. Over the years, discussions and arguments with family members, friends, and neighbours about episodes and personalities of the collective past also affect how individuals remember their own pasts.[16] By its very nature, the genre of autobiography likewise precluded the possibility of telling the entire story of Aitken's life, in all its richness and variety, and forced him to impose some kind of order on his memories. His life story, like all autobiographies, was, consequently, at best an incomplete and very selective account of his past. Aitken's personal circumstances in 1869 and the political and cultural context within which he organized and published his 'remembrances' were also crucial in determing how he told his readers the story of his life and gave it meaning. A creative and present-minded act of self-expression, the writing of his autobiography was thus mediated through and was influenced by the selective nature of memory and autobiography itself and by his relationship to the means of publication, the *Ashton News*, and to his audience. Together, these influences, some cultural, others personal and political, profoundly shaped Aitken's attempt to tell the truth about his life and one of its most dramatic episodes: the first great campaign for the People's Charter.

I

In the late 1860s the word 'autobiography', like the genre itself, was still relatively new. As a literary type, with its own distinctive style and conventions, it had only begun to emerge by the late eighteenth century; but, after 1800, the number of autobiographies that were published in Britain increased dramatically. This development pointed to a new belief in the relevance of what Buckley has called '"the subjective impulse", the writer's assumption that he or she may or even must confess, explain, divulge, or simply display an innermost self to a putative audience'.[17] In his own way, Aitken tried to follow the conventions of the new genre. Written in the first person, his autobiography took the form of a narrative about his past, from childhood and first memories onward. With the exception of a lengthy account of an 1862 trip to London during the early days of the 'Cotton Famine', his narrative proceeded chronologically up to his arrest in August 1839. There it ended abruptly; this was all that Aitken had written before his suicide. His autobiography was thus, in the most literal sense, an autobiographical fragment, one that left the story of much of his life untold and his final word on its meaning unsaid. And yet, the title that he chose, 'Remembrances and Struggles of a Working Man for Bread and Liberty', suggested something of his perspective on his life and its meaning. His autobiography sought, above all, to tell the story of 'a working man' and the political struggles of his public life.[18]

Precisely because the autobiography was a relatively new literary form, Aitken found himself with few models to draw upon in the writing of his narrative. This was particularly the case, since he chose to tell the story of a radical and 'a working man'. The most well-known and influential model of his day, the spiritual autobiography, had its obvious attractions. He, like many of the men and women of his generation, understood the development of the individual in moral terms; in his narrative he turned repeatedly to the importance of 'moral courage' and stressed the virtue of compassion and 'humane and Christian feelings' for fellow human beings, especially the poor and unfortunate. And yet, despite his respect for 'the simple and ennobling principles' of Christianity, he chose to avoid this model.[19] This decision by Aitken reflected, in part at least, his own uneasy relationship to the Christian faith. As a life-long critic of 'priestcraft and superstition' and someone of 'no particular religious sect', his life story did not match up very well with the conventions of the spiritual autobiography.[20] By the late 1860s, there was, however, an alternative model that closely fit the outlines of Aitken's life: the radical, and later, Chartist autobiography. Even here, though, the examples were few and far between. Of these, the best known in Aitken's Lancashire was the two-volume autobiography of Samuel Bamford, the weaver-poet, whose radical career unfolded during the stirring days of the Blanketeers and Peterloo.[21]

Drawing on a jumbled mass of memories, some intense, some half-forgotten, about persons, places, events, and books and poems, Aitken tried to create, through his narrative, a sense of stability of self.[22] It was his decision to portray his life story, in the words of his title, as the 'struggles of a working man for bread and liberty' that gave his narrative a sense of coherence and unity. By choosing to portray himself as 'a working man', Aitken moved beyond the material circumstances, if not of his childhood and youth, of his adult years as a 'highly respectable' schoolmaster and part-time accountant and writer.[23] His decision to adopt this persona enabled him to define himself as a working man and made the act of self-expression a political act, one that was consistent with a lifetime of struggle to gain political power and the right of self representation. In making his own a genre that had been reserved, like political representation itself, for the wealthy and powerful, Aitken proudly announced the entry of a new figure in the corridors of power as well as the pages of history. 'All things have a history,' he defiantly asserted in the opening lines of his autobiography. 'And the struggles of many of the working men of this country, if placed upon paper, would read as well, and be as interesting, as the lives of many a coronetted lord.'[24]

The sense of self-identity that this self-proclaimed 'working man' constructed out of his 'remembrances' took at once a very public and a radical form. It was significant that he described himself, not as a worker or a member of 'the working-classes', a term that he rarely used, even in its plural form, but as 'a working man'. His choice of words here suggested the extent to which the intertwining of class and masculinity informed his sense of self-identity.[25] Throughout his re-telling of his activities as 'a working man', he stressed in fact the centrality of manly exertion to the work place and political conflicts of the 1830s; again and again, he praised the role of the 'moral courage', the heroic spirit of self sacrifice, and 'the becoming fortitude' of those men who were 'engaged in a noble struggle for freedom'.[26] His was also a radical story of a lifetime of struggle for 'bread and liberty' that was based on 'moral power' and power of the spoken and written word, not 'brute force and secret mischief'.[27] Highly critical of the advocacy of political violence, whether by the Whiteboys or by trade unionists and Chartists, Aitken condemned their appeals to physical force as well as state violence and war making. 'Monarchial and aristocratic tyranny and ambition', he noted with disgust, had led to the steady growth of the military throughout Europe and 'needless wars of aggression'.[28]

Telling his story in this way inevitably meant that Aitken had to leave out certain memories about his personal life and family. He ultimately chose, like Bamford and the other radical autobiographers, to privilege the public and political over the private and personal; consequently, women, and children as well, were too often, as Eileen Yeo has noted, a 'missing presence' in his and other Chartist life stories.[29] Following the conventions of the autobiographical genre, Aitken discussed in some detail his childhood and 'first remembrances', but he said nothing about his mother and her family or about the 'mysterious', and no doubt traumatic, disappearance of his father in 1836. For the most part, he was even more reticent on the subjects of his own marriage and family and his private life as husband and father. Although the outgoing, sociable Aitken gave the names of many friends, personal and political, in his autobiography, he never mentioned his wife, Mary, by name; he never discussed their courtship or their life together and only alluded, in the most indirect way, to her contribution to his radical career. Nor did Aitken ever refer to their children in his autobiography.[30]

By their very nature, Aitken's memories about his public self were also highly selective; his attempt to understand and interpret the present in 1869 clearly shaped, to a certain extent, his 'remembrances' of the past.[31] Aitken tended to select, from among the sometimes conflicting memories of his past, the ones that most closely fit his emphasis on the role of 'moral suasion' in his struggles as 'a working man'. If the memories dealt with controversial events or undercut his interpretation, he typically only alluded to them indirectly or omitted them altogether. 'I have been told of acts of violence,' Aitken frankly admitted about local trade unions, 'and of violence contemplated, at which the mind shudders, but it is well to let them repose in the brain, and not bring them in here in these remembrances.'[32] One such set of memories that Aitken never directly mentioned dealt with the bitter 1830-31 strike in the Ashton and Stalybridge area. The *Ashton Reporter* obituary told a dramatic story of how the young Aitken had used his body as a shield to protect radical mill owner Charles Hindley from a group of angry strikers, armed with 'a considerable number of pistols'. For Aitken the autobiographer, keen to emphasize the triumph of 'moral power' and 'the growing intelligence of the many', the best approach was simply to pass over this, and similar episodes from his own Chartist past, in silence.[33]

By selecting certain memories, and setting aside others, Aitken thus tried to create a persona that he defined as that of 'a working man' who was radical in his political goals and moral in his political methods. Telling the story of the unfolding of this public self also involved something more—a search for a sense of purpose and meaning. What was the point of his years of sacrifice and hard work? Looking back over his life, he discovered a possible answer to this question in the 'healthful signs of progress' that he saw everywhere. Through his struggles, and the struggles of others like him, 'year after year,' he argued, 'a little is gained for the happiness of man'.[34] Throughout his narrative, Aitken paused to point out yet another example of the progress and changes that he had witnessed and indeed had contributed to over the course of his life: the passing of factory legislation, 'the growing intelligence of the many', the rise of rational trade unions, an end to taxes on knowledge and the corn laws, and the spread of democracy.[35]

What had made all this possible was the lonely struggles, often against enormous odds, of 'enthusiasts' and heroic individuals. 'It is well, indeed,' Aitken asserted, 'there are such beings born in the world, or where would progression seek for a shelter or a place to lift her all-ennobling head?'[36] For Aitken, and indeed many of his fellow Chartist activists, this turn to the Romantic cult of the hero came quite naturally. Drawing on his extensive knowledge of 'the writings of our best poets', Aitken often quoted poetry in his speeches and lectures and inserted lines and sometimes verses of poetry by Byron, Goldsmith, Burns, and

Cowper in the text of his autobiography.[37] In doing so, he was hardly unique. Running throughout many of the working-class autobiographies of this period was a fascination with poetry and personalities of great poets, especially Byron, 'that wonderful and wayward child of nature'.[38] There was as well, among those who were politically active, a tendency to cultivate a certain Romantic style of dress and oratory. The darkly handsome Peter McDouall, one of Aitken's close friends, liked to dress in black and wear a cape; this gave him, as W.E. Adams noted, the look of 'a hero of melodrama'.[39]

This emphasis on the role of the heroic, self-sacrificing individual was intimately linked to his own distinctive view of progress. In some cases, like the Ten Hours Act, progress came, he argued, as the result of 'the exertions of the working men themselves, and many others'. Here Aitken was careful to bring out the contributions of 'others', like the mill owner Charles Hindley and the Earl of Shaftesbury, to this great victory of 'the people'.[40] In other cases, the crucial figure was the high-minded patriot who struggled against the tyranny of the few and the apathy of the many. His was, Aitken believed, indeed an age of progress, but progress occurred only through the efforts, the sacrifices, and the 'moral courage' of the radical patriot, or hero: 'It has not been by timidity or fear that the battles of liberty have been won, but by a moral courage equalling, if not surpassing, the hero.'[41]

II

To set down on paper the story of one's life is a solitary, creative act of imagination and recollection, the usual object of which is to discover and interpret the meaning of one's life. This does not mean, however, that autobiographies represent purely individual accounts of past events; they involve the interplay between private memories and public representations and between past experiences and present situations.[42] 'It is in society,' as the sociologist Maurice Halbwachs has pointed out, 'that people normally acquire their memories. It is also in society that they recall, recognize, and localize their memories.'[43] In his search for the truth about his life, Aitken the autobiographer ultimately came to understand his past through a dialogue with his own present and with his prospective audience. His own difficult situation in 1869 inevitably affected his effort to create a sense of self and perhaps to reconnect, in some way, with the people and ideals that recurred in the telling of his life story. The medium of publication, a series of 'letters' in the Liberal *Ashton News*, and his awareness of the audience for his 'remembrances' also shaped how he told and understood the struggles of his past.

Alienated from Ashton Liberalism and many of his old friends by his support for the Confederacy during the American Civil War and by 'habits and associations' that he had formed, Aitken increasingly withdrew, in his final years, from public life. Well-known 'in his brighter days' for his wit and energy as a speaker and conversationalist, he was no longer able to speak in public for more than twenty minutes at a stretch; even reading, one of his great pleasures, was now a difficult chore. The waning of his intellectual powers and stamina, together with ill health, deepened his 'low desponding state' and forced him to give up in August 1869 his once flourishing school. The growing frequency of his bouts of depression and disturbing signs that 'his reasoning powers were leaving him' had begun to raise serious concerns among family members, friends, and neighbours. 'On the Friday before his death,' the *Ashton News* obituary noted, 'he called at the office of the *News* for a few minutes, and was apparently as cheerful and collected as usual, but his voice had a strange tone in it, and his eyes had a restless look.'[44]

It was against this background of bad health and a growing sense of personal and political isolation that Aitken set out to tell the story of his life. That he decided to do so reflected, in part, his longstanding belief in the importance of history to the struggle for political power. History, claimed Aitken in a lecture on Feargus O'Connor and democracy, 'was the light by which we could look upon past ages—the landmarks of what has gone before us; and by studying which with intentness, they would become wiser and more able to take part in the management of their country than they would be otherwise'.[45] Years later, this passion for history remained strong. In 1869, about the time that he began his autobiography, he published a cautionary but sympathetic account of the early years of the French Revolution; in this melodramatic tale, Aitken held up Camille Desmoulins, his central character and perhaps alter ego, as the voice of moderation, the very embodiment of the English tradition of 'liberty without licentiousness'.[46]

The autobiographical urge also represented in part an attempt to re-establish a connection to the people and ideals of his past and to establish a sense of stability of public self through all the twists and turns of a life in politics. To a certain extent, indeed, Aitken had come to see, by 1869, his career in politics as part of the unfolding of the Liberal vision. Speaking to a small meeting of Liberal activists on the eve of the 1868 general election, he described himself as 'an advocate of liberal principles when it was treason to love and death to acknowledge them'. He went on to praise the Liberal party for its consistent support for 'progressive measures' and for lowering taxes and establishing free trade. 'He was proud,' he concluded, 'to live in this grand historic age, and to help in improving the laws, so that the people might be better and happier in every respect. It was to the Liberals we were also indebted for liberty of conscience, free speech, and a free press, and he hoped those who had now the franchise for the first time would rally around the men who had consistently advocated those principles.'[47]

By re-interpreting the 'battles' of his public career as a struggle for 'liberal principles', Aitken fell in line with a political trend that had first emerged in his home town in the mid-1850s, with the founding of the *Ashton Reporter*. This advanced Liberal weekly, under the proprietorship of the impeccably radical Hobson family, pushed an ambitious, 'ultra' liberal reform agenda and devoted considerable time and space to covering and supporting the activities of trade unions and cooperative societies.[48] The *Reporter* took equal care, however, to graft the history and traditions of radicalism onto Liberalism. Through carefully selecting, muting, and re-interpreting key episodes, like Peterloo and the war of the unstamped, and ideas of the radical past, the paper began the process of converting old radicals and Chartists into what one editorial called 'The New Liberals'.[49] By 1869 the *Reporter* even eulogized the late Ernest Jones as an honest and sincere member of 'that section of the Liberal party for many years of which Mr. Feargus O'Connor was the leader'. Jones, the paper went on to admit, had been a follower of O'Connor, 'that noisy democrat', but he ultimately came to see 'the folly' of Chartism and took up 'the principles laid down by the advanced Liberals'.[50]

This interpretation of the life and career of Ernest Jones, with its remarkable transformation of Chartism into a 'section of the Liberal party', provides an invaluable insight into how 'advanced Liberals' tried to come to terms with the Chartist past. By distancing themselves from the noise and 'folly' of Chartism, its 'unruly meetings' and 'foolish songs' and appeals to physical force, they rendered the movement suitable for inclusion in the Liberal tradition and were also able to tap into 'the inert strength of that party'.[51] As Aitken cast about for models and themes to give a sense of unity and continuity to his public career, this way of tying together his life story had an obvious appeal. Once he decided to turn to the columns of the Liberal press as the forum for telling his story, the interpretative pull of this approach was, no doubt, almost irresistible.

But, despite his long history with the Hobson family, Aitken did not publish his autobiography with the *Reporter*, the oldest and most widely-circulated local paper in the Ashton and Stalybridge area. He turned instead to the *News*, a rival Liberal paper, a new weekly with financial ties to the wealthy and powerful Mason family.[52] The layout for page three, where each of his five instalments appeared, underscored, in a symbolic way, the extent to which his memories were embedded in and were shaped by the politics and business of Liberal journalism and by the interests and lives of his readers. Squeezed in between advertisements for Epps's Cocoa and Holloway's Ointment and Pills, local poetry and sensational fiction, articles on reform and free trade, and reports of local meetings and friendly society dinners, Aitken's life story made its public appearance in the form of a series of weekly 'letters'.[53] This very format, serialized weekly 'letters', as Aitken described them, imposed certain conventions and limitations on how he told his story. The serialization of autobiographies, as David Vincent has noted, often re-enforced the tendency to divide one's life into self-contained episodes; however, at the same time, serial publication required the autobiographer always to keep in mind the overall design and purpose of the narrative. This format also forced Aitken to meet deadlines and word counts and emphasized the importance of ending each episode at some dramatic, gripping point.[54]

Serialization in a local newspaper, in the form of weekly 'letters', almost inevitably made for a close relationship between autobiographer and audience. 'In a town like Manchester, though a large one,' Abel Heywood pointed out, 'the readers know the editor and all the parties connected with a paper.'[55] This kind of format enabled readers, moreover, to challenge points or to add new information and perspectives in the next weekly instalment. The audience that the *Ashton News* targeted was, like the one that Heywood described, a highly localized and politicized one; almost all, if not all, of the paper's readers lived in the immediate Ashton and Stalybridge area, or one of the outlying towns and villages, like Mossley, Hyde, Denton, and Droylsden. In this period, there was a growing sense of local patriotism that took the form of a new interest in dialect poetry and the history and 'folk' traditions, like Riding the Black Lad, of the area.[56] Aitken was well aware of the existence of this well-informed local audience for 'remembrances' about his public life. In the second sentence of the first instalment, he thanked the editor of the *News* for the opportunity 'to give your readers remembrances of the battles of a chequered life'.[57] But, he did not merely give his readers his own memories of the past; over the years, he had discussed and argued with the men and women of Ashton in their homes and in the pubs and public streets and markets of their town about the personalities and events of their collective past.

To a considerable degree, then, the 'remembrances' of his autobiography were deeply enmeshed in and were influenced by the memories of those who made up his audience. At two crucial points, Aitken the autobiographer paused and directly addressed his readership about events that loomed large in the collective memory of the townspeople of Ashton. The first of these had to do with the passing of the Ten Hours Act. Here Aitken explicitly referred to a contentious issue during the 1868 general election in Ashton: 'which party carried the bill?' His answer, then and now, Aitken argued, was 'that all parties alike, extreme Tory, Whig, Liberal, Radical, or any other name, added their weight, their eloquence, and their power to carry it'.[58] Two issues later, he once again stopped to address his 'gentle reader'; this time his subject was popular views about 'the absurdity of the men of 1838-39' and the first great mass campaign for the People's Charter. This was, even from 'the long vista of thirty years', still a living and controversial memory for Aitken and many of his 'gentle' readers.[59]

III

Turning to the turbulent days of the late 1830s, Aitken the autobiographer was acutely aware of the intensity of Chartist memories in Ashton and its environs. No doubt many of his readers ages forty and upwards had signed one of the petitions for the Six Points or had attended the mass meetings at Hyde or Kersal Moor that he described in his last two 'letters'. Over the course of the 1850s and 1860s, 'a few choice spirits' continued to display black flags on August 16 to commemorate the Peterloo massacre and met at public houses and inns to celebrate the birthdays of Henry Hunt and Thomas Paine and to toast 'The People's Charter' and 'the immortal memory of Feargus O'Connor'.[60] Through these kinds of commemorative events and rituals, and through participation in local politics and lectures and tea parties at the Chartist Institute or at the meeting room of the Ashton Secularist Society, a small but determined band of radical activists and plebeian intellectuals had struggled to keep alive the values and practices of Chartist democracy and an alternative set of memories about the recent past.[61]

Aitken clearly hoped to do justice to this very different set of collective memories of the movement and to give an honest account of what he called 'that much abused and misrepresented embodiment of the people's political rights'.[62] At several points, there was, however, clearly a tension between these goals and his desire to maintain a continuity of political self. Telling the truth about Chartism inevitably involved selecting some of the memories of the collective past and discarding or downplaying others. Even a cursory reading of his 'remembrances' revealed a Chartist world that was masculine and public in its politics and moral in its methods. In portraying the movement in this way, he tried to bring his Chartist past into line with the persona that he had so carefully crafted in his earlier 'letters'. And yet, even though this approach made Chartism more fit for inclusion in the Liberal tradition, Aitken was careful to stress aspects of the movement that were very much at odds with the Liberalism of his later years; he continued to emphasize, above all, the distinctiveness of the Chartist democratic vision and ultimately defined 'the people', in his account of 1838-39, in class terms.

For all his determination to give an evenhanded account of 'that much abused' movement, Aitken struggled, sometimes quite openly, over which 're-membrances' to include in his narrative of the 1839 campaign. He said almost nothing about the very public role of Ashton women in Chartism. There were, however, several allusions, though always in very general terms, to mass arming and the debate over the general strike, or 'SACRED MONTH', but he was careful to avoid any mention of the names of those local militants who had taken part in the insurrectionary side of the movement. One controversial memory that Aitken did discuss, though again without naming names, was the 'miserable dispute' between J.R. Stephens and McDouall that summer. It had, he sadly noted, 'serious consequences' for the movement, but he refused to go into the details of this incident. 'It would gratify,' he admitted, 'a morbid curiosity to know what it was, but that also will remain in the recesses of the brain, and shall never be printed with my sanction.'[63]

The fact that Stephens was still alive and well in 1869 probably contributed to Aitken's reticence here, but his silence was also consistent with his tendency to portray politics as a very masculine world that dealt with public, not private, matters. With the exception of his passing reference to the role of Mary Hobson in the war of the unstamped, Aitken the autobiographer never even alluded to the involvement of women in the radical politics of the 1830s.[64] He made no mention of the presence of women at the great Kersal Moor demonstrations or at the rowdy 20 April meeting at the marketplace in Ashton. Nor did he discuss their role in collecting the national rent and organizing exclusive dealing campaigns or their willingness support the mass platform's strategy of confrontation and intimidation.[65] These omissions in Aitken's account of 1839 were all the more striking because of his own introduction to radical culture. His earliest memory of Ashton radicalism, as he recalled in January 1869, was 'a Radical banquet of potato pies and home brewed ale' to commemorate Peterloo at 'Owd Nancy Clayton's'.[66]

This 'missing presence', to borrow Yeo's phrase, of women in Ashton Chartism was consistent, however, with Aitken's views on femininity in his autobiography and his definition of the political arena and work place as masculine domains. Throughout his narrative he used adjectives like 'kind', 'loving', and 'gentle' to describe women. Clearly, the proper place for 'frail women' was not the coal mine or the cotton mill.[67] Looking back on a visit to Wigan as a teenager, Aitken recalled with horror the sight of two miners, a husband and his 'gentle' wife, who had just returned to their home:

> Had it not been that the woman was suckling a child about six months old, I could not have told but that they were both male colliers. Yes, there this woman sat, dressed in the garb of a collier, and had been working the mine all day wagoning for her husband, yoked to coal wagons with a strap and chain like a beast of burden. As I had not then heard that females were employed in the mines,

it startled me the more coming on this exhibition so suddenly. It is needless to remark on the cruelty of such a system as that was, or the vast evils it inflicted on what should be gentle woman. It almost transformed woman into man, and took away that gentleness which is so high an attribute of her sex. This giant evil is now done away with, and I took a part with others, in after years, in laying these things before Parliament.[68]

For Aitken, indeed, the Ten Hours campaign had taken the form of 'a great moral effort' by men, like himself, to put an end to 'the evils of the long-hour system' and to protect 'frail women, and frailer children'.[69]

What was also 'missing' in his account of 1839 was any real discussion of the insurrectionary side of the movement. The emphasis by Aitken on the role of public meetings and the open, constitutional side of the movement was clearly one way of revising or at least avoiding, the most painful and controversial of the collective memories of Ashton Chartism; it reflected as well his conviction in 1869 about 'the folly of attempting to put down a Government like ours by physical force'. The proper way to bring about political change, he believed, was through moral power, 'the power of eloquence, the pen, and the press'.[70] This was possible in England, Aitken believed, because of its history and constitutional traditions. 'I hold that in a country like ours,' he wrote, 'where we have liberty of speech, liberty of the press, and what we call liberty without licentiousness, any means to accomplish a given end, however good it may be, other than moral power, must ultimately fail.'[71] For Aitken, the agent of moral change was the radical patriot or hero who struggled courageously against great odds in the cause of the people:

> All men who have hitherto taken the people's side of the question have had to sacrifice their own money and time. Their homes have been made desolate, themselves looked upon too often with scorn by the wealthy classes of society, their motives entirely mistaken, and they have been ostracised from what is called good society. Imprisonment and exile have too often been the lot of the men who have hitherto advocated the political and social rights of the people, but those days let us hope in this country and all others are gone.[72]

The consistency of Aitken the autobiographer's views on moral power and his identification with 'a country like ours' were at odds with the political actions and opinions of his Chartist past. While acknowledging 'a great many wild things said and done', Aitken chose to pass over in silence the drilling on secluded spots in the parish or the open sale of cutlasses, guns, and pike heads in the shops and market stalls in Stalybridge and Hyde. In a similar fashion he avoided any reference to '*secret meetings*' at Bush Inn, owned by James Duke, or to the involvement of fellow activists, like Timothy Higgins, in the mass arming campaign.[73] Unlike his close friends, Duke and McDouall, Aitken apparently steered clear of any direct involvement in 1839 in the buying and selling of firearms; however, Aitken, like most Chartists activists, made no hard and fast distinction between moral and physical force and always upheld the right of the people to bear arms.[74] Worried that 'the Government of this country intends to establish a military reign of despotism', Aitken urged his fellow Chartists to support the convention and to rely on 'the strength of your own right arm' to win their rights; he also defended mass arming as a way of applying pressure to the Whig government, 'the most bloodthirsty set of scoundrels in existence', and of preventing arbitrary arrests and another Peterloo massacre.[75] During the torchlight campaign in autumn 1838, his speeches took on an even more violent and threatening tone. 'Any man that would abuse my parent, kinsman, or child—(hear)—,' Aitken told his audience at a radical dinner, 'as those worthy Britons were treated at Peterloo, that man surely fall by my hand, let the consequence be what it may. (Loud cheers).'[76]

Dismissive alike of 'our "*glorious* Constitution"' and of the legitimacy of the Whigs' claim to political power, Aitken declared that it did not matter which faction was voted into office. 'Under the existing franchise,' he defiantly asserted in 1841, 'I consider it signifies nothing to the people who is returned to Parliament.'[77] These sentiments clearly clashed with his later identification with the Liberal party and the glorious constitutional traditions of England. They also put into perspective his willingness in 1839 to explore the potentially revolutionary question of the 'SACRED MONTH', or general strike, a tactic that he dismissed in his autobiography as a 'wild scheme'.[78] That summer Aitken was in fact at the centre of the debate among the Ashton and Stalybridge Chartists over the crucial issue of ulterior measures. Early on, in June, he apparently came out in favour of 'a cessation from labour for one month'. As the original day for launching the general strike, 12 August, drew close, Aitken continued to speak out and added his voice to the growing debate over this popular but controversial tactic.[79] His exact role during the three-day general strike in August remains unclear, but shortly after its conclusion he was arrested on charges of seditious conspiracy and speeches and unlawful assembly.[80]

By editing out these kinds of 'remembrances', Aitken began the process of bringing his interpretation of Chartism into line with the values and outlook of Ashton Liberalism and its own distinctive perspective on the recent Chartist past. But, at the same time, despite his description of the People's Charter as 'a document drawn up by five members of Parliament and five working men', he made no real attempt to recast the movement in the image of the cross class reform alliance of the Liberal party.[81] Thereafter, in his narrative of the 1839 campaign, he paused at several points to draw a distinction between 'the people' and what he referred to as 'the higher and middle classes', or 'the higher and well to do classes', or simply as 'the middle classes'.[82] In making this distinction, Aitken fell in line with a common contemporary usage of the phrase. 'The people,' as Thomas Wright remarked in *Our New Masters*, was often used in the early 1870s 'as a synonym for the working classes.'[83]

The hostility of the 'higher and middle classes' to democracy was, as Aitken the autobiographer pointed out, a formidable obstacle to reform both then and in the present. This was particularly true for the earlier period. 'Prejudice ran very high at that time,' he stressed about 1839, 'among the middle classes against the Chartists.'[84] Of course, such prejudice was still alive and well at the time that Aitken wrote the final lines of his 'remembrances'. When describing the ambitious, 'sweeping' democracy of the Six Points, he drew explicit parallels between middle-class 'prejudice' toward the People's Charter in the late 1830s and the continued strength of such feelings in the late 1860s:

> It was a document that provided for the election of members of Parliament on an equitable basis. In brief, a most extensive reform bill, going much further than the one we have just obtained. That the higher and middle classes of this country were not ready for so sweeping a measure of reform thirty years since, may easily be imagined, from the strong opposition we have seen within the last few years to the bills that have been before the country.[85]

One such liberal member of 'the higher and middle classes', John Stuart Mill, clearly found the coming of democracy deeply disturbing. Worried about the rights of 'minorities' (as well as the security of property) under majority rule, he was convinced that 'class feelings' would inevitably influence, if not determine, the politics of the working classes.[86] 'Every capitalist and property holder,' concluded a Mossley mill owner in 1866, 'will naturally become more Conservative who studies the aspect of the demagogues and radicals and the trades unions, strikes, and tyrannical interferences of working classes.'[87]

IV

For Aitken the autobiographer, 'the higher and middle classes' as a whole were not part of 'the people' in 1839. This did not mean, of course, that in his autobiography 'the people' always equalled 'the working class'. At several points, Aitken used the term as a sort of synonym for 'Chartists,' thus including, perhaps intentionally, individuals of 'a high social position', like John Frost or McDouall, who embraced and identified with the people's cause. If anything, then, his use of language in his autobiography points to the importance of context and the need to avoid univocal interpretations of this and other recurring tropes in radical rhetoric.[88] His life story also clearly underlined the ways in which empathy and imagination influenced the creation of individual and collective identities, like 'the people' or 'working man'. In defining himself in the latter way, Aitken transcended the social and economic realities of his daily life over the last thirty years and consciously chose this persona as a symbol of his democratic commitment and as a way of presenting and interpreting himself and his life story. This decision to portray himself as 'a working man', at once radical and moral in his politics, shaped how he told his story.

His relationship to his audience and to the medium of publication also affected how he ordered and interpreted his memories of a life in politics. Determined to create a continuity of public self, he downplayed or ignored some memories, selected other 'remembrances' for inclusion, and re-interpreted all of them in light of his Liberal present in 1869 and collective memories of the recent past. The Ashton men and women who made up his audience inevitably influenced his 'remembrances' of his struggles for 'bread and liberty', for, as the *Ashton News* stressed, Aitken had devoted his life to giving voice to 'what the many felt'.[89] Reaching out to this local readership through the columns of the Liberal *News*, Aitken also quite naturally began to lean toward the increasingly popular view of Chartism as a 'section of the Liberal party'.[90] This interpretation gave a sense of unity, mission, and consistency to his public self and also allowed him to smooth over many of the controversial (and illegal) aspects of the movement and to bring his life story into line with the prevailing Liberal perspective on the Chartist past.

One such example of this often subtle process of re-interpretation occurred in his re-telling of a story about an exchange that took place between himself and Colonel Wemyss in the Ashton marketplace in May 1839. In his autobiography, he recalled the incident almost with fondness:

A troop of dragoons had been over here and one piece of artillery on the Saturday previous, in consequence of anticipated disturbances which never took place. The troop was under the command of Colonel Wemyss, a fine, soldierly, kind, old gentleman as I have ever met with in all my travels. After he saw there was no occasion for this military display, he sent the soldiers back to Manchester, and on horseback he gathered the people round him and spoke to them of the constitutional methods to be used for the gaining of what they wanted. I being close to the Colonel got hold of his bridle, which hung loosely on his horse's neck, and he and I entered into a long discussion on the general topics which were then agitating the country, the Poor Laws, the Ten Hour's Bill and the Charter. The gallant old Colonel rode off with many compliments, good advice and the ringing cheers of the people.[91]

Aitken left his readers with a sense that 'the people' and 'the gallant old Colonel' had engaged in rational, far-ranging discussion of 'the constitutional methods to be used for the gaining of what they wanted'. A contemporary account in the *Northern Star*, reported by Richard Oastler, who was present at the scene, gave a somewhat different version, one that varied significantly from Aitken's 'remembrance'. The recent arrest by the Ashton police of four Chartists for drilling had created, Oastler noted, a tense situation in the town. Worried about the fate of the prisoners, all working men in their early twenties, crowds of men and women 'in great numbers' had begun to collect in the streets of Ashton on this wet, rainy Saturday; at least some of those who were present had heard rumours about plans for a rescue attempt. This volatile situation alarmed the Ashton magistrates, who sent out an urgent request to Manchester for troops. This was the immediate context for the 'conversation' in the marketplace between Wemyss and Aitken. For all the obvious reasons, Aitken the autobiographer chose not to recall his description, on this occasion, of the Ashton mill owners as 'a bloodthirsty set of monsters' or his curt dismissal of Wemyss' defense of English liberty. 'Liberty! The people of England,' he declared, 'have liberty to be worked to death in a cotton mill, and when they get so that they cannot perform the work required, to be starved to death in a Poor Law Bastile.' Nor did Aitken mention to his readers his final warning to Wemyss, amid 'great cheering' from the crowd, that 'the Government cannot put down the united voices and determination of the people of Great Britain'.[92]

This striking divergence between the account in the *Northern Star* and Aitken's own recounting of the incident some thirty years later points to some of the problems in trying to use the later careers and autobiographies of Chartist activists, like Aitken, as evidence for the 'currents of radicalism' approach to Chartism and Liberalism. On the one hand, he and other Chartist autobiographers selected and interpreted their memories of this period of their lives in light of their Liberal present; they also realized that in the case of certain painful or divisive 'remembrances', the best approach was simply to try to forget. 'Let the middle and working classes then…unite,' urged the former Chartist R.J. Richardson in 1848, 'let bygones be bygones; let Peterloo even be forgotten.'[93] On the other hand, Aitken and many of his fellow Chartist autobiographers often ignored Richardson's words of advice and went on to remind their readers about episodes, ideas, and traditions that fit uneasily with the Liberal vision of society and politics. For all his hard words about the convention and 'the very indiscreet conduct and language' of the Chartist leadership, he was candid about the 'state of incipient rebellion' in 1839 and the mass support for the Newport uprising; he was also critical of the heavy-handed response of the Whig government, especially of Lord John Russell, to the Chartist challenge.[94]

The entry of Aitken and other former Chartists into the world of Liberal and Conservative party politics was also a more troubled and contested passage than Biagini and Reid and like-minded historians have suggested. Their interpretation of Liberal politics overlooks, above all, the extent to which the mass movement for the Six Points transformed local and parliamentary politics in Ashton and Stalybridge and other former Chartist towns. The integration of plebeian intellectuals and activists into the party politics of the 1850s and 1860s was a two-way process, one which involved conflict as well as cooperation and affected the politicians of the emerging mass party system as well as 'owd' Chartists. While the Chartists drew back from the insurrectionary spirit and class confrontation of the late 1830s and early 1840s, many of the leaders of the emerging Liberal party retreated from their exposed ideological position as proponents of the harsh, utilitarian side of political economy and adopted some of the Chartist demands as well as some of the Chartists' methods of mobilization and forms of action. Out of this interplay between resistance and compromise and between forgetting and remembering, grew the conflict-ridden but stable society of mid-Victorian England.

In his 'remembrances' of things past, these tensions were always present; they emerged and then disappeared, only to resurface later on. Looking back over the ups and downs of 'a chequered life' in politics, Aitken the autobiographer sometimes chose to forget 'wild things said and done'; however, he continued to identify himself and the Chartist movement with the working classes and re-affirmed his commitment to the democratic vision of the Six Points, 'that much abused and misrepresented embodiment of the people's political rights'.[95] This way of defining 'the people' was at once an act of imagination and a reflection of the social position of Chartist followers (and most of the leaders) in his own militant locality. There was, however, a subtle shift in his 'remembrances' in his perspective on 'the people'. In his autobiography, the true agent of social and political change was the lonely, self-sacrificing hero or 'enthusiast' who led the way in 'the battles of liberty' against tyranny and injustice. Armed only with 'the powers of his eloquence and the prowess of his pen', the radical patriot struggled alone, with 'few, very few, to help him'. In the end, though, truth was sown in some hearts and minds. 'One unit of strength of mind keeps being added to another,' he triumphantly asserted, 'till like the avalanche descending from the mountain's top, it continues gathering strength till it bears down all before it; and truth stands enshrined in the hearts of men.'[96] For Aitken the autobiographer, the myth of 'the people' had taken on a new form.

Appendix

TABLE 1

POPULATION GROWTH, 1801-1861

	1801	1811	1821	1831	1841	1851	1861
Ashton	6,391	7,959	9,222	14,035	22,678	29,791	34,886
Glossop	3,625	4,012	6,112	9,631	14,557	19,587	21,200
Oldham	21,677	29,479	38,201	50,513	60,451	72,357	94,344

Proportional Change in Decennial Population, 1801-1861

	1801-11	1811-21	1821-31	1831-41	1841-51	1851-61
Ashton	1.245	1.158	1.521	1.615	1.313	1.171
Glossop	1.106	1.523	1.575	1.513	1.343	1.082
Oldham	1.359	1.290	1.322	1.196	1.196	1.303

SOURCES: *PP* (Commons) 1852-53 [1631] LXXXV: cxxvi; *PP* (Commons) 1852-53 [1632] LXXX-VI: 78; *PP (Commons)* 1862 [3056] L: 59, 541; *PP* (Commons) 1872 [c. 676] LXVI, pt. 1: 34, 187.

NOTE: Ashton has been defined as the municipality; Glossop as the townships of the manor; Oldham as the parliamentary borough.

TABLE 2

THE CARDING AND SPINNING DEPARTMENTS, WHITTAKER AND SONS, 1844

	Age and Upwards	Sex	Weekly Wages
Head Carders	25	Male	25s to 30s
Grinders	20	Male	13s to 16s
Strippers	18	Male	14s to 16s
Drawing Tenters	15	Female	8s to 10s
Bobbin Tenters	18	Female	8s to 10s
Stretchers	20	Male	13s to 20s
Spinners, First Class	25	Male	25s to 30s
Spinners, Second Class	18	Male	12s to 20s
Self-acting Mule Piecers	16	Male	14s to 16s
Overlookers	25	Male	25s to 35s

SOURCE: *Morning Chronicle*, 9 May 1844.

TABLE 3

ASHTON MULE SPINNERS IN 1841 AND 1851

	Male	Female	Married	Unmarried	English	Irish
1841	96%	4%	64%	36%	98%	2%
1851	98%	2%	79%	21%	96%	4%

Age Categories	1841	1851
10-19	11%	5%
20-29	43%	39%
30-39	30%	32%
40-49	12%	17%
50+	4%	7%

SOURCES: TNA, PRO, HO 107/532 and HO 107/2233.

NOTE: The 1841 figures are based on a one in five systematic sample of Ashton spinners; the 1851 figures are based on a one in two systematic sample.

TABLE 4

THE WEAVING DEPARTMENT, WHITTAKER AND SONS, 1844

	Age and Upwards	Sex	Weekly Wages
Weavers	15	Males & Females	10s to 12s
Winders	15	Females	10s to 12s
Warpers	18	Females	12s to 15s
Dressers	25	Males	30s to 40s
Overlookers	25	Males	25s to 32s
Mechanics	21	Males	24s to 30s

SOURCE: *Morning Chronicle*, 9 May 1844.

TABLE 5

CHARTIST LEADERSHIP IN ASHTON-UNDER-LYNE, 1838-1842

	Total Number	Percentage
Master Artisans	3	7.5%
Professionals	2	5%
Shopkeepers	5	12.5%
Publicans	1	2.5%
Newsagents and Printers	5	12.5%
Cotton Workers	17	42.5%
Journeymen Artisans	7	17.5%
	40	100%

SOURCE: This occupational profile draws primarily on published lists in the *Northern Star* of nominations to the NCA General Council; the prison interviews in TNA, PRO, HO 20/10; Pigot's 1841 directory; the 1841 census enumerators' books in PRO, HO 107/532.

NOTE: The totals for the lower middle class include five former factory workers: William Aitken (spinner), John Deegan (cardroom hand), John Williamson (spinner), Jame Duke (spinner), and Timothy Higgins (spinner). Two national figures, J.R. Stephens and Peter McDouall, have been excluded.

TABLE 6

CHARTIST LAND COMPANY SUBSCRIBERS IN ASHTON-UNDER-LYNE, 1847-1848

	Total Number of Adult Males	Percentage of Adult Males
Farmers and Gardeners	12	1%
Master Artisans	11	1%
Professionals and Clerks	10	1%
Shopkeepers	15	2%
Cotton Workers	549	62%
Journeymen Artisans	185	21%
Coal Miners	26	3%
Labourers	45	5%
Others	38	4%
	891	100%

SOURCE: TNA, PRO, Board of Trade, BT 41/474-76. I am indebted to Jamie Bronstein for a copy of her data on Land Company subscribers in Ashton and Stalybridge.

NOTE: The fifty-two women who appeared in the list of Land Company subscribers have been excluded. To distinguish between employers and employees, I looked up the names of subscribers who worked in the cotton industry or in one of the handicraft trades in Pigot's 1841 and Slater's 1848 directories for Ashton. If the name of the individual appeared in one of the directories, I assumed that he was an employer of labour. For all categories, percentages have been rounded off.

TABLE 7

THE SOCIAL STRUCTURE OF ASHTON-UNDER-LYNE IN 1841

	Total Number of Adult Males	Percentage of Adult Males
Farmers and Gardeners	54	1%
Agricultural Labourers	80	1%
Cotton Spinners and Manufacturers	65	1%
Master Artisans	224	4%
Professionals	82	2%
Shopkeepers	325	6%
Publicans	89	2%
Clerks	94	2%
Cotton Workers	2,250	43%
Journeymen Artisans	1,086	21%
Coal Miners	121	2%
Labourers	461	9%
Others	322	6%
	5,253	100%

SOURCE: *PP* (Commons) 1844 [587] XXVII: 68-96.

NOTE: The occupational abstract did not distinguish between employers and employees. I went through Pigot's 1841 directory to establish the number of cotton spinners and manufacturers and master artisans in Ashton and then subtracted the cotton masters and master artisans from the occupational abstract's totals for cotton workers and the handicraft trades. For all categories, percentages have been rounded off.

TABLE 8

COTTON YARN AND PIECE GOOD PRODUCTION, 1844-1861

(Pounds)

	1844-1846	1859-1861
Total Yarn Produced	523,300 lbs.	910,000 lbs.
Total Goods Produced	378,110 lbs.	720,870 lbs.

SOURCE: Thomas Ellison, *The Cotton Trade of Great Britain,* reprint ed., New York, 1968, p. 59.

TABLE 9

EXPANSION OF THE PRODUCTIVE CAPACITY OF THE COTTON INDUSTRY, 1850-1862

	1850	1856	1862
Total Number of Spindles	20,977,017	28,010,217	30,387,467
Total Number of Looms	249,627	298,847	399,992

SOURCE: *PP* (Commons) 1863 XVIII: 65.

NOTE: These figures represent the total number of spindles and looms in the cotton industry for the entire United Kingdom.

TABLE 10
WAGES IN THE COTTON INDUSTRY, MANCHESTER AREA, 1839-1859
(Shillings and Pence)

	1839	1849	1859
Self-acting Minders, 25s to 40s	18s	18s 6d	22s
Hand Mule Spinners, 40s, 800 Spindles	23s	21s	23s
Strippers	11s	12s	14s
Grinders	13s	13s	15s
Powerloom Weavers, 72 Reed Printers Cloth			
Two Looms	9s	9s	10s
Three Looms	—	13s	15s
Four Looms	17s	16s	18s

SOURCE: David Chadwick, 'On the Rate of Wages in Manchester and Salford, and the Manufacturing Districts of Lancashire, 1839-59', *Journal of the Royal Statistical Society* XXIII (March 1860): 23-24

TABLE 11
1841 ELECTION: VOTING BLOCS

	Hindley		Harrop	
	Votes	Percentage	Votes	Percentage
Cotton Masters	23	53%	20	47%
Master Artisans	45	56%	36	44%
Shopkeepers	92	62%	56	38%
Publicans	25	37%	43	63%
Working Class	49	64%	28	36%

SOURCE: Tameside, 'List of Persons who voted for Charles Hindley, Esq. List of Persons who voted for Jonah Harrop, Esq.', Ashton, 1841.

NOTE: These five voting blocs cast 75 percent of the total vote in the 1841 election. Although about 8 percent of the pollbook entries provided no information on occupation, the pollbook generally gave an occupation and a street address for each elector but made no explicit distinction between employer and employee. To sort out these cases, I turned to the 1841 directory and looked up all those electors who had an occupation which was related to the cotton industry or to one of the trades. If the elector was listed in Pigot's 1841 directory, I assumed that he was an employer of labour, a master spinner or a master artisan. In addition to those who appeared simply as 'shopkeeper', grocers, chandlers, mercers, bakers, pawnbrokers, and merchants, dealers, mongers, and sellers of all sorts were also included in this group. The voting bloc 'publicans' consisted largely of beersellers, publicans, tavern keepers, brewers, and assorted other members of the drink and lodging interest. The working-class electors included overlookers, warehousemen, spinners, dressers, labourers, mechanics, and journeymen from a dozen trades.

TABLE 12

THE 1851 RELIGIOUS CENSUS IN ASHTON

	Number of Places of Worship	Real Attendance
Church of England	6	4,169
New Connexion Methodist	5	1,552
Wesleyan Methodist	2	667
Primitive Methodist	3	426
Independent Methodist	1	84
Independent	2	1,630
Baptist	2	623
Swedenborgian	1	50
Stephenite	1	100
Christian Israelite	1	185
Mormon	1	300
Roman Catholic	1	725
	26	10,511

SOURCE: TNA, PRO, HO 129/474.

NOTE: The churches and chapels in the Knotts Lane division of the parish have been excluded. No attendance figures were given for Old and New St. George's, two Anglican places of worship. For the method of calculating 'real attendance', see Foster, *Class Struggle*, p. 313.

TABLE 13

OCCUPATIONS OF FATHERS OF CHILDREN BAPTIZED AT ALBION CHAPEL, 1818-1837

	Total	Percentage
Cotton Spinners and Manufacturers	9	4%
Master Artisans	12	6%
Shopkeepers	17	8%
Clerks and Schoolmasters	8	4%
Weavers	43	21%
Spinners	44	21%
Other Factory Workers	31	15%
Journeymen Artisans	42	21%
	206	100%

SOURCE: TNA, PRO, R 4 Register of Baptisms, Albion St., Independent chapel, Ashton-under-Lyne.

NOTE: Each individual was counted only once, even if he appeared several times; all those individuals who resided outside of the Ashton area were excluded. To distinguish between employer and employee, I looked up in local directories all weavers, spinners, and artisans; if the name of the individual appeared in the directories, I assumed that he was an employer of labour.

Notes

Introduction

1.   *London Democrat*, 18 May 1839. Dorothy Thompson, *The Chartists: Popular Politics in the Industrial Revolution*, London, 1984, pp. 61-62, 338-39; John K. Walton, *Chartism*, London, 1999, pp. 46-50. For book-length studies, see David Goodway, *London Chartism, 1838-1848*, Cambridge, 1982; Margot Finn, *After Chartism: Class and Nation in English Radical Politics, 1848-1874*, Cambridge, 1993; Paul Pickering, *Chartism and the Chartists in Manchester and Salford*, London, 1995.
2.   Thompson, *Chartists*, p. 62.
3.   J. Ginswick (ed.), *Labour and the Poor in England and Wales 1849-1851: The Letters to the Morning Chronicle*, eight volumes, London, 1983, 1: 86. One mile east of Ashton was Stalybridge; it was located on the edge of the Pennines. About one-half mile to the south of Ashton was the village of Dukinfield.
4.   Edwin Butterworth, *An Historical Account of the Towns of Ashton-under-Lyne, Stalybridge, and Dukinfield*, Ashton, 1842, pp. 53, 93-94.
5.   *Manchester Times and Gazette*, 11 June 1831.
6.   John Ross Coulthart, *A Report of the Sanatory Condition of the Town of Ashton-under-Lyne*, Ashton, 1844, pp. 8-13; Butterworth, *Historical Account*, pp. 69-72. Thompson, *Chartists*, p. 338; *Manchester Guardian*, 27 May 1840. In September 1847, when Ashton received its charter of incorporation, this system of local government came to an end. See George Foster, *Ashton-under-Lyne. Its Story Through the Ages*, Ashton, [1947], pp. 55-57.
7.   Thompson, *Chartists*, p. 133. Nicholas Cotton, 'Popular Movements in Ashton-under-Lyne and Stalybridge before 1832', Birmingham University, M.Litt. thesis, 1977.
8.   The National Archives, Public Record Office, Home Office 40/43, Shaw to Phillipps, 9 December 1839.
9.   Ginswick (ed.), *Labour and the Poor*, 1: 87.
10. *Northern Star*, 23 April 1842.
11. Jon Lawrence, *Speaking for the People: Party, Language and Popular Politics in England, 1867-1914*, Cambridge, 1998, pp. 3-6, 225-40, 266-67.
12. Barry Reay, *Microhistories: Demography, Society and Culture in Rural England, 1800-1930*, Cambridge, 1996, pp. 257-62; Giovanni Levi, 'On Microhistory', in Peter Burke (ed.), *New Perspectives on Historical Writing*, University Park, 2001, pp. 97-119. See also, Pickering, *Chartism and the Chartists*, pp. 1-3.
13. Gareth Stedman Jones, *Languages of Class: Studies in English Working Class History 1832-1982*, Cambridge, 1983, pp. 98-99.

14. Miles Taylor, 'Rethinking the Chartists: Searching for Synthesis in the Historiography of Chartism', *Historical Journal* 39 (June 1996): 492; Richard Price, *British Society, 1680-1880: Dynamism, Containment and Change*, Cambridge, 1999, pp. 155-59, 167-76.

15. TNA, PRO, HO 40/43, Shaw to Phillipps, 9 December 1839; Thompson, *Chartists*, pp. 341-68.

16. Pickering, *Chartism and the Chartists*, p. 34.

17. Miles Taylor, 'The Six Points: Chartism and the Reform of Parliament', in Owen Ashton, Robert Fyson and Stephen Roberts (eds.), *The Chartist Legacy*, Rendlesham, 1999, p. 1. See also, Logie Barrow and Ian Bullock, *Democratic Ideas and the British Labour Movement, 1880-1914*, Cambridge, 1996, pp. 1-5. For Chartist democracy, see Taylor, 'Six Points', in Ashton, Fyson and Roberts (eds.), *Chartist Legacy*, pp. 1-23; Eileen Yeo, 'Some Practices and Problems of Chartist Democracy', in James Epstein and Dorothy Thompson (eds.), *The Chartist Experience: Studies in Working-Class Radicalism and Culture, 1830-1860*, London, 1982, pp. 345-80.

18. Frederick Engels, *The Condition of the Working Class in England*, with an Introduction by Eric Hobsbawm, London, 1984, p. 261; Stedman Jones, *Languages of Class*, pp. 91-93.

19. Mark Hovell, *The Chartist Movement*, edited and completed by T.F. Tout, Manchester, 1918; reprint ed., New York, 1967, pp. 1-7. For critiques of Stedman Jones, see Neville Kirk, 'In Defence of Class: A Critique of Recent Revisionist Writing upon the Nineteenth-Century English Working Class', *International Review of Social History* 32 (1987): 2-47; James Epstein, *In Practice: Studies in the Language and Culture of Popular Politics in Modern Britain*, Stanford, 2003, pp. 15-33.

20. Taylor, 'Rethinking the Chartists', pp. 480-81, 491-95.

21. Joan Allen and Owen Ashton, 'Introduction', in Allen and Ashton (eds.), *Papers for the People: A Study of the Chartist Press*, London, 2005, pp. xii-xiii; Andrew Messner, 'Land, Leadership, Culture, and Emigration: Some Problems in Chartist Historiography', *Historical Journal* 42 (December 1999): 1093-1100.

22. John Garrard, *Democratisation in Britain: Elites, Civil Society and Reform Since 1800*, Basingstoke, 2002, pp. 93, 1-4, 37-42, 84-88. See also, Ian Machin, *The Rise of Democracy in Britain, 1830-1918*, Basingstoke, 2001, pp. vii-viii, 31-37, 150-51; Ruth Berins Collier, *Paths Toward Democracy: The Working Class and Elites in Western Europe and South America*, Cambridge, 1999, pp. 33-34, 61-66, 77-78, 96-101, 196-97. For a different view, see Charles Tilly, *Contention & Democracy in Europe, 1650-2000*, Cambridge, 2004, pp. 28-29, 34-35, 140-41, 163-65.

23. *Northern Star*, 27 October 1838. Tilly, *Contention & Democracy*, pp. 140-41, 163; Hugh Cunningham, *The Challenge of Democracy: Britain, 1832-1918*, London, 2001, pp. 1-3, 103, 128; Geoff Eley, *Forging Democracy: The History of the Left in Europe, 1850-2000*, Oxford, 2002, pp. 3-6.

24. *Northern Star*, 27 July 1839. For Thomas Cooper's lecture series on history and democracy, see *Northern Star*, 5 July 1845. See also, the series of 1841 articles in *McDouall's Chartist and Republican Journal*; William Lovett and John Collins, *Chartism: A New Organization of the People*, London, 1840; reprint ed., New York, 1969, pp. 7-10.

25. *The People*, no. 42, pp. 329-30. For negative comments about the American and French Revolutions, see *Ashton Reporter*, 11 December 1858 (Mason speech).

26. *Hansard's Parliamentary Debates* Third Series LXVI (1843): 1048-49. See also, Montague Gore, *A Letter to the Middle Classes, on the Present Disturbed State of the Country, especially with reference to the Chartist Meetings*, London, 1839, pp. 3-14.

27. Mill to De Tocqueville, 11 May 1840, in J.M. Robson (ed.), *The Collected Works of John Stuart Mill*, Vol. 13: *The Earlier Letters of John Stuart Mill, 1812-1848*, Toronto, 1963, p. 434.

28. E.P. Thompson, *The Poverty of Theory: or an Orrery of Errors*, London, 1995, pp. 201-204.

29. Finn, *After Chartism*, p. 11.

30. TNA, PRO, HO 45/650, Arbuthnot to Phillipps, 8 February 1844.

31. *Parliamentary Papers* (Commons) 1842 [158] XXXV: 18.

32. *Voice of the People*, 19 February 1831; Robert G. Hall, 'Tyranny, Work and Politics: The 1818 Strike Wave in the English Cotton District', *International Review of Social History* 34 (1989): 435-36, 455-57.

33. *Manchester Observer*, 3 October 1818.

34. TNA, PRO, HO 20/10. For the spinners and radicalism, see Hall, 'Tyranny, Work and Politics', pp. 440-41, 458, 469-70; Marc W. Steinberg, *Fighting Words: Working-Class Formation, Collective Action, and Discourse in Early Nineteenth-Century England*, Ithaca, 1999, pp. 181-86; Robert Sykes, 'Early Chartism and Trade Unionism in South-East Lancashire', in Epstein and Thompson (eds.), *Chartist Experience*, pp. 152-93.

35. John Bates, *A Sketch of His Life*, Queensbury, 1895.

36. John James Bezer, *The Autobiography of One of the Chartist Rebels of 1848*, 1851, in David Vincent (ed.), *Testaments of Radicalism*, London, 1977, p. 187; British Library, Add Mss 34,245A, Lowery and Duncan to the Convention, 12 March 1839, in Brian Harrison and Patricia Hollis (eds.), *Robert Lowery: Radical and Chartist*, London, 1979, p. 233.

37. John Belchem, *'Orator' Hunt: Henry Hunt and English Working-Class Radicalism*, Oxford, 1985, pp. 4, 43, 58, 64; James Epstein, *The Lion of Freedom: Feargus O'Connor and the Chartist Movement 1832-1842*, London, 1982, pp. 90-93, 110-31. Henry Jephson defines 'the Platform' as 'every political speech at a public meeting, excluding those from the Pulpit and those in Courts of Justice'. See *The Platform: Its Rise and Progress*, two volumes, 1892; reprint ed., New York, 1971, 1: xix.

38. Clive Behagg, *Politics and Production in the Early Nineteenth Century*, London, 1990, p. 226.

39. This was on a Rochdale banner at Kersal Moor. See *Northern Star*, 29 September 1838.

40. Charles Tilly, *Social Movements, 1768-2004*, Boulder, 2004, p. 48.

41. *Ashton News*, 2 October 1869. James Epstein, '"Bred as a Mechanic": Plebeian Intellectuals and Popular Politics in Early Nineteenth-Century England', in Leon Fink, Stephen T. Leonard, and Donald Reid (eds.), *Intellectuals and Public Life: Between Radicalism and Reform*, Ithaca, 1996, pp. 53-73; E.P. Thompson, *The Making of the English Working Class*, New York, 1966, pp. 711-46.

42. *Northern Star*, 11 June 1842.

43. In 1869 he entitled his autobiography 'Remembrances and Struggles of a Working Man for Bread and Liberty'. See Robert G. Hall and Stephen Roberts (eds.), *William Aitken: The Writings of a Nineteenth Century Working Man*, Tameside, 1996.

44. *Northern Star*, 18 May 1839; Hall and Roberts (eds.), *William Aitken*, p. 28.

45. Hall and Roberts (eds.), *William Aitken*, p. 39.

Chapter I

1. For copies of this address, see *Black Dwarf*, 30 September 1818 and *Manchester Observer*, 3 October 1818.

2. TNA, PRO, HO 20/10, Interview with Timothy Higgins.

3. I.J. Prothero, *Artisans and Politics in Early Nineteenth-Century London: John Gast and His Times*, Folkestone, 1979, pp. 336, 2-3; Thompson, *The Making of the English Working Class*, pp. 191-93. Michael Hanagan, 'Artisan and Skilled Worker: The Problem of Definition', *International Labor and Working-Class History* 12 (1977): 28-31; Richard Price, *Masters, Unions and Men: Work Control in Building and the Rise of Labour, 1830-1914*, Cambridge, 1980, pp. 9-11; Steinberg, *Fighting Words*, pp. 26-27, 136-46.

4. Charles More, *Skill and the English Working Class, 1870-1914*, New York, 1980, pp. 15-16, 20, 25. See also, Jutta Schwarzkopf, *Unpicking Gender: The Social Construction of Gender in the Lancashire Cotton Weaving Industry, 1880-1914*, Aldershot, 2004, pp. 53-56, 73-74.

5. Cynthia Cockburn, *Brothers: Male Dominance and Technological Change*, London, 1983, pp. 132-33. Anne Phillips and Barbara Taylor, 'Sex and Skill: Notes Toward a Feminist Economics', *Feminist Review* 6 (October 1980): 79, 85-86. See also, Sonya Rose, *Limited Livelihoods: Gender and Class in Nineteenth-Century England*, Berkeley, 1992, pp. 22-23; Schwarzkopf, *Unpicking Gender*, pp. 53-81.

6. John Rule, 'Artisan Attitudes: A Comparative Survey of Skilled Labour and Proletarianization Before 1848', *Bulletin of the Society for the Study of Labour History* 50 (Spring 1985): 22-31; Prothero, *Artisans and Politics*, pp. 28-40; Hanagan, 'Artisan and Skilled Worker', pp. 28-31.

7. *A Report of the Proceedings of a Delegate Meeting of the Operative Spinners of England, Ireland, and Scotland*, Manchester, 1829, p. 6. Sally Alexander, 'Women, Class, and Sexual Differences in the 1830s and 1840s: Some Reflections on the Writing of a Feminist History', *History Workshop Journal* 17 (Spring 1984): 136-39; John Rule, 'The Property of Skill in the Period of Manufacture', in Patrick Joyce (ed.), *The Historical Meanings of Work*, Cambridge, 1987, pp. 99-118; John Tosh, 'What Should Historians Do with Masculinity? Reflections on Nineteenth-Century Britain', *History Workshop Journal* 38 (Autumn 1994): 184-87; Eileen Janes Yeo, 'Taking It Like A Man', *Labour History Review* 69 (August 2004): 129-30.

8. TNA, PRO, HO 20/10, Interview with Timothy Higgins.

9. Thomas Laqueur, *Making Sex: Body and Gender from the Greeks to Freud*, Cambridge, 1990, p. 6.

10. Michael Kimmel, 'The Contemporary "Crisis" of Masculinity in Historical Perspective', in Harry Brod (ed.), *The Making of Masculinities: The New Men's Studies*, Boston, 1987, p. 122. Rose, *Limited Livelihoods*, p. 17. See also, Leonore Davidoff

and Catherine Hall, *Family Fortunes: Men and Women of the English Middle Class, 1780-1850*, Chicago, 1987; Joan Scott, *Gender and the Politics of History*, New York, 1988, pp. 93-112; Anna Clark, *The Struggle for the Breeches: Gender and the Making of the British Working Class*, Berkeley, 1995.

11. Michael Kimmel, *Manhood in America: A Cultural History*, New York, 1996, p. 120. Tosh, 'What Should Historians Do', pp. 192-94, 198; Michael Roper and John Tosh, 'Introduction: Historians and the Politics of Masculinity', in Roper and Tosh (eds.), *Manful Assertions: Masculinities in Britain Since 1800*, London, 1991, pp. 17-19.

12. Ginswick (ed.), *Labour and the Poor*, 1: 56.

13. *PP* (Commons) 1833 XX [450] D2: 2-3.

14. Ibid., pp. 59-60.

15. TNA, PRO, HO 40/27(3), Chappell to Peel, 20 October 1830; Barrie Ratcliffe and W.H. Chaloner (eds.), *A French Sociologist Looks at Britain: Gustave d'Eichthal and British Society in 1828*, translated by Ratcliffe and Chaloner, Manchester, 1977, p. 97; Robert Hyde Greg, 'The Factory Question', London, 1837, pp. 57-58.

16. W.E. Adams, *Memoirs of a Social Atom*, London, 1903; reprint ed., New York, 1967, p. 81. David Vincent, *Bread, Knowledge and Freedom: A Study of Nineteenth-Century Working Class Autobiography*, London, 1981, pp. 67-74; Keith McClelland, 'Some Thoughts on Masculinity and the "Representative Artisan" in Britain, 1850-1880', *Gender and History* 1 (Summer 1989): 164-77.

17. James Dawson Burn, *The Autobiography of a Beggar Boy*, edited with an Introduction by David Vincent, 1855; reprint ed., London, 1978, pp. 200, 120, 123.

18. Victor Neuburg (ed.), *London Labour and the London Poor*, Harmondsworth, 1985, p. 392. [James Leach] *Stubborn Facts from the Factories*, London, 1844, pp. 29-30.

19. Hall and Roberts (eds.), *William Aitken*, pp. 18-19, 21-22. See also, James Bradley, *Reminiscences in the Life of Joshua Bradley... From Little Piecer to Manager*, Oldham, 1904; reprint ed., Mottram, 1974, pp. 18-19, 28-29, 38, 44-45; William Marcroft, *The Marcroft Family and the Inner Circle of Human Life*, Rochdale, 1888, pp. 92-93.

20. *PP* (Commons) 1816 [397] III: 355; *PP* (Lords) 1818 [90] XCVI: 186; *PP* (Lords) 1819 [24] CX: 237, 342, 400, 436; *United Trades' Co-operative Journal*, 3 April 1830; *Poor Man's Advocate*, 25 February 1832; *PP* (Commons) 1837-38 [488] VIII: 259.

21. TNA, PRO, HO 42/179, 'At A Meeting of Deputies, from the Cotton Weavers', broadside, 22 August 1818. Hardman to Fletcher, 22 August 1818.

22. *A Report of the Proceedings of a Delegate Meeting*, p. 6.

23. Barbara Taylor, *Eve and the New Jerusalem: Socialism and Feminism in the Nineteenth Century*, Cambridge, 1993, p. 35; Davidoff and Hall, *Family Fortunes*, pp. 210, 275-79; Jane Rendall, *Women in Industrializing Society: England, 1750-1880*, Oxford, 1990, pp. 34-35, 79-80.

24. *United Trades' Co-operative Journal*, 1 May 1830. For 'respectability', see Prothero, *Artisans and Politics*, pp. 26-28; Hall, 'Tyranny, Work and Politics', pp. 435-36, 456-57, 467-68; Sonya Rose, 'Respectable Men, Disorderly Others: the Language of Gender and the Lancashire Weavers' Strike of 1878 in Britain', *Gender and History* 5 (Autumn 1993): 383-87; 'A Respectable Mon' in Samuel Laycock, *Lancashire Songs*, Manchester, 1866, pp. 49-51.

25. *United Trades' Co-operative Journal*, 14 August 1830.

26. *PP* (Commons) 1842 [158] XXXV: 18. See also, *United Trades' Co-operative Journal*, 6 March 1830; *Manchester Chronicle*, 17 September 1842. For the male bread-winner, see Rose, *Limited Livelihoods*, pp. 130-32; 138-44; Clark, *Struggle for the Breeches*, pp. 20-21, 197-98, 203-204, 218-19, 266-67.

27. Rule, 'Artisan Attitudes', pp. 25-26; George Jacob Holyoake, *Sixty Years of an Agitator's Life*, two volumes, London, 1882, 1: 23; [Leach], *Stubborn Facts*, pp. 11-12.

28. *Manchester Observer*, 18 April 1818.

29. *United Trades' Co-operative Journal*, 6 March 1830.

30. Richard Marsden, *Cotton Spinning: Its Development, Principles, and Practice*, London, 1891, pp. 224-25; *United Trades' Co-operative Journal*, 6 March 1830; *PP* (Commons) 1837-38 [488] VIII: 259.

31. *PP* (Commons) 1837-38 [488] VIII: 67.

32. George White, *A Practical Treatise on Weaving, By Hand and Power Looms*, Glasgow, 1846, pp. 197-98; James Latham, *The Art of Managing the Patent Power Loom; or the Overlookers and Weavers' Assistant*, Bury, n.d., pp. 36-38. For a critique, see Schwarzkopf, *Unpicking Gender*, pp. 53-81.

33. *The Pioneer*, 8 February 1834.

34. Rose, *Limited Livelihoods*, pp. 22-49. See also, Jane Humphries, "'… The Most Free from Objection …" The Sexual Division of Labor and Women's Work in Nineteenth Century England', *Journal of Economic History* 47 (December 1987): 930, 936-37; Robert Gray, 'Factory Legislation and the Gendering of Jobs in the North of England, 1830-1860', *Gender and History* 5 (Spring 1993): 56-57.

35. TNA, PRO, HO 40/23(3), Humphreys to Peel, 29 May 1829; Robert Sykes, 'Popular Politics and Trade Unionism in South-East Lancashire 1829-42', University of Manchester, Ph.D. dissertation, 1982, pp. 164-68.

36. *PP* (Commons) 1831-32 [706] XV: 323; *PP* (Commons) 1837-38 [488] VIII: 259. For female piecers, see also *PP* (Lords) 1819 [24] CX, Appendix 22; *PP* (Commons) 1833 [450] XX D1: 44. For practice of hiring women on small mules, see *PP* (Commons) 1816 [397] III: 355; *PP* (Lords) 1818 [90] XCVI: 186; *PP* (Lords) 1819 [24] CX: 237, 342, 400, 420, 436; *Manchester Guardian*, 12 February 1825.

37. Place to James Turner, 29 September 1835, quoted by Wanda F. Neff, *Victorian Working Women: An Historical and Literary Study of Women in British Industries and Professions, 1832-1850*, 1929; reprint ed., London, 1966, p. 31. For the spinners' strategy of 'patriarchial cooperation', see Clark, *Struggle For the Breeches*, pp. 5, 20-21, 24, 134-39.

38. *Poor Man's Advocate*, 25 February 1832; *United Trades' Co-operative Journal*, 3 April 1830.

39. Prothero identifies four key institutions: the friendly society, the house of call, tramping, and apprenticeship. See *Artisans and Politics*, pp. 22-50.

40. John Kennedy, 'A Brief Memoir of Samuel Crompton', *Memoirs of the Literary and Philosophical Society of Manchester* (1831): 335-36; *PP* (Commons) 1834 [167] XIX D1: 169.

41. *PP* (Commons) 1842 [158] XXXV: 14-15; *Oddfellows' Magazine* (October 1844): 217; P.H.J.H. Gosden, *The Friendly Societies in England 1815-1875*, Manchester, 1961, pp. 76-77, 221-23.

42. *PP* (Commons) 1824 [51] V: 610; Gosden, *Friendly Societies*, pp. 9-11, 71. See also, Hall, 'Tyranny, Work and Politics', pp. 454-57.

43. *PP* (Commons) 1837-38 [488] VIII: 44, 66, 258. *A Report of the Proceedings of a Delegate Meeting*, pp. 9-10, 48, 51. In the appendix to the latter, the delegates recommended in resolution 24 that female spinners become members of an association 'to be formed exclusively for themselves'.

44. *A Report of the Proceedings of a Delegate Meeting*, pp. 10, 15.

45. *PP* (Commons) 1837-38 [488] VIII: 273, 250-51, 280-82, 258. [John Doherty] *The Quinquarticular System of Organization. To the Operative Spinners of Manchester and Salford*, Manchester, 1834.

46. *Poor Man's Advocate*, 10 November 1832.

47. *PP* (Lords) 1819 [24] CX: 377; Andrew Ure, *The Cotton Manufacture of Great Britain*, two volumes, London, 1836; reprint ed., New York, 1970, 2: 448.

48. John Dunlop, *Artificial Drinking Usages of North Britain*, fourth ed., Greenock, 1836, pp. 5-10.

49. *Poor Man's Advocate*, 21 January 1832; Dunlop, *Artificial Drinking Usages*, pp. 5-10.

50. William Chadwick, *Reminiscences of Mottram*, reprint ed., 1972, p. 9.

51. Sim Schofield, *Short Stories about Failsworth Folk*, Blackpool, 1905, pp. 58-59; for the decline of St. Monday among spinners, see *PP* (Lords) 1819 [24] CX: 344; *PP* (Commons) 1833 [519] XXI D2: 36.

52. *PP* (Lords) 1819 [24] CX: 330, 341; William Lazonick, 'Industrial Relations and Technical Change: The Case of the Self-Acting Mule', *Cambridge Journal of Economics* 3 (1979): 233-34; Harold Catling, *The Spinning Mule*, Newton Abbot, 1970, pp. 32-34, 44-45; Kennedy, 'Brief Memoir', pp. 324-29.

53. Kennedy, 'Brief Memoir', pp. 335-36; Michael M. Edwards, *The Growth of the British Cotton Trade 1780-1815*, New York, 1967, p. 201.

54. *PP* (Lords) 1819 [24] CX: 348-49, 377; *PP* (Commons) 1834 [167] XIX D1: 168-69; *PP* (Commons) 1833 [519] XXI D2: 36; S. J. Chapman, *The Lancashire Cotton Industry: A Study in Economic Development*, Manchester, 1904, pp. 262-63; *idem*, 'The Regulation of Wages by Lists in the Spinning Industry', *Economic Journal* 9 (1899): 592-93.

55. For the rise of the two mule system, see Edward Baines, *History of the Cotton Manufacture in Great Britain*, London, 1835; reprint ed., New York, 1966, pp. 205-206; Kennedy, 'Brief Memoir', pp. 337-38; Catling, *Spinning Mule*, pp. 44-46; G.N. von Tunzelman, *Steam Power and British Industrialization to 1860*, Oxford, 1978, pp. 176-79.

56. *PP* (Commons) 1834 [167] XIX D1: 119e; Catling, *Spinning Mule*, pp. 166, 175; *PP* (Lords) 1819 [24] CX: 38-40; *Northern Star*, 11 May 1844.

57. *PP* (Commons) 1837-38 [488] VIII: 306-307; see also, James Montgomery, *The Theory and Practice of Cotton Spinning; or the Carding and Spinning Master's Assistant*, third ed., Glasgow, 1836, pp. 178-79.

58. Bradley, *Reminiscences*, p. 47; see also, the letter from 'A Persecuted Cotton Spinner', in *Northern Star*, 20 August 1842; Manchester Central Library, Higson Mss (microfilm copy), H52 Omnibus Book, p. 29.

59. Ure, *Cotton Manufacture*, 2: 172; *PP* (Commons) 1873 [C.754] LV: 11-12; *PP* (Commons) 1837-38 [488] VIII: 306-307.

60. *PP* (Commons) 1886 [C-4715] XXI: 177, 173; Montgomery, *Theory and Practice*, pp. 48-50; J. Lomax, *Fine Cotton Spinning: A Practical Manual*, Manchester, 1913, pp. 110, 116.

61. Bradley, *Reminiscences*, pp. 46-47; *PP* (Lords) 1819 [24] CX: 6, 35-37, 417.

62. Michael Huberman, *Escape from the Market: Negotiating Work in Lancashire*, Cambridge, 1996, pp. 49-60; Lazonick, 'Industrial Relations', pp. 242-46; Montgomery, *Theory and Practice*, pp. 272-73; *PP* (Commons) 1833 [450] XX D1: 52-53; Bradley, *Reminiscences*, pp. 92-95.

63. *PP* (Lords) 1818 [90] XCVI: 169; *PP* (Lords) 1819 [24] CX: 11-13, 343, 480-81; *PP* (Commons) 1833 [450] XX D1: 53-55. For piecers spinning, see *A Report of the Proceedings of a Delegate Meeting*, pp. 17, 37-38; Hall and Roberts (eds.), *William Aitken*, p. 19.

64. *PP* (Commons) 1833 [450] XX D1: 53, 2, 5, 8, 42-44. For the controversy over this question, see Neil J. Smelser, *Social Change in the Industrial Revolution: An Application of Theory to the British Cotton Industry*, Chicago, 1959; Michael Anderson, 'Sociological History and the Working-Class Family: Smelser Revisited', *Social History* 1 (October 1976): 317-34.

65. *PP* (Commons) 1834 [167] XIX D1 : 119e.

66. *PP* (Lords) 1819 [24] CX: 6, 11-13, 35-37, 41-46, 343; *PP* (Commons) 1834 [167] XIX D1: 119e-g; *Manchester Observer*, 8 August and 12 September 1818.

67. Mary Freifeld, 'Technological Change and the "Self-Acting" Mule: A Study of Skill and the Sexual Division of Labour', *Social History* 11 (October 1986): 320-31; John Foster, *Class Struggle and the Industrial Revolution: Early Industrial Capitalism in Three English Towns*, London, 1974, pp. 83, 296-97; Patrick Joyce, *Work, Society and Politics: the Culture of the Factory in Later Victorian England*, London, 1982, pp. 55-56, 61-63, 313-14; William Lazonick, *Competitive Advantage on the Shop Floor*, Cambridge, 1990, pp. 82-88.

68. E.C. Tufnell, *Character, Object, and Effects of Trades' Unions*, London, 1834, pp. 17-20; R.G. Kirby and A.E. Musson, *The Voice of the People: John Doherty, 1798-1854 Trade Unionist, Radical, and Factory Reformer*, Manchester, 1975, pp. 28-32.

69. *PP* (Commons) 1837-38 [488] VIII: 271; Bradley, *Reminiscences*, pp. 44-45.

70. *PP* (Commons) 1837-38 [488] VIII: 271-72, 252; *United Trades' Co-operative Journal*, 3 April 1830; see also, Kirby and Musson, *Voice of the People*, pp. 28, 60, 109, 142.

71. *PP* (Commons) 1837-38 [488] VIII: 271-72, 275-76; for a discussion of double decker mules, see Montgomery, *Theory and Practice*, pp. 192-94; Thomas Thornley, *Practical Treatise upon Self-Acting Mules*, Manchester, n.d., pp. 200-201.

72. [Leach], *Stubborn Facts*, pp. 29-30. See also, *Northern Star*, 9 April 1842 and 11 May 1844; *Ashton Reporter*, 25 October 1856.

73. *PP* (Commons) 1837-38 [488] VIII: 259; Marsden, *Cotton Spinning*, pp. 224-25.

74. Samuel Smiles, *Industrial Biography: Iron-Workers and Tool-Makers*, Chicago, 1890, pp. 324-27; Baines, *Cotton Manufacture*, pp. 206-208; Ure, *Cotton Manufacture*, 2: 194-98.

75. Ure, *Cotton Manufacture*, 2: 199; Tufnell, *Character, Object, and Effects*, pp. 107-109; Montgomery, *Theory and Practice*, p. 204; see also, W. Cooke Taylor, *Notes of a Tour in the Manufacturing Districts of Lancashire*, London, 1842; reprint ed., New York, 1968, p.110.

76. *PP* (Commons) 1833 [690] VI: 323. See also, Eleanor Gordon, *Women and the Labour Movement in Scotland, 1850-1914*, Oxford, 1991, pp. 44-45.

77. *Bolton Free Press*, 22 June 1839; *PP* (Commons) 1842 [31] XXII: 29.

78. *PP* (Commons) 1833 XX [450] D1: 46.

79. [Leach], *Stubborn Facts*, pp. 28-33.

80. Neuburg (ed.), *London Labour and the London Poor*, p. 392. See also, MCL, OB 360/72 Edwin Butterworth Mss (microfilm copy), November 1841; *Northern Star*, 11 May 1844; *PP* (Commons) 1842 [158] XXXV: 18, 107.

81. Kurt Neste, *The Mule Spinning Process, and the Machinery Employed in It*, Manchester, 1865, p. 62; *PP* (Commons) 1873 [C.754] LV: 10, 14; Marsden, *Cotton Spinning*, pp. 275, 289-90; George Henry Wood, 'The Statistics of Wages in the United Kingdom during the Nineteenth Century (Part XV) The Cotton Industry', *Journal of the Royal Statistical Society* (February 1910): 134; *idem*, 'The Statistics of Wages in the Nineteenth Century, Part XIX. The Cotton Industry', *Journal of the Royal Statistical Society* (June 1910): 612; Catling, *Spinning Mule*, pp. 115-19.

82. Ratcliffe and Chaloner (eds.), *A French Sociologist*, p. 99. For the price of new self actors, *PP* (Commons) 1835 [500] XXXV: 190; James Montgomery, *The Cotton Manufacture of the United States Contrasted and Compared with that of Great Britain*, Glasgow, 1840; reprint ed., New York, 1968, p. 76; *Manchester Guardian*, 22 May 1841; for energy costs, von Tunzelman, *Steam Power*, pp. 186-88, 192-93, 211, 290; Ure, *Cotton Manufacture*, 1: 304; Montgomery, *Theory and Practice*, p. 220.

83. Samuel Andrew, *Fifty Years' Cotton Trade*, Oldham, 1887, p. 6.

84. MCL, Mayall Mss, L43 Box 41 Memorandum Book 1845-90.

85. Wood, 'The Statistics of Wages', (February 1910): 134; *idem*, 'The Statistics of Wages', (June 1910): 612.

86. Marcroft, *Marcroft Family and the Inner Circle of Human Life*, p. 96. See also, Tufnell, *Character, Object, and Effects*, pp. 17-18; *The Economist*, 4 March 1848: 257.

87. *PP* (Commons) 1892 [C-6708-VI] XXXV, Group C: 28-29; Huberman, *Escape from the Market*, pp. 49-60; Lazonick, 'Industrial Relations', pp. 242-46.

88. Alan Fowler and Terry Wyke (eds.), *The Barefoot Aristocrats: A History of the Amalgamated Association of Operative Cotton Spinners*, Littleborough, 1987, pp. 36-58. In the late 1870s the spinners at the giant Britannia Mill in Mossley were, with only one or two exceptions, all union members. See MCL, Higson Mss (microfilm copy) H52 Omnibus Book, pp. 27-29; British Library of Political and Economic Science, Webb Trade Union Collection, Section A: XXXV: 291-98.

89. Catling, *Spinning Mule*, pp. 75-84, 97-113, 149; Freifeld, 'Technological Change', pp. 324-28.

90. Marsden, *Cotton Spinning*, pp. 256-57; Catling, *Spinning Mule*, p. 149; Thornley, *Practical Treatise*, p. 198.

91. Neste, quoted by, Catling, *Spinning Mule*, pp. 109-10; see also, Catling, pp. 75-77, 83-84, 98, 100-102, 107-10.

92. Bradley, *Reminiscences*, pp. 92-94; see also, Freifeld, 'Technological Change', pp. 325-27.

93. Catling, *Spinning Mule*, pp. 149, 161.

94. British Association for the Advancement of Science, *On the Regulation of Wages by Means of Lists in the Cotton Industry. Spinning*, Manchester, 1887, p. 7.

95. Lomax, *Fine Cotton Spinning*, pp. 110, 116; British Association, *On the Regulation of Wages*, p. 7; Catling, *Spinning Mule*, pp. 161-64.

96. *PP* (Commons) 1833 [450] XX D1: 50. See Jacques Rancière, 'The Myth of the Artisan: Critical Reflections on a Category of Social History', *International Labor and Working-Class History* 24 (Fall 1983): 1-16.

97. Bradley, *Reminiscences*, pp. 46, 44-45.

98. Hall and Roberts (eds.), *William Aitken*, pp. 21-22; TNA, PRO, HO 20/10, Interview with William Aitken.

99. Ginswick (ed.), *Labour and the Poor*, 1: 86-87; Edwin Butterworth, *Historical Sketches of Oldham*, Oldham, 1856; reprint ed., Manchester, 1981, pp. 177-78; *HD* Third series 1847 LXXXIX: 492. For examples of the 'self-made' man, see *Ashton Chronicle*, 27 January 1849; *Ashton Reporter*, 1 September 1866 (Abel and James Buckley). Ibid., 20 February 1886 (Hugh Mason). Ibid., 25 April 1868 (Thomas Mason). Ibid., 11 March 1876 (John Mayall).

100. *Morning Chronicle*, 9 May 1844. TNA, PRO, HO 20/10, Interview with James Duke; *PP* (Commons) 1833 [450] XX D2: 134.

101. TNA, PRO, HO 20/10, Interview with Timothy Higgins. In the 1841 census Ireland was listed as his birthplace. See TNA, PRO, HO 107/532.

102. Behagg, *Politics and Production*, pp. 1, 155-56, 224-26. Clark, *Struggle For the Breeches*, pp. 220-27; Pickering, *Chartism and the Chartists*, pp. 34-55.

103. *The Champion*, 5 January 1850. *PP* (Commons) 1835 [500] XXXV: 185-86. In 1841 Irish spinners represented only about 2 per cent of the spinners in Ashton (see Table 3).

104. *PP* (Commons) 1836 XXXIV, Appendix G: 84-85.

105. TNA, PRO, HO 20/10, Interview with Timothy Higgins. Dorothy Thompson, 'Ireland and the Irish in English Radicalism', in Epstein and Thompson (eds.), *Chartist Experience*, p. 122.

106. Kirby and Musson, *Voice of the People*, pp. 52, 58, 214, 355; Ratcliffe and Chaloner (eds.), *A French Sociologist*, p. 95.

107. *A Report of the Proceedings of a Delegate Meeting*, pp. 12, 4, 8-10, 25.

108. Harry Pollitt, *Serving My Time: An Apprenticeship to Politics*, London, 1940, p. 57. Born in 1890, Pollitt grew up in Droylsden. His father was a blacksmith's striker; his mother worked in the weaving shed. See also, Thomas Cooper, *Eight Letters to the Young Men of the Working Classes*, London, 1850 in Gregory Claeys (ed.), *The Chartist Movement in Britain, 1838-1850*, six volumes, London, 2001, 5: 412-13.

109. Alexander Somerville, *The Autobiography of A Working Man*, 1848; reprint ed., London, 1951, p. 110.

110. Bradley, *Reminiscences*, p. 273.

111. *Manchester Guardian*, 18 December 1847. For the high level of turnover among piecers, see *PP* (Lords) 1819 [24] CX: 480-81; *PP* (Commons) 1892 [C-6708-VI] XXXV Group C: 28-29.

112. TNA, PRO, HO 107/532.

113. *Ashton Reporter*, 18 May 1889.

114. *Northern Star*, 9 April 1842. [Leach,] *Stubborn Facts*, pp. 42-44; Eileen Yeo and E.P. Thompson (eds.), *The Unknown Mayhew*, New York, 1971, pp. 323-24, 328; Sykes, 'Popular Politics', pp. 332-38.

115. *The Trial of Feargus O'Connor and Fifty-Eight Others on a Charge of Sedition, Conspiracy, Tumult, & Riot*, Manchester, 1843; reprint ed., New York, 1970, p. 279.

116. TNA, PRO, HO 42/180, 'At a Meeting of Deputies from the Undermentioned Trades', broadside.

Chapter II

1.   Finsbury Tract Society, 'The Question "What is a Chartist?" Answered', 1839, in Dorothy Thompson (ed.), *The Early Chartists*, Columbia, 1971, p. 89.

2.   Ibid. It was priced at 1s. 6d. per hundred, or five for a 1d.

3.   Ibid., pp. 89-92.

4.   Ibid., p. 89.

5.   Ibid., p. 92.

6.   John Belchem, 'Republicanism, Popular Constitutionalism and the Radical Platform in Early Nineteenth-Century England', *Social History* 6 (January 1981): 1-32; James Epstein, *Radical Expression: Political Language, Ritual, and Symbol in England, 1790-1850*, New York, 1994, pp. 3-28; James Vernon, *Politics and the People: A Study in English Political Culture, c. 1815-1867*, Cambridge, 1993.

7.   For two different views, see Stedman Jones, *Languages of Class*, pp. 93-95, 101-4, 107-8, 177-78; Patrick Joyce, *Democratic Subjects: The Self and the Social in Nineteenth-Century England*, Cambridge, 1994, pp. 1-20.

8.   Epstein, *Radical Expression*, p. 71.

9.   Taylor, 'Rethinking the Chartists', p. 492. Michael Savage, 'Space, Networks and Class Formation', in Neville Kirk (ed.), *Social Class and Marxism: Defences and Challenges*, Aldershot, 1996, pp. 59, 67-69, 75-80.

10. *Northern Star*, 29 December 1838. Taylor, 'The Six Points', in Ashton, Fyson, and Roberts (eds.), *Chartist Legacy*, pp. 1-3, 7-12; Thompson, *The Making of the English Working Class*, pp. 821-26; Thompson, *Chartists*, pp. 11-36.

11. R.C.O. Matthews, *A Study in Trade-Cycle History: Economic Fluctuations in Great Britain 1833-1842*, Cambridge, 1954, pp. 141-46; Sykes, 'Popular Politics', pp. 332-38.

12. *Manchester and Salford Advertiser*, 27 January 1838.

13. Lawrence, *Speaking for the People*, pp. 3-6.

14. Belchem, *'Orator' Hunt*, pp. 4, 43, 58, 64; Epstein, *Lion of Freedom*, pp. 90-93, 110-31.

15. Epstein, *Radical Expression*, p. 27; Vernon, *Politics and the People*, pp. 9-10.

16. The Popular Memory Group, 'Popular Memory: Theory, Politics, Method', in Richard Johnson et al. (eds.), *Making Histories: Studies in History-Writing and Politics*, Minneapolis, 1982, pp. 213-14; Vernon, *Politics and the People*, pp. 207-8.

17. Bonnie Smith, *The Gender of History: Men, Women, and Historical Practice*, Cambridge, 1998, pp. 19-20, 104-5, 117-18, 130.
18. *HD*, Third Series, XIX (1833): 752-53. Vernon, *Politics and the People*, pp. 304-5; Epstein, *Radical Expression*, pp. 13-14, 177.
19. *Manchester and Salford Advertiser*, 29 July 1837. Vernon, *Politics and the People*, pp. 298-302; Epstein, *Radical Expression*, pp. 27, 152-53. For one such Manchester dinner, see *Manchester and Salford Advertiser*, 3 June 1837.
20. Robson (ed.), *Collected Works*, Vol. 18: *Essays on Politics and Society*, Toronto, 1977, 18: 121. See also, Dror Wahrman, *Imagining the Middle Class: The Political Representation of Class in Britain, c. 1780-1840*, Cambridge, 1995, pp. 352-61.
21. *People's Paper*, 30 August 1856.
22. Ibid., 22 December 1855.
23. William Cobbett, *Advice to Young Men*, London, 1830; reprint ed., Oxford, 1980, p. 301. See also, Ian Dyck, *William Cobbett and Rural Popular Culture*, Cambridge, 1992, pp. 125-51.
24. For this latter division in Ashton Chartism, see *Northern Star*, 30 September 1843 and 13 November 1841.
25. *McDouall's Chartist and Republican Journal*, 31 July 1841.
26. *Northern Star*, 28 April 1838.
27. *Manchester Guardian* and *Manchester Times and Gazette*, 29 January 1831.
28. *Manchester and Salford Advertiser*, 2 June and 22 September 1838.
29. TNA, PRO, HO 40/47, Report of the Speeches Delivered at Public Meeting of the Chartists, held on Nottingham Forest, 22 May 1839; *Northern Star*, 1 June 1839.
30. *Northern Star*, 1 June 1839.
31. Ibid., 16 November 1839.
32. Ibid.
33. Epstein, *Radical Expression*, pp. 149-55; E.J. Hobsbawm, 'Introduction: Inventing Traditions', in Hobsbawm and Terence Ranger (eds.), *The Invention of Tradition*, Cambridge, 1992, pp. 1-14.
34. Cotton, 'Popular Movements', pp. 124-25; Epstein, *Radical Expression*, pp. 82-86; Samuel Bamford, *Passages in the Life of a Radical*, 1884; reprint ed., Oxford, 1984, p. 146.
35. John Rylands University Library, Peterloo Relief Fund, English Mss no. 172; Cotton, 'Popular Movements', pp. 124-25; Thompson, *The Making of the English Working Class*, pp. 679-89.
36. For Higson's role, see his obituary in *Ashton Reporter*, 9 April 1859; *Manchester Observer*, 19 August 1820.
37. The Ashton radicals noted that their Peterloo procession had attracted 'double' the attendance of the coronation procession. Henry Hunt, *Memoirs of Henry Hunt*, three volumes, London, 1820-22, 2: 25.
38. *Northern Star*, 22 August 1840 and 24 August 1844.
39. *National Reformer*, 14 June 1868.
40. Hunt, *Memoirs*, 2: 25.
41. *Ashton Reporter*, 30 January 1869.
42. TNA, PRO, HO 42/177, Brother of No. 2 to Fletcher, 10 May 1818. Bamford, *Passages*, pp. 123-25.

43. *Northern Star*, 16 November 1839.

44. *Northern Star*, 16 November 1839; 14 November 1840; 16 November 1844; 13 November 1847. The phrase 'village Hampden' appeared in Thomas Gray's 'Elegy Written in a Country Church-Yard'. Several lines were reprinted on the title page. See John Stafford, *Songs Comic and Sentimental*, Ashton, 1840.

45. Stafford, *Songs*, title page and preface, 'To The Public'.

46. Ibid., 'To The Public'.

47. Ibid., pp. 3-8, 15-17, 17-22.

48. Ibid., pp. 6, 21-22, 15.

49. For other Chartist theatre groups, see Thompson, *Chartists*, pp. 117-18.

50. *Poor Man's Guardian and Repealer's Friend*, no. 4.

51. William Farish, *The Autobiography of Wiliam Farish: The Struggles of A Handloom Weaver*, 1889; reprint ed., London, 1996, p. 50.

52. *Northern Star*, 31 October 1840. See also, Ibid., 19 December 1840; 21 August 1841.

53. *Manchester and Salford Advertiser*, 30 June 1838.

54. While in prison William Aitken wrote a short life of the Tyrolean patriot Andreas Hofer (1767-1810). See *Ashton Reporter*, 2 October 1869.

55. David Geggus, 'British Opinion and the Emergence of Haiti, 1791-1805', in James Walvin (ed.), *Slavery and British Society, 1776-1846*, Baton Rouge, 1982, pp. 123-49; for the radical careers of Wedderburn and Davidson, see Peter Fryer, *Staying Power: The History of Black People in Britain*, Atlantic Highlands, 1984, pp. 214-27; Patricia Hollis, 'Anti-Slavery and British Working-Class Radicalism in the Years of Reform', in Christine Bolt and Seymour Drescher (eds.), *Anti-Slavery, Religion, and Reform*, Folkestone, 1980, pp. 294-315.

56. *Northern Star*, 2 February 1839. For the role of women in the commemoration of Peterloo, see Ibid., 22 August 1840 and 19 August 1843; *Ashton Reporter*, 30 January 1869.

57. Stedman Jones, *Languages of Class*, pp. 96, 102, 104-5.

58. *Northern Star*, 1 December 1838.

59. Ibid., 3 April 1841 (O'Connor) and 26 October 1850 (Ernest Jones).

60. 'A Constant Reader' described party politics in Rochdale: 'There are here, as in most other boroughs, three parties—the tories, the liberals, and the radicals.' *Manchester and Salford Advertiser*, 6 May 1837. See also, T.A. Jenkins, *Parliament, Party and Politics in Victorian Britain*, Manchester, 1996; Miles Taylor, *The Decline of British Radicalism, 1847-1860*, Oxford, 1995.

61. *Isis*, 16 June 1832. Between 1832 and 1841 electors who voted in parliamentary elections ranged between 372 and 557. See J. Vincent and M. Stenton (eds.), *McCalmont's Parliamentary Poll Book: British Election Results 1832-1918*, eighth ed., Brighton, 1971, p. 8.

62. W.O. Aydelotte, 'Parties and Issues in Early Victorian England', *Journal of British Studies* 5 (1966): 108-14; W.R. Ward, *Religion and Society in England 1790-1850*, New York, 1973, pp. 178-92. For party disputes over revising the lists of electors, see *Manchester Guardian*, 25 April and 3 October 1835, 9 September 1843, and 5 September 1846.

63. Tameside Local Studies and Archives Centre, L324.1 'To the Independent Electors of the Borough of Ashton' (1841); BL, Robert Peel Papers, Add Mss 40,613, f. 47, Mellor to Peel, 6 December 1841; *The Times*, 20 September 1837. For the Ashton Operative Conservative society, see *Manchester and Salford Advertiser*, 5 and 12 December 1835; William Paul, *A History of the Origin and Progress of Operative Conservative Societies*, second ed., Leeds, 1839, pp. 8-10. *Stockport Advertiser*, 3 July 1835; *Manchester Guardian*, 16 July 1845.

64. *Manchester Times and Gazette*, 5 January 1833; *Manchester Times*, 21 April 1838; *Manchester and Salford Advertiser*, 21 February 1835.

65. *Manchester Guardian*, 16 February 1833. Educated for the pulpit, Hindley took over the management of the family spinning mill at Dukinfield and married into the mill owning Buckley family. He served as MP for Ashton from1835 until 1857. See *Ashton Reporter*, 5 December 1857; John Evans, *Lancashire Authors and Orators*, London, 1850, pp. 132-35.

66. William Glover, *History of Ashton-under-Lyne and the Surrounding District*, Ashton, 1884, pp. 39-41. See also, Stewart Angas Weaver, *John Fielden and the Politics of Popular Radicalism 1832-1847*, Oxford, 1987, pp. 142-47; Cecil Driver, *Tory Radical: The Life of Richard Oastler*, New York, 1946, pp. 310-30.

67. *Manchester and Salford Advertiser*, 17 and 31 October 1835; 4 June and 22 October 1836.

68. Michael S. Edwards, *Purge This Realm: A Life of Joseph Rayner Stephens*, London, 1994, pp. 21-86; Eileen Groth Lyon, *Politicians in the Pulpit: Christian Radicalism in Britain from the Fall of the Bastille to the Disintegration of Chartism*, Aldershot, 1999, pp. 168-70, 182-86.

69. Sykes, 'Popular Politics', pp. 462-64.

70. E.A. Rose, *Methodism in Ashton-under-Lyne, Part Two: 1797-1914*, Ashton, 1969, pp. 46-52; Eileen Yeo, 'Christianity in the Chartist Struggle 1838-1842', *Past and Present* 91 (May 1981): 115; Edwards, *Purge This Realm*, pp. 17-20, 146-54.

71. *Manchester Guardian*, 7 January 1837; *Northern Star*, 17 February and 17 March 1838.

72. Alfred [Samuel H. G. Kydd], *The History of the Factory Movement*, two volumes, London, 1857; reprint ed., New York, 1966, 2: 78-79; *A Report of the Important Proceedings of a Public Meeting, held in…Oldham on…the 11th…of November, 1836: On the Subject of Shortening the Time of Labour in the Cotton, Woollen, Silk and Other Factories in Great Britain and Ireland*, Oldham, 1836, pp. 25-33; T.M. Kemnitz and F. Jacques, 'J.R. Stephens and the Chartist Movement', *International Review of Social History* 19 (1974): 218-19.

73. For Stephens on universal suffrage, see *Northern Star*, 3 February and 6 October 1838; 1 June 1839; 6 March 1841.

74. *Manchester and Salford Advertiser*, 22 September 1838.

75. *New Moral World*, 20 April 1839. Eileen Yeo, 'Robert Owen and Radical Culture', in Sidney Pollard and John Salt (eds.), *Robert Owen: Prophet of the Poor*, Lewisburg, 1971, pp. 95-103.

76. *New Moral World*, 20 April 1839; 5 January, 9 February, 14 December 1839; 26 December 1840; see also, ibid., 26 May, 25 August, 6 October 1838; 8 June 1839;

16 April 1842 (lectures); 26 December 1840; 16 September and 23 December 1843 (Sunday School and friendly society); 9 February and 20 April 1839 (festivals).

77. *What is Socialism? and What would be its Practical Effects upon Society? A Correct Report of the Public Discussion between Robert Owen & Mr. John Brindley*, London, 1841, pp. 47, 7-8. See also, Taylor, *Eve and the New Jerusalem*, pp. 272-73; Edward Royle, *Victorian Infidels: The Origins of the British Secularist Movement, 1791-1866*, Manchester, 1974, pp. 61-65.

78. *Northern Star*, 17 March 1849. See also, Gregory Claeys, *Citizens and Saints: Politics and Anti-Politics in Early British Socialism*, Cambridge, 1989, pp. 212-18.

79. *Trial of Feargus O'Connor and Fifty-Eight Others*, p. ix. *Northern Star*, 1 August 1840 and 27 February 1841; Finsbury Tract Society, 'What is a Chartist?', in Thompson (ed.), *The Early Chartists*, p. 89.

80. *Northern Star*, 17 November 1838 and 16 November 1839.

81. Ibid., 6 January and 27 October 1838.

82. Sidney Tarrow, *Power in Movement: Social Movements, Collective Action and Politics*, Cambridge, 1994, pp. 7-8, 24-25, 153-55; Charles Tilly, *Popular Contention in Great Britain, 1758-1834*, Cambridge, 1995, pp. 37-38, 288-89, 331, 338-39, 375-76; Epstein, *Lion of Freedom*, pp. 115, 134-35.

83. *Northern Star*, 24 August 1839. See also, Ibid., 8 December 1838 (Higgins); 10 November 1838 and 1 June 1839 (Deegan); 2 February 1839 (Ashton Female Association).

84. *HD*, Third Series LXIII (1842): 77. Antony Taylor, 'Medium and Messages: Republicanism's Traditions and Preoccupations', in David Nash and Antony Taylor (eds.), *Republicanism in Victorian Society*, Phoenix Mill, 2000, pp. 2-3; Paul Pickering, '"The Hearts of the Millions": Chartism and Popular Monarchism in the 1840s', *History* 88 (April 2003): 227-48.

85. William Lovett, *Life and Struggles of William Lovett in his Pursuit of Bread, Knowledge & Freedom*, London, 1876; reprint ed., London, 1967, Appendix A: 'Petition Agreed to at the "Crown and Anchor" Meeting, February 28th, 1837', p. 311; Finsbury Tract Society, 'What is a Chartist?' in Thompson (ed.), *The Early Chartists*, pp. 91-92.

86. Lovett, *Life and Struggles*, Appendix A, p. 313. Anna Clark, 'Manhood, Womanhood, and the Politics of Class in Britain, 1790-1845', in Laura L. Frader and Sonya O. Rose (eds.), *Gender and Class in Modern Europe*, Ithaca, 1996, pp. 276-77.

87. *Bolton Chronicle*, 1 April 1848. Behagg, *Politics and Production*, pp. 224-26.

88. Taylor, 'Six Points', in Ashton, Fyson, and Roberts (eds.), *Chartist Legacy*, pp. 11-13. Jephson, *The Platform*, 2: 133-39, 142, 146.

89. *Manchester and Salford Advertiser*, 27 October 1838.

90. *Northern Star*, 27 October 1838.

91. Flora Tristan, *London Journal: A Survey of London Life in the 1830s*, translated by Dennis Palmer and Giselle Pincetl, Paris, 1840; London, 1980, pp. 199-200, 227, 240-42.

92. For contradictory statements by O'Connor, see *Northern Star*, 14 September 1839 and 1 July 1843; R.J. Richardson, *The Rights of Woman*, Manchester, 1840.

93. Mrs. Hugo Reid [Marion Reid], *A Plea for Woman: Being a Vindication of the Importance and Extent of Her Natural Sphere of Action*, Edinburgh, 1843, pp. 17-18.

94. Clark, *Struggle for the Breeches*, pp. 271, 220-21, 230-34; Jutta Schwarzkopf, *Women in the Chartist Movement*, London, 1991, pp. 58, 76-77, 264-69. For different perspectives, see Thompson, *Chartists*, pp. 120-51; Michelle De Larrabeiti, 'Conspicuous Before the World: the Political Rhetoric of the Chartist Women', in Eileen Janes Yeo (ed.), *Radical Femininity: Women's Self-Representation in the Public Sphere*, Manchester, 1998, pp. 106-26.

95. Lovett, *Life and Struggles*, p. 141.

96. *The People's Charter*, third ed., 1838, p. 9, quoted by Thompson, *Chartists*, p. 124.

97. *Northern Star*, 3 November 1838.

98. Ibid., 30 January 1841.

99. *Operative*, 4 November 1838; *New Moral World*, 15 May 1841.

100. *Northern Star*, 1 July 1843 and 14 September 1839.

101. *Bolton Chronicle*, 1 April 1848 (Parkinson); *Northern Star*, 5 September 1840 (McDouall).

102. *Northern Star*, 16 May 1840.

103. Finsbury Tract Society, 'What is a Chartist?' in Thompson (ed.), *The Early Chartists*, pp. 92-93.

104. *Northern Star*, 2 February 1839.

105. Ben Brierley, *Home Memories and Recollections of a Life*, Manchester, 1886, pp. 23-24.

106. *Northern Star*, 22 August 1840.

107. *Northern Star*, 8 April 1843, quoted by Edward Royle, 'Chartists and Owenites—Many Parts but One Body', *Labour History Review* 65 (2000): 10-11.

108. *New Moral World*, 25 November 1843. See also, Neville Kirk, 'In Defence of Class', pp. 16-25; Claeys, *Citizens and Saints*, pp. 208-60; Royle, 'Chartists and Owenites', pp. 2-21.

109. Yeo, 'Chartist Democracy', in Epstein and Thompson (eds.), *Chartist Experience*, pp. 345-80; Paul Pickering, 'Chartism and the "Trade of Agitation" in Early Victorian England', *History* 76 (June 1991): 221-37; Epstein, *Lion of Freedom*, pp. 220-35; Taylor, 'Rethinking the Chartists', p. 492; Philip Howell, '"Diffusing the Light of Liberty": The Geography of Political Lecturing in the Chartist Movement', *Journal of Historical Geography* 21 (January 1995): 23-27, 35-36.

110. Bates, *A Sketch of His Life*.

111. *Northern Star*, 1 August 1840; *Manchester and Salford Advertiser*, 22 September 1838.

112. *Manchester and Salford Advertiser*, 28 September 1839. Pickering, *Chartism and the Chartists*, pp. 49-53; Behagg, *Politics and Production*, pp.1, 156-57, 224-26.

113. *Poor Man's Guardian and Repealer's Friend*, no. 8.

114. Yeo, 'Chartist Democracy', in Epstein and Thompson (eds.), *Chartist Experience*, pp. 351-54. For the Sturges Bourne Acts as 'a death blow to their rights and privileges' and the use of the class system, see TNA, PRO, HO 42/177, Thackery to Fletcher, 16 May 1818 and and *Northern Star*, 13 July 1839; Robert Wearmouth, *Methodism and the Working-Class Movements in England, 1800-1850*, London, 1937, pp. 100-129.

115. *Northern Star*, 3 February, 10 and 24 March, and 1 September 1838.

116. Ibid., 27 April and 29 June 1839. 'There were,' Storer and Pilling later explained, 'two Associations in the town, the Senior and Junior; the former for middle-aged men, the latter for young men.' The members of the 'Juvenile Radical Association' were expelled from the original Fleet Street association because of their involvement in drilling. See Ibid., 13 November 1841 and 11 May 1839.

117. Ibid., 10 October 1840; there were also NCA localities in Stalybridge, Dukinfield, Mossley, and Hooley Hill. See Ibid., 11 December 1841; 1 and 15 January 1842; 18 June 1842.

118. Ibid., 27 February 1841. After an Ashton meeting, O'Connor called on men and women to come forward and join the NCA. See Ibid., 4 December 1841.

119. Ibid., 13 November 1841 and 7 August 1841.

120. *The Life Boat*, 16 December 1843.

121. Jephson, *The Platform*, 2: 134-39, 142, 146.

122. *National* (1839): 52-53.

123. *Northern Star*, 26 February 1842.

124. Ibid., 22 May 1841; 11 September 1841; 16 July 1842; 5 November 1842.

125. *Manchester and Salford Advertiser*, 21 February 1835.

126. *Northern Star*, 13 July 1839 and *Manchester and Salford Advertiser*, 29 June 1839. On the question of 'the sacred month', Deegan voted in obedience to the wishes of his constituents, but against his own opinions. See *North Cheshire Reformer*, 16 August 1839; BL, Place Papers, Add Mss 34,245B, Deegan to Fletcher, 6 August 1839.

127. *Northern Star*, 26 June and 3 July 1841.

128. *Manchester Political Register*, 4 January 1817. Epstein, *Lion of Freedom*, pp. 90-137; Vernon, *Politics and the People*, pp. 208-14.

129. *Northern Star*, 6 January and 28 April 1838.

130. *Northern Star*, 18 May 1839. Butterworth, *Historical Account*, pp. 108-10; for unsuccessful efforts of Stalybridge radicals to use town hall, see *Northern Star*, 12 May 1838.

131. Butterworth, *Historical Account*, pp. 120-21; Coulthart, *A Report of the Sanatory Condition*, p. 15. For meetings at Ashton Moss, see Hall, 'Tyranny, Work and Politics', pp. 460-62.

132. *Manchester Guardian*, 24 April 1839; *Northern Star*, 13 April 1839. For meetings near Thacker's foundry during the 1842 strike, see TNA, PRO, Treasury Solicitor's Papers, TS 11/813/2677.

133. Lovett and Collins, *Chartism*, p. 46.

134. *Northern Star*, 2 February and 20 April 1839; 22 August 1840. Of the 6312 signatures from Ashton to the first national petition, 1312 were by women. See Thompson, *Chartists*, p. 342.

135. *Northern Star*, 16 November 1839 and 22 September 1838; *Manchester Guardian*, 24 April 1839.

136. *Northern Star*, 2 February, 27 April, and 1 June 1839.

137. Ibid., 2 February 1839.

138. *People's Paper*, 9 October 1852.

139. *Northern Star*, 4 August 1838; *Bolton Free Press*, 22 June 1839; *Northern Star*, 24 November 1838.

140. For differing party uses of 'the people', see Vernon, *Politics and the People*, pp. 298-305.

141. Taylor, 'Rethinking the Chartists', pp. 486-87, 479-82; Stedman Jones, *Languages of Class*, pp. 93-96, 103-104. For critiques of Stedman Jones, see Kirk, 'In Defence of Class', pp. 2-47; Epstein, *In Practice*, pp. 16-29.

142. Robert Tucker (ed.), *The Marx-Engels Reader*, second ed., New York, 1978, pp. 608, 218. See also, R.J. Morris, *Class and Class Consciousness in the Industrial Revolution, 1780-1850*, London, 1979, pp. 24-25.

143. *Northern Star*, 4 August 1838. Dorothy Thompson, 'Who were "the People" in 1842?', in Malcolm Chase and Ian Dyck (eds.), *Living and Learning: Essays in Honour of J.F.C. Harrison*, Aldershot, 1996, pp. 119-23, 127, 131.

144. Edward Baines, *The Designs of the Chartists, and their Probable Consequences: A Letter Addressed to Mr. James Ibbetson, Bookseller, Bradford*, Leeds, 1839, pp. 6-7.

145. For a discussion of the social composition of Ashton Chartism, see Chapter Four.

146. *Annual Register* (1839), quoted by Edward Royle, *Modern Britain: A Social History, 1750-1985*, London, 1987, p. 125.

147. *United Trades' Co-operative Journal*, 8 May 1830.

148. W. Clarke, *A Reply to 'An Appeal to Members of Parliament, and the Working Classes on the Ten Hours' Factory Bill'; or the 'Doctor Dissected'*, Ashton, 1837, p. 15.

149. *Northern Star*, 3 March 1838. For the Stephenites' address, see Ibid., 13 October 1838.

150. Ibid., 3 February 1838.

151. Ibid., 1 June 1839.

152. BL, Place Papers, Add Mss 27,810, Place to Harrison, 21 February 1842. For similar views, see Baines, *Designs of the Chartists*, pp. 3-7; Gore, *Letter to the Middle Classes*, pp. 3-4, 7.

153. TNA, PRO, HO 40/38, Hyde magistrates to Russell, 16 November 1838; HO 40/38, Anonymous to Jowett, 4 December 1838; *Manchester Guardian*, 19 December 1838.

154. *Manchester Guardian*, 27 May 1840. For the 1830-31 strike, see evidence of Samuel Robinson and Thomas Ashton in *PP* (Commons) 1839 [169] XIX: 78-83; Steinberg, *Fighting Words*, pp. 206-26.

155. TNA, PRO, HO 40/43, Shaw to Phillipps, 9 December 1839.

156. *Manchester and Salford Advertiser*, 15 January 1842; *Northern Star*, 18 May 1839. Tameside, L322, William Aitken, 'To the Non-Electors and Electors of the Borough of Ashton-under-Lyne' [1841].

157. *Northern Star*, 5 March 1842.

158. *Northern Liberator*, 29 August 1840; *English Chartist Circular*, vol. 1, no. 50.

159. *Northern Star*, 2 July 1842.

160. See the Halifax speech by Matthew Fletcher in *Northern Star*, 4 August 1838.

161. Belchem, *'Orator' Hunt*, pp. 4, 43, 58, 64; Epstein, *Lion of Freedom*, pp. 90-93, 110-31; Jephson, *The Platform*, 1: xix.

162. William Lindsay, *Some Notes: Personal and Public*, Aberdeen, 1898, pp. 149-50. TNA, PRO, TS 11/1030/4424A, Queen vs Timothy Higgins; *Northern Star*, 8 December 1838.

163. *Northern Liberator*, 21 March 1840. For Chartist petitions, see Epstein, *Lion of Freedom*, pp. 104-110; *idem, Radical Expression*, pp. 17-18; Paul Pickering, '"And Your Petitioners &c": Chartist Petitioning in Popular Politics 1838-48', *English Historical Review* 116 (April 2001): 378-80.

164. BL, Add Mss 34,245A, Lowery and Duncan to the Convention, 12 and 22 March 1839, in Harrison and Hollis (eds.), *Robert Lowery*, pp. 233, 235-36.

165. Epstein, *Lion of Freedom*, pp. 138-39; T.M. Parssinen, 'Association, Convention and Anti-Parliament in British Radical Politics, 1771-1848', *English Historical Review* 88 (July 1973): 521-33.

166. For a discussion of these tactics, see Richard Pilling's speech at Stockport, *Northern Star*, 27 July 1839. See also, Epstein, *Lion of Freedom*, pp. 157-58; I.J. Prothero, 'William Benbow and the Concept of the "General Strike"', *Past and Present* 63 (May 1974): 149-55.

167. *Northern Star*, 1 June 1839.

168. William Benbow, *Grand National Holiday, and Congress of the Productive Classes*, London, [1832], p. 7. Prothero, 'William Benbow', pp. 170-71; Epstein, *Lion of Freedom*, pp. 164-81; Robert Sykes, 'Physical-Force Chartism: The Cotton District and the Chartist Crisis of 1839', *International Review of Social History* 30 (1985): 224-27.

169. Harrison and Hollis (eds.), *Robert Lowery*, p. 142.

170. Philip Snowden, *An Autobiography*, two volumes, London, 1934, 1: 83-84. Florence Boos (ed.), *William Morris's Socialist Diary*, London, 1982, pp. 26-27, 49, 53; Owen Ashton, 'Orator and Oratory in the Chartist Movement, 1840-1848', in Ashton, Fyson, and Roberts (eds.), *Chartist Legacy*, pp. 48-79; Paul Pickering, 'Class Without Words: Symbolic Communication in the Chartist Movement', *Past and Present* 112 (August 1986): 144-47, 152-54.

171. Lindsay, *Some Notes*, pp. 149-50.

172. Ingrid and Peter Kuczynski (eds.), *A Young Revolutionary in Nineteenth-Century England: Selected Writings of Georg Weerth*, Berlin, 1971, p. 67. Weerth quoted here his Bradford friend John Jackson.

173. For the responses of a Chartist crowd at Ashton, see *Northern Star*, 27 April 1839; TNA, PRO, HO 40/37, Meeting of Chartists at Ashton-under-Lyne, 20 April 1839. See also, John Belchem and James Epstein, 'The Nineteenth-Century Gentleman Leader Revisited', *Social History* 22 (May 1997): 181-85, 188; Boos (ed.), *William Morris's Socialist Diary*, pp. 33, 42, 45.

174. Harrison and Hollis (eds.), *Robert Lowery*, p. 96.

175. Ingrid and Peter Kuczynski (eds.), *A Young Revolutionary*, p. 111.

176. *Northern Star*, 2 June 1849. See also, Harrison and Hollis (eds.), *Robert Lowery*, p. 96.

177. For an example of O'Connor's use of this phrase, see *Northern Star*, 16 May 1840.

178. Raphael Samuel and Paul Thompson, 'Introduction', in Samuel and Thompson (eds.), *The Myths We Live By*, London, 1990, pp. 4-5; Jon Lawrence, 'Labour—The Myths It Has Lived By', in Duncan Tanner, Pat Thane, and Nick Tiratsoo (eds.), *Labour's First Century*, Cambridge, 2000, pp. 341-66.

179. See William Aitken's letter in *Northern Liberator*, 14 November 1840.

180. At Kersal Moor, the Stalybridge association carried a banner with Lafayette's quote. *Northern Star*, 1 June 1839. His lines appeared on the masthead of the *Chartist Circular*. See also, the editorial 'The Nation's Will', in the *Northern Star*, 4 August 1838.

181. *Northern Star*, 25 March 1848.

182. C.F. Volney, *The Ruins, or the Meditation on the Revolutions of Empires: and the Law of Nature*, Paris, 1802; New York, 1950, pp. 63-66. Epstein, *Radical Expression*, pp. 115, 143, 161-62; Prothero, 'William Benbow', pp. 161-62.

183. *Northern Star*, 18 May 1839; *McDouall's Chartist and Republican Journal*, 31 July 1841.

184. *Northern Star*, 17 July 1841.

185. *Manchester and Salford Advertiser*, 20 August 1842.

186. *Northern Star*, 16 May 1840; *Trial of O'Connor and Fifty-Eight Others*, p. 279.

187. David Ross, *The State of the Country, as the Effect of Class Legislation; and the Charter as the Remedy*, Manchester, [1842], in Gregory Claeys (ed.), *The Chartist Movement in Britain, 1838-1850*, six volumes, London, 2001, 3: 107.

Chapter III

1. *Northern Star*, 29 December 1838; Thompson, *Chartists*, pp. 11-36. For the radicals' response in Ashton to the 1832 Act, see *Poor Man's Guardian*, 3 November 1832 and 12 April 1834.

2. TNA, PRO, HO 40/38, 'To the Officers and Members of Trades' Unions', Manchester, 25 August 1838, placard.

3. Matthews, *A Study in Trade-Cycle History*, pp. 141-46; *Northern Star*, 9 April 1842; [Leach] *Stubborn Facts*, pp. 42-44; Yeo and Thompson (eds.), *The Unknown Mayhew*, pp. 323-24, 328, 334; Sykes, 'Popular Politics', pp. 332-38.

4. *Manchester and Salford Advertiser*, 27 January 1838.

5. *Northern Star*, 13 October 1838.

6. *Manchester Guardian*, 18 June 1842; *Northern Star*, 26 March 1842.

7. Epstein, *In Practice*, pp. 28-29; John Saville, *1848: The British State and the Chartist Movement*, Cambridge, 1987, pp. 217-23. For a different perspective, see Stedman Jones, *Languages of Class*, pp. 173-78. See also, Edward Royle, *Revolutionary Britannia? Reflections on the Threat of Revolution in Britain, 1789-1848*, Manchester, 2000, pp. 168-89.

8. Miles Taylor has estimated that in the late 1840s the reform party in the Commons came to about sixty to seventy MPs. See *The Decline of British Radicalism*, pp. 9-10. In 1839 parliament voted against the Charter 235 to 46. See Thompson, *Chartists*, p. 69. See also, David Nicholls, 'Friends of the People: Parliamentary Supporters of Popular Radicalism', *Labour History Review* 62 (Summer 1997): 128-30, 135, 141-42.

9. W.F.P. Napier, *The Life and Opinions of General Sir Charles James Napier*, four volumes, London, 1857, 2: 69.

10. *Northern Star*, 30 May 1840 and 3 November 1838 (Bolton and Hyde).

11. Address of the Provisional Executive Council in *Northern Liberator*, 22 August 1840.

12. Christopher Hill, *The Experience of Defeat: Milton and Some Contemporaries*, New York, 1984, p. 17. See also, Wolfgang Schivelbusch, *The Culture of Defeat: On National Trauma, Mourning, and Recovery*, translated by Jefferson Chase, New York, 2003.

13. *Operative*, 16 December 1838. See also, TNA, PRO, HO 42/180, Brother to No. 2 to Chippendale, 2 September 1818.

14. *Manchester Guardian*, 26 September 1838; Sykes, 'Physical-Force Chartism', pp. 209-10; Epstein, *Lion of Freedom*, pp. 110-16.

15. R.G. Gammage, *History of the Chartist Movement 1837-1854*, second ed., London, 1894; reprint ed., New York, 1969, pp. 94-95.

16. TNA, PRO, HO 40/38, Hyde magistrates to Russell, 16 November 1838; *Northern Star*, 17 November 1838.

17. *Northern Star*, 8 December 1838. Sykes, 'Physical-Force Chartism', pp. 214-19. Epstein, *Lion of Freedom*, pp. 124-26; Thompson (ed.), *The Early Chartists*, pp. 16-27.

18. *Northern Star*, 11 April 1840; See also, Ibid., 17 November 1838.

19. Ibid., 8 December 1838.

20. Harrison and Hollis (eds.), *Robert Lowery*, p. 120.

21. Robert Gray, *The Factory Question and Industrial England, 1830-1860*, Cambridge, 1996, pp. 37-47; Clark, *Struggle for the Breeches*, pp. 224-26.

22. *Northern Star*, 10 November 1838. TNA, PRO, HO 40/37, Meeting of Chartists at Ashton-under-Lyne, 20 April 1839 (Wilde's speech).

23. *Northern Star*, 24 August 1839.

24. Francis Maceroni, *A New System of Defensive Instructions for the People*, third ed., London, n.d., p. 6. A copy of this edition appears in TNA, PRO, HO 40/37.

25. Sykes, 'Physical-Force Chartism', pp. 214-18; *Manchester Guardian*, 16 March 1839.

26. On the title page, Hobson and Williamson appear in a list of vendors. See TNA, PRO, HO 40/37. A copy was also found in Higgins' home. See *Northern Star*, 20 July 1839.

27. *Manchester Guardian*, 8 May 1839; TNA, PRO, Treasury Solicitor's Papers 11/1030/4424C-E, Queen vs William Cox, Queen vs Samuel Bardsley, and Queen vs John Bardsley.

28. *Manchester and Salford Advertiser*, 27 April 1839. Harrison and Hollis (eds.), *Robert Lowery*, p. 143; *Northern Star*, 24 August 1839. The first estimate was by McDouall; the latter appears in a document at the Chester Assizes. See also, Sykes, 'Physical-Force Chartism', pp. 217-18.

29. TNA, PRO, HO 20/10, Interview of John Broadbent; *Northern Star*, 24 August 1839; Sykes, 'Physical-Force Chartism', pp. 216-17.

30. TNA, PRO, HO 40/50, Deposition of Joseph Westwood, 9 May 1839; Sykes, 'Physical-Force Chartism', pp. 216-17; *Northern Star*, 24 August 1839; HO 40/37, Jowett to Russell, 3 July 1839; TNA, PRO, TS 11/1030/4424A, Queen vs Timothy Higgins.

31. *Northern Star*, 1 June 1839.

32. Sykes, 'Physical-Force Chartism', pp. 213, 219-26; Epstein, *Lion of Freedom*, pp. 148-51, 157-58; for Ashton Chartists and the convention, see *Northern Star*, 9 March, 13 April, and 13 July 1839.

33. BL, Place Papers, Add Mss 34,245B, Deegan to Fletcher, 6 August 1839; Epstein, *Lion of Freedom*, pp. 164-81; Sykes, 'Physical-Force Chartism', pp. 224-27.

34. *Manchester Guardian* and *Manchester and Salford Advertiser*, 29 June 1839.

35. *Manchester and Salford Advertiser*, 29 June 1839. On June 21, the question of ulterior measures was discussed at a meeting of over five thousand; Aitken, Higgins, and others had spoken out strongly in favour of 'a cessation from labour for one month'. Ibid., 22 June 1839.

36. *Manchester Guardian*, 29 June 1839; *Manchester and Salford Advertiser*, 29 June and 6 July 1839; *Stockport Advertiser*, 28 June 1839; Hall and Roberts (eds.), *William Aitken*, pp. 35, 38. For a later version by O'Connor, see *Northern Star*, 10 May 1845. On July 7, his church heard his explanation and restored him to his ministry. Edwards, *Purge This Realm*, pp. 63-64.

37. Hall and Roberts (eds.), *William Aitken*, p. 38.

38. Harrison and Hollis (eds.), *Robert Lowery*, p. 143; *Northern Star*, 6, 20, and 27 July 1839; 'Mr. Stephens's Last Sermon', *Northern Star*, 17 August 1839.

39. *Northern Star*, 11 May 1839 and 13 November 1841.

40. Sykes, 'Physical-Force Chartism', pp. 227-33.

41. *Manchester Guardian*, 17 August 1839. During the national holiday (12-14 August 1839) and its aftermath, John Broadbent, John Williamson, William Aitken, George Johnson, John Wilde, and John Deegan were arrested. See *Manchester Guardian*, 17 August 1839; Hall and Roberts (eds.), *William Aitken*, pp. 40-42; TNA, PRO, HO 40/37, Examinations of John Cragg, James Butterworth, and William Bentley, Rochdale, 12 August 1839.

42. *Manchester Guardian*, 17 August 1839; *North Cheshire Reformer*, 16 August 1839. For an Ashton meeting, see *Manchester Chronicle*, 10 August 1839.

43. *Stockport Advertiser*, 16 August 1839; *Manchester and Salford Advertiser*, 17 August 1839.

44. *Manchester Guardian*, 17 and 21 August 1839.

45. *Northern Star*, 22 August 1840.

46. *Manchester and Salford Advertiser*, 28 September 1839.

47. *Northern Star*, 18 May 1839.

48. Ibid., 27 July 1839.

49. For 'premature' outbreaks, see *Manchester Times*, 11 May 1839; Harrison and Hollis (eds.), *Robert Lowery*, pp. 242-43.

50. Harrison and Hollis (eds.), *Robert Lowery*, p. 242. For other assessments, see *Manchester and Salford Advertiser*, 28 September 1839 (Matthew Fletcher); *Northern Liberator*, 8 February 1840 (T.R. Smart). See also, Epstein, *Lion of Freedom*, pp. 183-86; Parssinen, 'Association, Convention, and Anti-Parliament', pp. 532-33.

51. BL, Place Papers, Add Mss 34,245B, Deegan to Fletcher, 6 August 1839.

52. Matthews, *A Study in Trade-Cycle History*, pp. 141-46.

53. TNA, PRO, HO 45/350, Hindley to the Earl of Derby, 4 January 1843.

54. *PP* (Commons) 1842 [31] XXII: 26.

55. *McDouall's Chartist and Republican Journal*, 3, 10, 24 July 1841; [Leach] *Stubborn Facts*, pp. 11-12, 29-34, 42-49; W. Kenworthy, *Inventions and Hours of Labour. A Letter to Master Cotton Spinners, Manufacturers, and Mill-Owners in general*, second ed., Blackburn, 1842, pp. 42-44; TNA, PRO, HO 45/650, Arbuthnot to Phillipps, 8 February 1844.

56. *Northern Star*, 9 April 1842. See also, *Manchester Chronicle*, 17 September 1842.

57. *Stockport Advertiser*, 27 April 1838.

58. *The Oddfellow*, 8 October 1842. For a similar argument by O'Connor, see *Northern Star*, 28 March 1840.

59. Thompson, *Chartists*, pp. 279-81. For the published figures on NCA cards that were taken out in Ashton, Stalybridge, Hyde, Mossley, Dukinfield, and Hooley Hill, see *Northern Star*, 20 March 1841; 24 July 1841; 18 December 1841; 8 January 1842; 5 March 1842; 9 April 1842; 2 July 1842; 12 November 1842. For signatures to the 1842 petition, see Ibid., 23 April 1842; *HD*, Third Series (1842) LXII: 1374-75.

60. *Northern Star*, 9 July 1842.

61. Ibid., 17 September 1842.

62. Norman McCord, *The Anti-Corn Law League 1838-1846*, London, 1958, pp. 121-24.

63. *Trial of Feargus O'Connor and Fifty-Eight Others*, p. 404; TNA, PRO, TS 11/813/2677: 44-45; McCord, *Anti-Corn Law League*, pp. 125-26. See also, Paul A. Pickering and Alex Tyrrell, *The People's Bread: A History of the Anti-Corn Law League*, London, 2000, pp. 139-64.

64. TNA, PRO, TS 11/813/2677: 46-47. In early 1842 Gregory had tried unsuccessfully to arrange an agreement between the local ACLL and the Chartists. The only thing that came of this overture was a corn law repeal meeting that the Chartists quickly took over and dominated. See PRO, TS 11/813/2677: 46-49; *Manchester Guardian*, 2 March 1842.

65. Mick Jenkins, *The General Strike of 1842*, London, 1980, pp. 64-66; *Northern Star*, 17 September 1842 and 17 February 1844.

66. F.C. Mather, 'The General Strike of 1842: A Study in Leadership, Organisation, and the Threat of Revolution during the Plug Plot Disturbances', in R. Quinault and J. Stevenson (eds.), *Popular Protest and Public Order: Six Studies in British History*, New York, 1975, pp. 115-16.

67. *Trial of Feargus O'Connor and Fifty-Eight Others*, p. 13; *Northern Star*, 17 September and 30 July 1842.

68. *Trial of Feargus O'Connor and Fifty-Eight Others*, pp. 16-17 (Stalybridge) and pp. 17, 73 (Dukinfield); *Northern Star*, 6 August 1842 (Hyde). See also, *Manchester and Salford Advertiser*, 6 August 1842.

69. For letters and addresses from Ashton operatives, see *Northern Star*, 20 August and 10 September 1842; *Manchester Guardian*, 13 August 1842. See also, TNA, PRO, HO 45/249, Resolutions of a Meeting of the Cotton Spinners of Bolton and Vicinity, 15 August 1842, placard.

70. *Northern Star*, 30 August 1845.

71. See Deegan's speeches in TNA, PRO, HO 40/47, Report of Speeches delivered at Chartist Public Meeting at Nottingham, 22 May 1839; *Northern Star*, 10 Novem-

ber 1838 and 1 June 1839. For accounts that overstate the Chartist embrace of the male breadwinner ideal, see Taylor, *Eve and the New Jerusalem*, pp. 268-69; Clark, *Struggle for the Breeches*, pp. 220-47; Schwarzkopf, *Women in the Chartist Movement*, pp. 58, 246, 281-82, 264-69.

72. *Replies of Sir Charles Shaw to Lord Ashley, M.P. Regarding the Education, and Moral and Physical Condition of the Labouring Classes*, London, 1843, pp. 31-32.

73. *Northern Star*, 10 September 1842.

74. TNA, PRO, Records of the Palatinate of Lancaster 27/11, part 2, Deposition of John Robinson.

75. *Northern Star*, 17 September 1842.

76. The six delegates were: William Aitken and Alexander Challenger (Preston), Richard Pilling and Thomas Storer (Bolton), and George Johnson and James Taylor (Saddleworth). TNA, PRO, TS 11/813/2677: 55-56; TNA, PRO, PL 27/11, pt. 2, Deposition of Joseph Armitage.

77. TNA, PRO, HO 45/264, Mayor of Hull to Graham, 16 August 1842; Jenkins, *General Strike*, pp. 90-95.

78. *Manchester Guardian*, 13 August 1842. For the 'run for gold', see *Northern Star*, 20 August 1842 (Manchester) and 27 August 1842 (Ashton and Failsworth). For general unionism, see Sykes, 'Early Chartism and Trade Unionism', in Epstein and Thompson (eds.), *Chartist Experience*, pp. 155-56; Hall, 'Tyranny, Work and Politics', pp. 455-57.

79. Epstein, *Lion of Freedom*, pp. 295-96; Jenkins, *General Strike*, pp. 115, 162-63; Owen Ashton and Paul Pickering, *Friends of the People: Uneasy Radicals in the Age of the Chartists*, London, 2002, pp. 101-102.

80. Thomas Cooper, *The Life of Thomas Cooper*, London, 1872; reprint ed., New York,
1971, p. 208; *Northern Star*, 20 August 1842.

81. Cooper, *Life*, pp. 209-11; Jenkins, *General Strike*, pp. 270-75; *Northern Star* and *Manchester and Salford Advertiser*, 20 August 1842.

82. *Northern Star*, 20 August 1842.

83. Cooper, *Life*, p. 211; Ashton and Pickering, *Friends of the People*, pp. 16-17.

84. *Manchester Guardian*, 17 August 1842.

85. *Northern Star*, 20 August 1842; Jenkins, *General Strike*, pp. 150-59.

86. *Manchester Guardian*, 17 August 1842.

87. *Northern Star* and *British Statesman*, 20 August 1842.

88. *British Statesman*, 20 August 1842.

89. *Manchester Guardian*, 17 August 1842; TNA, PRO, PL 27/11, pt. 2, Deposition of John Robinson.

90. Epstein, *Lion of Freedom*, pp. 295-98; Jenkins, *General Strike*, pp. 205-206, 152-59.

91. TNA, PRO, HO 45/249, Wanklyn to Graham, 17 August 1842; Jowett to Graham, 11 August 1842.

92. *Manchester Guardian*, 5 October 1842; *Northern Star*, 27 August 1842; *Manchester Guardian*, 3 September 1842; *Northern Star*, 10 and 17 September 1842.

93. *Northern Star*, 27 August 1842; *Manchester Guardian*, 7, 17, and 21 September and 5 October 1842; William Aitken, *A Journey up the Mississippi River from its Mouth*

to Nauvoo, the City of the Latter Day Saints, Ashton, n.d., pp. 5, 11, 14; see also, *Northern Star,* 15 July 1843.

94. *Northern Star,* 24 September 1842.

95. *Manchester Guardian,* 21 September 1842.

96. Graham to Croker, 1 September 1842, in Louis J. Jennings (ed.), *The Correspondence and Diaries of John Wilson Croker,* three volumes, second ed., London, 1885, 2: 387.

97. *HD,* Third series, LXIV (1842): 1217.

98. MCL, Ministry to the Poor, Sixth Report (1840): 29-30; Ninth Report (1843): 23-25.

99. MCL, Ministry to the Poor, Eighth Report (1842): 18-19. See also, Rev. Richard Parkinson, *On the Present Condition of the Labouring Poor in Manchester,* Manchester, 1841, pp. 12-13.

100. MCL, Ministry to the Poor, Ninth Report (1843): 7-8, 23; *Nonconformist,* 9 November 1842.

101. Magdalen Goffin (ed.), *The Diaries of Absalom Watkin: A Manchester Man 1787-1861,* Phoenix Mill, 1993, p. 226.

102. Ibid.

103. *Manchester Guardian,* 5 December 1846.

104. *HD,* Third Series LXVIII (1843): 102.

105. Cooke Taylor, *Notes of a Tour,* p. 316.

106. MCL, Ministry to the Poor, Eighth Report (1842): 19; Ninth Report (1843): 24-25. See also, Parkinson, *Labouring Poor in Manchester,* pp. 15-18.

107. Raymond Williams, *Keywords: A Vocabulary of Culture and Society,* revised ed., New York, 1985, pp. 93-98; Gregory Claeys, 'The Example of America a Warning to England? The Transformation of America in British Radicalism and Socialism, 1790-1850', in Chase and Dyck (eds.), *Living and Learning,* pp. 68-69; Epstein, *Radical Expression,* pp. 11-14.

108. Thompson, *The Making of the English Working Class,* pp. 88-89; Epstein, *Radical Expression,* pp. 22-23. For one attempt to do so, see Richardson, *The Rights of Woman,* pp. 12-13.

109. *Northern Star,* 26 March 1842.

110. Ibid., 3 September 1842.

111. Ibid., 27 August 1842.

112. For the angry letter of 'An Old Chartist' from Manchester, see Ibid., 3 September 1842.

113. *Trial of Feargus O'Connor and Fifty-Eight Others,* p. 279.

114. *Northern Star,* 20 August 1842.

115. Ibid., 27 August 1842.

116. *English Chartist Circular,* vol. 1, no. 50; *Northern Star,* 5 March 1842.

117. Brian Harrison and Patricia Hollis, 'Chartism, Liberalism, and the Life of Robert Lowery', *English Historical Review* 82 (July 1967): 503-35; Eugenio Biagini, *Liberty, Retrenchment and Reform: Popular Liberalism in the Age of Gladstone, 1860-1880,* Cambridge, 1992, pp. 6-11, 97-102, 297.

118. 'Many people—we are afraid the majority of the middle classes—think that woman's duties are comprised in good humour and attention to her husband, keeping

her children neat and clean, and attending to domestic arrangements.' See [Reid], *A Plea for Woman*, p. 23.

119. *Manchester and Salford Advertiser*, 20 August 1842.
120. *British Statesman*, 3 September 1842.
121. *Northern Star*, 17 September 1842.

Chapter IV

1.   *Northern Star*, 29 August 1840.
2.   Harrison and Hollis (eds.), *Robert Lowery*, p. 96; *Northern Star*, 2 June 1849.
3.   Pickering, *Chartism and the Chartists*; Clark, *Struggle for the Breeches*; Foster, *Class Struggle*.
4.   For the problem of democratic leadership, see Epstein, *Lion of Freedom*, pp. 90-94; Thompson, *Chartists*, pp. 95-101; Yeo, 'Chartist Democracy', in Epstein and Thompson (eds.), *Chartist Experience*, pp. 345-80; Pickering, 'Trade of Agitation', pp. 221-37; Belchem and Epstein, 'Gentleman Leader Revisited', pp. 173-93; Miles Taylor, *Ernest Jones, Chartism, and the Romance of Politics 1819-1869*, Oxford, 2003; Glenn Airey, 'Feargus O'Connor 1842-1855: A Study in Chartist Leadership', Staffordshire University, Ph.D. dissertation, 2003.
5.   Antonio Gramsci, *Prison Notebooks*, edited and translated by Quintin Hoare and Geoffrey Nowell Smith, London, 1971, pp. 3, 5-23. Epstein, 'Bred as a Mechanic', in Fink, Leonard, and Reid (eds.), *Intellectuals and Public Life*, pp. 53-58. For examples of this approach, see Thompson, *Chartists*, pp. 91-233; Christopher B. Godfrey, 'Chartist Lives: The Anatomy of a Working-Class Movement', Harvard University, Ph.D. dissertation, 1978, pp. 9-190; Pickering, *Chartism and the Chartists*, pp. 139-72.
6.   Lovett and Collins, *Chartism*, pp. 17-18; *Democrat and Labour Advocate*, 10 November 1855. Pickering, *Chartism and the Chartists*, pp. 152, 189-210; Thompson, *Chartists*, pp. 152-72; Kate Tiller, 'Late Chartism: Halifax, 1847-1858', in Epstein and Thompson (eds.), *Chartist Experience*, pp. 335-37; Ashton and Pickering, *Friends of the People*.
7.   Rancière, 'The Myth of the Artisan', pp. 4-5, 10-11. For examples of the influence of Rancière's work, see Iain McCalman, *Radical Underworld: Prophets, Revolutionaries and Pornographers in London, 1795-1840*, Cambridge, 1988, pp. 48-49, 152-53; Epstein, 'Bred as a Mechanic', in Fink, Leonard, and Reid (eds.), *Intellectuals and Public Life*, pp. 53-73; Miles Taylor, 'The Knife and Fork Question', *London Review of Books* 23 (29 November 2001): 28-29.
8.   For portrayals of John Deegan and Timothy Higgins in this way, see *Manchester Times*, 9 June 1838; *Manchester Guardian*, 3 July 1839.
9.   Samuel Bamford, *Walks in South Lancashire*, Blackley, 1844; reprint ed., Brighton, 1972, p. 17.
10. *Northern Star*, 11 April 1840.
11. For George Julian Harney on this issue, see ibid., 6 January 1849.
12. See also, TNA, PRO, HO 20/10, Interviews of William Aitken, John Broadbent, James Duke, Timothy Higgins, John Hilton, George Johnson, John Wilde.
13. *Lion*, 24 July 1829.

14. *Northern Star*, 11 June 1842. Associates and friends of Aitken included local people as well as national figures, like O'Connor, McDouall, and Oastler. See Hall and Roberts (eds.), *William Aitken*.

15. There were two women in the group of sixty-five: Mrs. Williamson and Miss Mary Ann Hughes. They chaired meetings of women Chartists. *Northern Star*, 2 February and 1 June 1839.

16. Hall and Roberts (eds.), *William Aitken*, p. 14; *Northern Star*, 22 August 1840; in the 1841 census, Higgins gave Ireland as his birthplace. See TNA, PRO, HO 107/532. The two other Irishmen were James Milligan and Bernard Treanor.

17. By multiplying data on the native 'country' of heads of working-class families times its estimate of average family size, I came up with a *rough* estimate of the ethnic composition of Ashton's working classes: English (87 per cent), Irish (11.5 per cent), Scottish (1 per cent), Welsh and 'foreigners' (0.5 per cent). See *Report of a Committee of the Manchester Statistical Society, on the Condition of the Working Classes, in an Extensive District in 1834, 1835, and 1836*, London, 1838, pp. xi, xiv.

18. Mann meant that most working men and women never or only rarely attended church services. *PP* (Commons) 1852-53 [1690] LXXXIX: clviii. See Chapter Five. 'Conscious' secularists included: James Duke, Edward Hobson, Timothy Higgins, Thomas Storer, John Williamson. For the three Stephenites (John Broadbent, George Johnson, Abel Swann), see Edwards, *Purge This Realm*, pp. 154-57.

19. These estimates are based mainly on information in TNA, PRO, HO 20/10 and the 1841 census enumerators' books, PRO, HO 107/532. In sixteen out of twenty cases where reliable information on age and marital status has been discovered, the individuals were married men.

20. Peter Taylor, *Popular Politics in Early Industrial Britain: Bolton, 1825-1850*, Keele, 1995, pp. 107-13.

21. *Northern Star*, 1 December 1838; TNA, PRO, HO 40/38, Bentley to Russell, 17 December 1838.

22. For occupations of former mule spinners in Ashton, see *Morning Chronicle*, 9 May 1844.

23. *Northern Star*, 5 January 1839; TNA, PRO, HO 20/10, Interviews of William Aitken and John Wilde. Aitken made about three pounds a week from his school.

24. The most common occupations were powerloom weaver (eight), mule spinner (three), and clogger and shoemaker (three).

25. The Board of Trade list gives the names, addresses, and occupations of some 25,000 to 30,000 Land Company subscribers. Yeo, 'Chartist Democracy', in Epstein and Thompson (eds.), *Chartist Experience*, pp. 370-71; Alan Little, 'Appendix: Liverpool Chartists; Subscribers to the National Land Company, 1847-8', in John Belchem (ed.), *Popular Politics, Riot and Labour: Essays in Liverpool History 1790-1940*, Liverpool, 1992, pp. 247-49.

26. *Northern Star*, 13 December 1845. Thompson, *Chartists*, pp. 93-94.

27. *Northern Star*, 10 April 1847 and 8 January 1848. Only about 23 per cent (fifteen in number) of the sixty-five leaders and activists during the years 1838 to 1842 appear in the Board of Trade list; the most well-known of these were Richard Pilling, Thomas Storer, and James Taylor.

28. Little, 'Appendix: Liverpool Chartists', in Belchem (ed.), *Popular Politics*, pp. 248-49. See also, Airey, 'Feargus O'Connor', pp. 66-71.

29. Jamie Bronstein, '"Under Their Own Vine and Fig Tree": Land Reform and Working-Class Experience in Britain and America, 1830-1860', Stanford University, Ph.D. dissertation, 1996, Appendix 1, pp. 376-86; *idem, Land Reform and Working-Class Experience in Britain and the United States, 1800-1862*, Stanford, 1999, pp. 185-87, 308.

30. Pickering, 'Trade of Agitation', pp. 221-37. *Northern Star*, 23 February 1839. For Stephens' collectibles, see TNA, PRO, HO 73/55, Mott to Lefevre, 22 March 1839.

31. Lindsay, *Some Notes*, pp. 241-42. Pickering, 'Trade of Agitation', pp. 228-29; W.H. Maehl (ed.), *Robert Gammage: Reminiscences of a Chartist*, Manchester, 1983, pp. 12-15; Harrison and Hollis (eds.), *Robert Lowery*, pp. 173, 107-08. Newton Heath and Hollinwood paid lecturers respectively nine pence and one shilling and three pence. See *Northern Star*, 3 December 1842.

32. *Ashton Reporter*, 2 October 1869. Between 1839 and 1842, four of the most active lecturers were William Aitken, Timothy Higgins, Thomas Storer, and James Taylor.

33. Yeo, 'Chartist Democracy', in Epstein and Thompson (eds.), *Chartist Experience*, pp. 345-80; Pickering, *Chartism and the Chartists*, pp. 49-55.

34. Martin Hewitt and Robert Poole (eds.), *The Diaries of Samuel Bamford*, New York, 2000, p. 23; *Northern Star*, 3 December 1842 and 1 June 1839.

35. *Northern Star*, 27 April 1839.

36. Ibid., 1 June 1839 and 6 January 1838.

37. *Reasoner*, 20 December 1848.

38. For 1839-40, these include John Deegan, John Williamson, and the seven Ashton Chartists in HO 20/10. In 1842 Abel Duke, Albert Wolfenden, Richard Pilling, George Johnson, William Woodruffe, Thomas Storer, and Samuel Sigley were arrested. See also, Pickering, *Chartism and the Chartists*, pp. 148-51.

39. McDouall made this charge in a letter 'To the Men of Ashton' in the *Northern Star*, 21 December 1839. See also, Hall and Roberts (eds.), *William Aitken*, pp. 29-30.

40. TNA, PRO, HO 20/10, Interview of Timothy Higgins; *Northern Star*, 17 April 1841; *Stephens' Monthly Magazine* (August 1840): 187-89.

41. *Northern Star*, 17 April 1841.

42. Ibid., 22 February 1840.

43. Tameside, L322, Aitken, 'To the Non-Electors and Electors'; Aitken, *Journey*, p. 29.

44. Cooper to Gammage, 26 February 1855, in Gammage, *History*, pp. 407-408.

45. Epstein, 'Bred as a Mechanic', in Fink, Leonard, and Reid (eds.), *Intellectuals and Public Life*, pp. 64-65.

46. *Oddfellows' Magazine* (July 1857): 129-30.

47. TNA, PRO, HO 20/10, Interview of William Aitken; Aitken, *Journey*, pp. 29, 25-26.

48. Aitken, *Journey*, p. 26.

49. Ibid., p. 29.

50. *Loyal Ancient Shepherds' Quarterly Magazine* (July 1847): 288.

51. *Ashton News*, 2 October 1869; Aitken, *Journey*, p. 29.

52. *Northern Star*, 23 January 1841; 23 April 1842; 17 October 1846; 8 January 1848; *McDouall's Chartist and Republican Journal*, 10 April-28 August 1841.

53. *Ashton News*, 2 October 1869.

54. *Manchester Guardian*, 1 August 1846; *McDouall's Chartist and Republican Journal*, 10 April 1841; Aitken, *Journey*, pp. 8, 11, 21, 29.

55. *McDouall's Chartist and Republican Journal*, 10 April 1841. Aitken, *Journey*, pp. 30, 38.

56. Samuel Bamford, *Early Days*, London, 1849, p. 91.

57. Brierley, *Home Memories*, pp. 11-12, 21, 23, 32, 38.

58. Alain Kahan, Patricia Arnison, and Helen Bowyer, 'Samuel Collins' Library', *Working Class Movement Library Bulletin* 2 (1992): 56-63.

59. TNA, PRO, HO 20/10. For this source, see James Epstein and Christopher Godfrey, 'H.O. 20/10: Interviews of Chartist Prisoners 1840-41', *Bulletin of the Society for the Study of Labour History* 34 (1977): 27-34; Christopher Godfrey, 'The Chartist Prisoners, 1839-41', *International Review of Social History* 24 (1979): 189-236. These Chartist prisoners were residents of Manchester, Ashton, Stockport, Bolton and Newton. The majority were members of the working classes, but this group also included a number of lower middle-class figures as well. J.R. Stephens and William Benbow were excluded.

60. TNA, PRO, HO 20/10. John Hilton and George Wareham could neither read nor write; Charles Morris and Daniel Ball could read but not write. Of the other twenty-one Chartist prisoners, five could read and write only 'indifferently' or 'imperfectly'.

61. TNA, PRO, HO 20/10, Interviews of Timothy Higgins and James Duke.

62. TNA, PRO, HO 20/10, Interview of Christopher Doyle.

63. W.B. Stephens, *Education, Literacy and Society, 1830-70: The Geography of Diversity in Provincial England*, Manchester, 1987, pp. 94-95.

64. Coulthart, *A Report of the Sanatory Condition*, p. 42.

65. Ginswick (ed.), *Labour and the Poor*, 1: 68; Frederic Hill, *National Education; Its Present State and Prospects*, two volumes, London, 1836, 1: 17, 104; Martin Hewitt, 'Confronting the Modern City: the Manchester Free Public Library, 1850-80', *Urban History* 27 (2000): 64-65.

66. 'Report of a Committee of the Manchester Statistical Society, on the State of Education in the Township of Pendleton, 1838', *Journal of the Statistical Society of London* 2 (March 1839): 73.

67. *Report on the Condition of the Working Classes, in an Extensive District*, p. xii.

68. *PP* (Commons) 1849 [548] XVII: 125.

69. *PP* (Commons) 1867-68 [402] XIV: 383; 'Autobiography of Samuel Fielden', in Philip S. Foner (ed.), *The Autobiographies of the Haymarket Martyrs*, New York, 1969, p. 136.

70. *Manchester Guardian*, 16 July 1845 and 5 October 1844; *Northern Star*, 29 October 1842; *Slater's Directory, 1848; Loyal Ancient Shepherds' Quarterly Magazine* (April 1855): 103. See Gideon Reuveni, 'Reading Sites as Sights for Reading. The Sale of Newspapers in Germany before 1933: Bookshops in Railway Stations, Kiosks and Street Vendors', *Social History* 27 (October 2002): 273-87.

71. *PP* (Commons) 1849 [548] XVII: 179, 129; *Manchester Guardian*, 5 October 1844; 'On the State of Education in the Township of Pendleton, 1838', pp. 67-68.

72. James Heywood, 'Report of an Enquiry, Conducted from House to House, into the State of 176 Families in Miles Platting, within the Borough of Manchester in 1837', *Journal of the Statistical Society of London* 1 (May 1838): 35. Hill, *National Education*, 1: 17, 104.

73. Walter Lowe Clay (ed.), *The Prison Chaplain: A Memoir of the Rev. John Clay*, Cambridge, 1861; reprint ed., Montclair, 1969, p. 509.

74. Ibid., pp. 509-10.

75. Thomas Frost, *Forty Years' Recollections: Literary and Political*, London, 1880, p. 79.

76. *Manchester Guardian*, 5 October 1844; Tameside, MI 1/1/1, Ashton and Dukinfield Mechanics' Institution, Minute Books, 1825-44, Annual Report (1844): 2. The books in the greatest demand at the Dukinfield Village Library, a lending library that catered to a working-class audience, were travel narratives and 'works of light reading'. See *Manchester Guardian*, 5 October 1844.

77. Tameside, MI 1/1/1, Annual Report (1844): 2; Ginswick (ed.), *Labour and the Poor*, 1: 61-64; Brierley, *Home Memories*, p. 32.

78. Bamford, *Early Days*, p. 90; Brierley, *Home Memories*, p. 32.

79. *Ashton Reporter*, 26 September 1857; Edwin Waugh, *Sketches of Lancashire Life and Localities*, London, 1855, pp. 213-14.

80. Waugh, *Sketches of Lancashire Life*, pp. 213-14. W.E.A. Axon, *The Black Knight of Ashton*, Manchester, [1870], pp. 4-5.

81. Axon, *Black Knight*, pp. 4-5; Waugh, *Sketches of Lancashire Life*, pp. 213-14; Bamford, *Walks in South Lancashire*, pp. 205-10.

82. MCL, Ministry to the Poor, Sixth Report (1840): 20.

83. Aitken, *Journey*, pp. 46-47.

84. *McDouall's Chartist and Republican Journal*, 10 April 1841; Aitken, *Journey*, p. 30. See also David Vincent, 'The Decline of the Oral Tradition in Popular Culture', in Robert D. Storch (ed.), *Popular Culture and Custom in Nineteenth-Century England*, London, 1982, pp. 33-36.

85. Aitken, *Journey*, p. 38.

86. Vincent, 'Oral Tradition', in Storch (ed.), *Popular Culture*, p. 42.

87. Robert Roberts, *The Classic Slum: Salford Life in the First Quarter of the Century*, Harmondsworth, 1986, pp. 50-51, 54-55. See also J.R. Clynes, *Memoirs*, two volumes, London, 1937, 1: 45.

88. Aitken, *Journey*, pp. 15-16.

89. Henry Mayhew, *London Labour and the London Poor*, four volumes, London, 1861-62, 1: 22, 8, 27.

90. *PP* (Commons) 1843 [517] XXV and XXVI: 67-68.

91. *Herald to the Trades' Advocate*, no. 36 [28 May 1831].

92. Harrison and Hollis (eds.), *Robert Lowery*, p. 128.

93. BL, Add Mss 34, 245A, Duncan and Lowery to the Convention, 12 March 1839, in Harrison and Hollis (eds.), *Robert Lowery*, p. 233. *True Scotsman*, 30 March 1839; Harrison and Hollis (eds.), *Robert Lowery*, p. 130.

94. *Northern Star*, 6 January 1849.

95. Ibid.,16 November 1839. For Pilling on this issue, see *Trial of Feargus O'Connor and Fifty-Eight Others*, p. 252.

96. *Northern Star*, 27 April 1839.

97. *McDouall's Chartist and Republican Journal*, 31 July 1841. For the riots and street brawls during the 1841 election, see *Manchester Guardian*, 3 July 1841; TNA, PRO, HO 45/43, Wemyss to Phillipps, 30 June 1841.

98. Rancière, 'The Myth of the Artisan', pp. 10-11.

99. TNA, PRO, TS 11/813/2677: 46-49.

100. *Ashton Reporter* and *Ashton News*, 2 October 1869; *PP* (Commons) 1867-68 [402] XIV: 382.

101. *Northern Star*, 4 December 1841.

102. *Ashton News*, 2 October 1869. Tameside, L322, Aitken, 'To the Non-Electors and Electors'. Reference is to the political 'friends' of Charles Hindley, Liberal MP for Ashton.

103. Hall and Roberts (eds.), *William Aitken; Ashton News* and *Ashton Reporter*, 2 October 1869; TNA, PRO, HO 107/532.

104. William Neild, 'Comparative Statement of the Income and Expenditure of Certain Families of the Working Classes in Manchester and Dukinfield, in the years 1836 and 1841', *Journal of the Statistical Society of London* 4 (January 1842): 322.

105. *Morning Chronicle*, 9 May 1844; TNA, PRO, HO 20/10, Interview of James Duke. By 1841 John A. Stewart, radical and former handloom weaver, had taken a shop in Wellington Street. Two of his daughters were powerloom weavers; a teenage son was a cotton piecer. PRO, HO 107/532.

106. Maehl (ed.), *Robert Gammage*, p. 49; Clynes, *Memoirs*, 1: 62. For the role of 'superior speaking or argumentative powers' and education in the selection of leaders, see John Bedford Leno, *The Aftermath*, London, 1892, p. 53; *PP* (Commons) 1833 [450] XX E: 18; Clynes, *Memoirs*, 1: 62.

107. Bamford, *Walks in South Lancashire*, p. 17.

108. *Northern Star*, 17 September 1842.

109. *McDouall's Chartist and Republican Journal*, 15 May 1841.

110. *Northern Star*, 27 April 1839 and 3 December 1842.

111. Thompson (ed.), *Early Chartists*, pp. 57-66; Taylor, 'The Six Points', in Ashton, Fyson, and Roberts (eds.), *Chartist Legacy*, pp. 1-2, 19-20.

112. *Northern Star*, 22 December 1838.

113. Ibid., 1 December 1838 and 17 September 1842.

114. Frost, *Forty Years' Recollections*, p. 225.

115. Maehl (ed.), *Robert Gammage*, p. 64.

116. George J. Holyoake, *The History of Co-operation in England*, two volumes, London, 1879; reprint ed., New York, 1971, 2: 18.

117. *English Republic* (1851), vol. 1: 175.

118. *Northern Star*, 11 November 1848.

119. Thompson, *The Making of the English Working Class*, pp. 17-22; *The Advocate, and Merthyr Free Press*, 1 February 1841, in TNA, PRO, HO 45/54.

Chapter V

1. [R.G. Gammage], *The Charter: What It Is, And Why We Want It*, Stoke-on-Trent, 1854, in Claeys (ed.), *Chartist Movement*, 6: 31.
2. Ibid., pp. 33-35.
3. Ibid., p. 40.
4. Ibid., pp. 39-40. See Epstein, *Lion of Freedom*, pp. 263-76.
5. [Gammage,] *The Charter*, in Claeys (ed.), *Chartist Movement*, 6: 40-45.
6. *Northern Star*, 1 February 1851.
7. For critical surveys of Chartism's decline, see Thompson, *Chartists*, pp. 330-35; Neville Kirk, *The Growth of Working Class Reformism in Mid-Victorian England*, London, 1985, pp. 1-26; Walton, *Chartism*, pp. 65-79; Stedman Jones, *Languages of Class*, pp. 90-178. For liberalization, see Foster, *Class Struggle*, pp. 1-3, 201-50; Epstein, *Lion of Freedom*, pp. 299, 310; R.J. Morris, *Class, Sect and Party: The Making of the British Middle Class, Leeds 1820-1850*, Manchester, 1990, pp. 163-65, 249-63; Martin Hewitt, *The Emergence of Stability in the Industrial City: Manchester, 1832-67*, Aldershot, 1996, pp. 66-91; Neville Kirk, *Change, Continuity and Class: Labour in British Society, 1850-1920*, Manchester, 1998, pp. 35-37, 84-107.
8. *Manchester and Salford Advertiser*, 27 January 1838.
9. Thomas Clark, *Reflections upon the Past Policy, and Future Prospects of the Chartist Party*, London, 1850, in Claeys (ed.), *Chartist Movement*, 6: 15.
10. *Manchester Times*, 16 September 1848. See also, *National Reformer and Manx Weekly Review*, 22 May 1847 (O'Brien); *Northern Star*, 6 January 1849 (Harney).
11. John Belchem, *Industrialization and the Working Class: the English Experience, 1750-1900*, Aldershot, 1990, pp. 144, 138-41; John Saville, 'Introduction', in Saville (ed.), *Ernest Jones: Chartist*, London, 1952, pp. 44-49. For a critical view, see Taylor, *Ernest Jones*, pp. 140-47. For a different view of Chartist ideology and Liberalism, see Eugenio F. Biagini and Alastair J. Reid (eds.), *Currents of Radicalism: Popular Radicalism, Organised Labour, and Party Politics in Britain, 1850-1914*, Cambridge, 1991, pp. 1-12; Patrick Joyce, *Visions of the People: Industrial England and the Question of Class, 1840-1914*, Cambridge, 1991, pp. 27-55.
12. Finn, *After Chartism*, pp. 83-92, 112-15.
13. Mill to Fox, 9 September 1842, in Robson (ed.), *Collected Works*, 13: 544. For Richard Cobden on 'social dissolution', see *HD* Third Series, LXIV (1842): 1217.
14. Disraeli to Sarah D, 19 August 1842, in M.G. Wiebe (ed.), *Benjamin Disraeli Letters*, vol. 4, *1842-1847*, Toronto, 1989, p. 55.
15. Epstein, *Lion of Freedom*, pp. 299, 310; Foster, *Class Struggle*, pp. 1-3, 204, 209-11, 251; Kirk, *Change, Continuity and Class*, pp. 35-38.
16. For an exception, see Finn, *After Chartism*, pp. 4-7, 303-307.
17. *Ashton Reporter*, 20 September 1856.
18. *Manchester Guardian*, 2 March 1842; *Northern Star*, 5 March 1842; *Ashton Reporter*, 8 September 1866.
19. Stedman Jones, *Languages of Class*, pp. 177-78; Clark, *Struggle for the Breeches*, pp. 244-45. For critiques of Stedman Jones, see Saville, *1848*, pp. 217-29; Epstein, *In Practice*, pp. 28-29.

20. *PP* (Commons) 1850 [1239] XXIII: 4; *PP* (Commons) 1852 [1439] XXI: 6-7; *Manchester Guardian*, 11 November 1848 and 18 April 1849. See also, J.T. Ward, *The Factory Movement 1830-1855*, London, 1962, pp. 346-90; Gray, *Factory Question*, pp. 195-209; G.R. Searle, *Entrepreneurial Politics in Mid-Victorian Britain*, Oxford, 1993, pp. 271-77. For strikes, see *Manchester Guardian*, 7-18 April 1849; 20 and 23 April 1853.

21. *Manchester Guardian*, 20 May 1848.

22. Ibid., 14 January 1854.

23. *Ashton Reporter*, 7 November 1857.

24. Kirk, *Growth*, pp. 83-115; Gray, *Factory Question*, pp. 213-15.

25. See Table 3; BLPES, Webb Trade Union Collection, A/XXXV: 158, 160-62, 178; Fowler and Wyke (eds.), *Barefoot Aristocrats*, pp. 39-74.

26. British Association, *On the Regulation of Wages by Means*, pp. 3-4, 9. For wage lists in Ashton, see Ibid., pp. 201, 180; *Ashton Reporter*, 31 March, 7 and 21 April 1860. See also, Huberman, *Escape from the Market*, pp. 132-48; Mary Rose, *Firms, Networks and Business Values: The British and American Cotton Industries Since 1750*, Cambridge, 2000, pp. 125-27.

27. *PP* (Commons) 1843 [431] XIV: B32. See also Table 10.

28. *PP* (Commons) 1824 [51] V: 302; *PP* (Commons) 1833 [690] VI: 622-23; *Morning Chronicle*, 9 May 1844. See also, Schwarzkopf, *Unpicking Gender*, pp. 64-69.

29. MCL, Mayall Mss, L43 Box 41 Memorandum Book 1845-90.

30. *Northern Star*, 20 August 1842. See also, Chapter One.

31. *Manchester Guardian*, 15 September 1847; 8 July 1846; 9 December 1843.

32. Ibid., 27 October 1847. For critical views of the 1842 strike, see *Ashton Reporter*, 23 March and 4 May 1861.

33. Bezer, *Autobiography*, in Vincent (ed.), *Testaments of Radicalism*, p.187.

34. Ibid., p. 187. Fowler and Wyke (eds.), *Barefoot Aristocrats*, pp. 44-45; Saville, *1848*, pp. 58-59.

35. Epstein, *Lion of Freedom*, pp. 276-86; *Northern Star*, 17 July 1841; 24 July and 7 August 1847.

36. *Northern Star*, 28 August and 4 September 1847.

37. Ibid., 25 March 1848 (Pilling's speech); *Manchester Guardian*, 12 April 1848 (Nixon's speech). For a different view, see Taylor, *Ernest Jones*, pp. v-vi, 7, 107-08, 114, 118-20.

38. Saville, *1848*, pp. 9-10; Tiller, 'Late Chartism', in Epstein and Thompson (eds.), *Chartist Experience*, pp. 316-17; Theodore Koditschek, *Class Formation and Urban-Industrial Society: Bradford, 1750-1850*, Cambridge, 1990, pp. 552-61.

39. *Manchester Guardian*, 18 March and 15 April 1848.

40. *Northern Star*, 8 April 1848.

41. Ibid., 25 April 1846; 4 December 1847; *Manchester Guardian*, 25 April 1846; 13 January, 1 and 8 December 1847. In 1846 members of Young Ireland seceded from the Repeal Association and formed the Irish Confederation; in 1848 a Confederate club flourished in Stalybridge under the leadership of Bernard Treanor.

42. TNA, PRO, HO 45/2410B, Deposition of Bartholomew Hickey; *Manchester Guardian*, 22 March 1848; *Northern Star*, 25 March 1848.

43. *Manchester Guardian*, 22 March 1848. See also, *Northern Star*, 25 March 1848.

44. *Manchester Guardian*, 18 March 1848. See also, 5 and 12 April 1848; *Northern Star*, 8 April 1848; TNA, PRO, HO 45/2410B, Trafford to the Home Office, 3 April 1848. At the national convention Robert Wild claimed that local Chartists had collected around 60,000 to 70,000 signatures. *Northern Star*, 8 April 1848; *Manchester Guardian*, 8 April 1848.

45. *Northern Star*, 8 April 1848.

46. TNA, PRO, HO 45/2410B, Armitage to Grey, 4 April 1848. See also, HO 45/2410B, Buckley, Whittaker, and Jowett to Grey, 7 April 1848.

47. *Bury Times*, 24 February 1894. *Manchester Guardian*, 12 April 1848.

48. *Manchester Guardian*, 12 and 15 April 1848.

49. Ibid., 22 April, 3 and 10 May 1848; *Northern Star*, 22 April 1848.

50. *Manchester Guardian*, 17 May 1848.

51. *Northern Star*, 20 May 1848. For Pilling's speech at the National Assembly, see *Northern Star*, 20 May 1848.

52. On 7 May, at Stalybridge, James Milligan claimed that at Ashton they had formed an armed 'Protection of Life and Property Society'. See *Manchester Guardian*, 10 May 1848; *Northern Star*, 22 April 1848 (Aberdeen and Nottingham); Gammage, *History*, pp. 320, 332.

53. TNA, PRO, HO 45/2410B, Hall and Taylor to Grey, 16 June 1848. While on a speaking tour, George Holyoake received information that 700 were enrolled in the National Guard in Ashton. See *The Reasoner*, 2 August 1848.

54. Richard Davis, *The Young Ireland Movement*, Dublin, 1987, pp. 156-62; Cecil Woodham-Smith, *The Great Hunger: Ireland 1845-1849*, New York, 1962, pp. 348-50, 357-59.

55. Saville, *1848*, pp. 132-33; Woodham-Smith, *The Great Hunger*, pp. 345-46; Davis, *Young Ireland Movement*, pp. 156-62.

56. Goodway, *London Chartism*, pp. 89-95; John Belchem, '1848: Feargus O'Connor and the Collapse of the Mass Platform', in Epstein and Thompson (eds.), *Chartist Experience*, pp. 294-98.

57. TNA, PRO, HO 48/40, no. 34, Deposition of John Latimer, 8 September 1848. For delegate meetings in Manchester, see also HO 45/2410AB, Higgs to Arbuthnot, 11 August 1848; Goodway, *London Chartism*, pp. 91-92.

58. TNA, PRO, HO 48/40, no. 34, Deposition of John Latimer, 8 September 1848.

59. Ibid.; HO 45/2410B, Mayor and Magistrates of Ashton to Grey, 15 August 1848; *Manchester Guardian*, 16 and 19 August 1848. Joseph Radcliffe was convicted for the murder; his death sentence was commuted to transportation for life. See his obituary *Ashton Reporter*, 18 May 1889; John Belchem, 'The Spy-System in 1848: Chartists and Informers—An Australian Connection', *Labour History* 39 (1980): 20-21, 24-26.

60. *Manchester Guardian*, 9 December 1848. See also, TNA, PRO, HO 48/40, no. 31, Deposition of Thomas Brown; no. 35, Deposition of Thomas Winterbottom.

61. *Northern Star*, 30 December 1848; Koditschek, *Class Formation*, pp. 513-14, 554-65.

62. *Manchester Guardian*, 19 August 1848; TNA, PRO, TS 11/141, Deposition of Richard Beswick.

63. John Belchem, 'English Working-Class Radicalism and the Irish, 1815-50', in Roger Swift and Sheridan Gilley (eds.), *The Irish in the Victorian City*, London, 1985, pp. 93-94; Saville, *1848*, pp. 119-20, 200-202.

64. *English Patriot and Irish Repealer*, 5 August 1848; *Manchester Guardian*, 15 March 1848; *Manchester Examiner*, 29 July 1848.

65. *Manchester Examiner*, 29 July 1848. See also, Ibid., 5 August 1848.

66. Ibid., 19 August 1848; *Bolton Chronicle*, 26 August and 7 October 1848. In 1848 William Cuffay was involved in insurrectionary plotting in London. His father was a slave, born in St. Kitts. For a biographical sketch, see *Reynold's Political Instructor*, 13 April 1850.

67. *English Republic*, (1851), volume 1: 85.

68. *Northern Star*, 11 November 1848. For the age and occupation of those arrested, see *Manchester Guardian*, 9 and 20 September 1848.

69. J.K., *History of the Ashton-under-Lyne Mutual Improvement Society*, Ashton, 1858, pp. 5, 9-11, 13.

70. *Ashton Chronicle*, 19 August 1848. J.R. Stephens edited the newspaper; L. Swallow and later the Chartist Edward Hobson were its printers. See Philip Martin Williams and David L. Williams, *Extra, Extra, Read All About It. A Brief History of Newspapers of Ashton-under-Lyne 1847-1990*, Ashton, 1991.

71. Thompson, *The Making of the English Working Class*, pp. 17-22.

72. *Red Republican*, 19 October 1850.

73. Donald Read and Eric Glasgow, *Feargus O'Connor: Irishman and Chartist*, London, 1961, pp. 137-43; Gammage, *History*, pp. 380, 390; *Northern Star*, 23 August 1851; 3 January; 14 February; 5 and 12 June 1852. See also, Laurence M. Geary, 'O'Connorite Bedlam: Feargus and his Grand-Nephew, Arthur', *Medical History* 34 (1990): 125-43; Airey, 'Feargus O'Connor', pp. 155-59.

74. *Northern Star*, 7 June 1851. For the Ashton subscription campaign to raise money for a monument in honour of O'Connor, see *Ashton Reporter*, 5, 12, and 27 October 1855.

75. *Ashton Reporter*, 10 November 1855; *Northern Star*, 29 June and 27 July 1850. For the state and the Land Plan, see Yeo, 'Chartist Democracy', in Epstein and Thompson (eds.), *Chartist Experience*, pp. 367-73; Bronstein, *Land Reform and Working-Class Experience*, pp. 220-31.

76. *Trial of Feargus O'Connor and Fifty-Eight Others*, pp. 75-76; Thompson, *Chartists*, p. 216.

77. Belchem, 'The Spy-System', pp. 20-24. For Pilling, Treanor, and Sigley, see *Northern Star*, 16 December 1848; TNA, PRO, TS 11/137/374, pt. 1, Queen vs George Archdeacon and Others, p. 43a; Herbert G. Gutman, *Work, Culture, and Society in Industrializing America: Essays in American Working-Class and Social History*, New York, 1976, pp. 43, 274. After about two years in the United States, Pilling returned in 1850 to Ashton. See *Ashton Reporter*, 5 December 1874.

78. Hall and Roberts (eds.), *William Aitken*, p. 42.

79. *Northern Star*, 11 June 1842.

80. *Star of Freedom*, 24 July 1852.

81. For an early manifesto, see *Red Republican*, 22 June 1850.

82. *Northern Star*, 27 January and 17 March 1849; 17 August 1850. Belchem, *Industrialization*, pp. 138-44; Saville, 'Introduction', in Saville (ed.), *Ernest Jones*, pp. 44-49.

83. *Northern Star*, 19 October 1850.

84. Ibid., 5 April 1851. Hewitt, *Emergence*, pp. 249-53.

85. *Northern Star*, 8 March 1851.

86. Ibid., 19 April 1851.

87. *Manchester Guardian*, 16 February 1850. Nicholas Edsall, *Richard Cobden: Independent Radical*, Cambridge, 1986, pp. 192-93, 201-11; Saville, 'Introduction', in Saville (ed.), *Ernest Jones*, pp. 35-37.

88. For O'Connor's views, see *Northern Star*, 26 May; 21 July; 18 August 1849; 5 January; 27 April; 19 October 1850; 1 February 1851. Airey, 'Feargus O'Connor', pp. 89-104.

89. *Friend of the People*, 24 May 1851; *Northern Star*, 10 August 1850; *Red Republican*, 26 October and 23 November 1850.

90. *Northern Star*, 8 March 1851. For the Manchester debate, see Ibid., 11 January; 15 February; 19 April 1851; Hewitt, *Emergence*, pp. 249-53.

91. *Ashton Reporter*, 13 August 1859; 14 November 1857. See also, Epstein, *Radical Expression*, pp. 147-65.

92. *Ashton Reporter*, 14 November 1857; 5 February and 20 August 1859; *National Reformer*, 13 February 1864.

93. *People's Paper*, 17 November 1855; 11 October 1856.

94. Ibid., 17 November 1855.

95. *Northern Star*, 5 April 1851 and 9 November 1850.

96. *People's Paper*, 12 February 1853 and 17 February 1855.

97. Ibid., 17 February 1855 and 27 January 1855; *Ashton Reporter*, 31 March 1860.

98. *People's Paper*, 17 February 1855 and 9 February 1856. It was later renamed the People's Educational Institute. See *Ashton Reporter*, 30 March 1861 and 28 March 1868.

99. *National Reformer*, 30 January 1864; *Reasoner*, 30 September 1857.

100. *Reasoner*, 30 September 1857; *National Reformer*, 8 February 1862; *Ashton Reporter*, 17 November 1855. For the creation of the Institute of the Ashton Secularist Society, see *Ashton Reporter*, 26 September 1863; *National Reformer*, 30 January 1864.

101. *Reasoner*, 13 February 1859; *Ashton Reporter*, 10 August 1861; J. Thompson, *History of the Ashton-under-Lyne Working Men's Co-operative Society, 1857-1907*, Manchester, 1907, p. 19; *The Co-operator*, August 1860. See also, Edward Royle, *Radicals, Secularists and Republicans: Popular Free Thought in Britain, 1866-1915*, Manchester, 1980, p. 229.

102. *The Co-operator*, August 1860.

103. Ibid., June 1860.

104. *Ashton Reporter*, 6 July 1861.

105. Ibid., 9 October 1869; *Oddfellows' Magazine* (July 1857): 129-32; Garrard, *Democratisation in Britain*, pp. 183-84. Aitken thought that cooperatives tended to focus on profits. See *Ashton Reporter*, 8 May 1858.

106. *Northern Star*, 20 April 1844. See also, Ibid., 29 October 1842.

107. *Manchester Guardian*, 27 February 1847. Incorporation led to a substantial extension of the franchise; in 1848 there were almost 2100 burgesses. Tameside, *The List of Burgesses of the Borough of Ashton-under-Lyne*, Ashton, 1848.

108. *Ashton Reporter*, 27 October 1860; 1 November 1862; *Rochdale Observer*, 12 July 1856.

109. *People's Paper*, 8 October 1853; *Northern Star*, 3 April 1841.

110. *Ashton Reporter*, 25 May 1861.

111. Peter Gurney, 'Labor's Great Arch: Cooperation and Cultural Revolution in Britain, 1795-1926', in Ellen Furlough and Carl Strikwerda (eds.), *Consumers Against Capitalism? Consumer Cooperation in Europe, North America, and Japan, 1840-1990*, Lanham, 1999, pp. 138-39.

112. *Northern Star*, 18 January 1851; 17 August 1850. See also, Pickering, 'The Hearts of the Millions', pp. 229-30, 243-48.

113. See Gray's speech in *Northern Star*, 5 April 1851.

114. *PP* (Commons) 1843 [429] XXVII: 21.

115. Joyce, *Work*, pp. 240-43; Morris, *Class, Sect and Party*, pp. 165-67, 264-79. In the Ashton area in 1842, Anglican masters owned thirty-six mills with a total workforce of 6,575; Dissenters owned twenty-seven mills, with a workforce of 14,400. See *PP* (Commons) 1843 [429] XXVII: 6. See Table 11.

116. *HD*, Third series, LXIV (1842): 1217. Searle, *Entrepreneurial Politics*, pp. 2-3, 17-21, 209-10.

117. Forster to his mother, 4 April 1848, quoted by T. Wemyss Reid, *Life of the Rt. Hon. W.E. Forster*, London, 1888; reprint ed., New York, 1970, p. 223. See also, Koditschek, *Class Formation*, pp. 519-21, 554.

118. *Manchester Spectator*, 10 February 1849. For the radical manufacturer Thomasson, see Taylor, *Popular Politics in Early Industrial Britain*, pp. 63-64, 114-15.

119. *Manchester Spectator*, 2 February 1850.

120. *Manchester Guardian*, 21 January 1846.

121. *PP* (Commons) 1866 [3626] LVII: 73; *Isis*, 16 June 1832; *Ashton Reporter*, 2 February and 26 January 1861.

122. *PP* (Commons) 1854 [69] LIII: 5, 9; *PP* (Common) 1859, Session 2 [56] VII, Appendix A: 154-55.

123. Forster to his father, n.d. (April 1848), quoted by Reid, *Life*, p. 227.

124. For the concerns of Charles Hindley and Samuel Robinson, see *Manchester Guardian*, 16 February 1833; Samuel Robinson, *An Address Delivered at a Public Meeting of the Inhabitants of Ashton-under-Lyne and Dukinfield to Advocate the Claims of the Mechanics' Institution*, Manchester, 1836, p. 62. See also, Hewitt, *Emergence*, pp. 87-88, 92-122.

125. MCL, Ministry to the Poor, Seventeenth Report (1851): 38-39.

126. *Report on the Condition of the Working Classes in an Extensive District*, pp. 13-14.

127. *PP* (Commons) 1852-53 [1690] LXXXIX: clviii. K.S. Inglis, 'Patterns of Religious Worship in 1851', *Journal of Ecclesiastical History* 11 (1960): 79-86; Joyce, *Work*, pp. 243-46.

128. Algernon Wells, 'Thoughts on the Need for Increased Efforts to Promote the Religious Welfare of the Working Classes in England, by the Independent Churches and their Pastors', *Congregational Year Book* (1848), in Richard Helmstader and

Paul T. Phillips (eds.), *Religion in Victorian Society: A Sourcebook of Documents*, New York, 1985, p. 216.

129. James Guinness Rogers, *An Autobiography*, London, 1903, pp. 112, 114. Mill owners who worshipped at Albion chapel in the 1830s included Abel Buckley, Alfred and Frederick Reyner, James Lees, John Knott, Edward Redfern, and John Cheetham; Hugh Mason later joined Albion. See also, Glover, *History*, p. 256; Tameside, NC 2/18 'Proceedings and Resolutions of the Trustees of the Albion Chapel, Ashton-under-Lyne', 5 March 1835.

130. Rogers, *Autobiography*, pp. 109-16; *Ashton Reporter*, 10 April and 12 May 1858; Tameside, NC 1/8/15 Records of Albion Congregational Church; Ginswick (ed.), *Labour and the Poor*, 1: 91-92.

131. Rogers, *Autobiography*, pp. 112, 114, 109-10, 115-16.

132. Marjorie A. Cruickshank, 'The Anglican Revival and Education: A Study of School Expansion in the Cotton Manufacturing Areas of North-West England, 1840-1850', *Northern History* XV (1979): 179, 186, 188; William Farrer and J. Brownbill (eds.), *The Victoria History of the County of Lancaster*, seven volumes, London, 1911; reprint ed., London, 1966, 4: 350. For the Church and education, see Butterworth, *Historical Account*, p. 104; *Ashton Reporter*, 28 March and 18 April 1857; 10 April 1858; S.D. Ashton, 'A Survey of Educational Development in the Borough of Ashton-under-Lyne 1840-1938', M.Ed. thesis, 1938, pp. 26, 30-34, 38, 41-45.

133. *Ashton Reporter*, 20 November 1858; Tameside, DD 13/24/11 'The Weavers' Strike: The Labourer's Friend in the Poor Man's Temple', broadside; Joyce, *Work*, pp. 253-54; Kirk, *Growth*, pp. 205-206, 338-41.

134. Ashton mill owners included the Mellors, the Heginbottoms, Ralph Kershaw, and Oldham Whittaker; Jonah Harrop and Henry Lees were both Anglican coal masters. See *Ashton Herald*, 20 June 1891; *Ashton Reporter*, 22 February 1902; H. Heginbottom, *Thomas Heginbottom: A Few Slight Impressions of His Life and Times*, Hyde, 1913, pp. 4-8, 31-32, 36-37; *Ashton Herald*, 27 December 1890; *Ashton Reporter*, 24 May 1862 and 6 January 1872; Glover, *History*, pp. 25-27; *Ashton Reporter*, 8 October 1859.

135. *PP* (Commons) 1854 [1796] XIX: 4-5. *PP* (Commons) 1842 [410] XXII: 5. See Chapter Four.

136. 'A Magistrate' [Robert Brook Aspland] *Public Instruction and Moral Improvement*, London, 1846, pp. 34-35. Aspland served for many years as a Unitarian minister at Dukinfield.

137. *PP* (Commons) 1846 [681] XX: 8-9; *Ashton Reporter*, 28 March 1857.

138. Rogers, *Autobiography*, pp. 109, 115-16; Ginswick (ed.), *Labour and the Poor*, 1: 68.

139. For mill owners' opposition to the Stalybridge races and the wakes, see *Manchester Guardian*, 29 July 1846; *Ashton Chronicle*, 19 April and 5 August 1848. See also, William Chadwick, *Reminiscences of a Chief Constable*, Manchester, [1900]; reprint ed., Longdendale, 1974, pp. 115-19, 137-38; Hewitt, *Emergence*, pp. 156-69.

140. William Hone, *The Every-Day Book*, two volumes, London, 1827; reprint ed., Detroit, 1967, 2: 467-69; Bamford, *Early Days*, pp. 141-43; *Ashton Reporter*, 31 March and 8 September 1866. See also, Steinberg, *Fighting Words*, pp. 154-57.

141. *Ashton Reporter*, 8 September 1866.

142. *Manchester Guardian*, 4 April 1849 and 7 April 1847; *Manchester Examiner and Times*, 23 April 1851; *Ashton Reporter*, 14 April 1855; 31 March and 8 September 1866.

143. Axon, *Black Knight*, pp. 20-21.

144. *Ashton Reporter*, 7 February 1857; 1 January; 5 February; 9 July; 27 August; 8 October 1859. Lancashire Record Office, DDX 350/12, illuminated address presented to Hugh Mason, February 1859.

145. Ginswick (ed.), *Labour and the Poor*, 1: 91-92; Owen Ashmore, 'Hugh Mason and the Oxford Mills and Community, Ashton-under-Lyne', *Transactions of the Lancashire and Cheshire Antiquarian Society* 78 (1975): 38-50.

146. Ginswick (ed.), *Labour and the Poor*, 1: 91-92.

147. *Northern Star*, 17 February 1844. Joyce, *Work*, pp. 134-57; R.J. Morris, 'The Industrial Town', in Philip Waller (ed.), *The English Urban Landscape*, Oxford, 2000, pp. 197-203.

148. *Ashton Reporter*, 5 February 1859.

149. John Teer, *Silent Musings*, Manchester, 1869, pp. 55-56, 45-47.

150. *Ashton Reporter*, 4 September 1858.

151. Ibid., 6 March 1858 and 4 July 1857.

152. Anthony Howe, *The Cotton Masters, 1830-1860*, Oxford, 1984, pp. 178-93; Judy Lown, *Women and Industrialization: Gender at Work in Nineteenth-Century England*, Cambridge, 1990, pp. 3-4, 8-9, 200-201; Rose, *Limited Livelihoods*, pp. 33-36, 41, 47-48.

153. *Ashton Reporter*, 30 March 1861 and 18 April 1868; *The Bee-Hive*, 4 March 1876. See also, *Ashton Reporter*, 20 February 1886; *Ten Hours' Advocate*, 13 March 1847.

154. *Ashton Reporter*, 22 August 1857; *Ashton Chronicle*, 19 August 1848.

155. *Ashton Reporter*, 13 April 1861.

156. Ibid., 1 June 1861.

157. *Ashton Standard*, 23 June 1860, quoted by Joyce, *Work*, p. 149.

158. *Ashton Reporter*, 30 January 1869; Benjamin Grime, *Memory Sketches*, Oldham, 1887, p. 12; Paul, *Operative Conservative Societies*, pp. 8-10, 14-16, 25-28.

159. *PP* (Commons) 1836 XXXIV, Appendix G: 84; *PP* (Commons) 1852-53 [1691-II] LXXXVIII, pt. 2: 615, 662; *The Champion*, 5 January 1850; *Manchester Guardian*, 3 July 1852.

160. *Ashton Reporter*, 19 February 1859; 28 March 1857; 2, 9, and 23 January 1858; LRO, QJD 1/241; *Manchester Guardian*, 16 September 1854.

161. Tameside, *Revised Rules of the Ashton-under-Lyne Working Men's Church and Conservative Association*, Ashton, 1868. See also, Kirk, *Change, Continuity and Class*, pp. 95-97.

162. Rev. F.H. Williams, *Second Lecture, delivered in Reply to the Rev. J.G. Rogers*, Manchester, 1861, pp. 23, 15.

163. *Ashton Reporter*, 12 December 1857. See also, his obituaries in *Ashton Reporter*, 8 September 1888; *Manchester Guardian*, 11 September 1888.

164. William Haslam Mills, *Sir Charles W. Macara, Bart.: A Study of Modern Lancashire*, second ed., Manchester, 1917, pp. 66-67.

165. *Manchester Spectator*, 3 February 1849; *Manchester Guardian*, 31 July 1847.

166. *Ashton Reporter*, 21 June 1856. For the Radcliffe case, see *Ashton Chronicle*, 20 January and 12 May 1849; *Manchester Guardian*, 28 April 1849.

167. *Ashton Reporter*, 5 and 12 December 1857. For favourable comments by William Hill and Thomas Storer, see *People's Paper*, 27 February 1858; *Ashton Reporter*, 17 July 1858.

168. *Ashton Reporter*, 8 September and 3 March 1860. For the Hobson family and radicalism, see *Ashton Reporter*, 17 August 1867; Hall and Roberts (eds.), *William Aitken*, p. 30.

169. *Ashton Reporter*, 26 December 1857. See also, Ibid., 12 January and 5 October 1861.

170. *Manchester Guardian*, 5 December 1846. See also, *Manchester and Salford Advertiser*, 28 December 1844.

171. *Ashton Reporter*, 21 September 1861.

172. Ibid., 18 April 1868. See also, Kirk, *Change, Continuity and Class*, pp. 84-85; Searle, *Entrepreneurial Politics*, pp. 277-86.

173. Jephson, *The Platform*, 2: 423-24, 427-29. John Vincent, The *Formation of the British Liberal Party*, New York, 1966, pp. 142-43, 162-63.

174. Belchem and Epstein, 'The Gentleman Leader Revisited', pp. 189-93; John Breuilly, Gottfried Niedhart, and Antony Taylor (eds.), *The Era of the Reform League: English Labour and Radical Politics, 1857-1872. Documents Selected by Gustav Mayer*, Mannheim, 1995, pp. 19-20; Grime, *Memory Sketches*, pp. 122, 207, 216-25; Vernon, *Politics and the People*, pp. 235-36.

175. *Northern Star*, 6 April 1839 (Bradford); 1 December 1838 (Keighley); 13 April 1839 (Barnsley); 4 July 1840 and 1 October 1842 (Ashton).

176. Farish, *Autobiography*, p. 35. Trygve Tholfsen, 'The Origins of the Birmingham Caucus', *Historical Journal* 2 (1959): 161-84; Biagini, *Liberty, Retrenchment and Reform*, pp. 328-37.

177. *Bury Times*, 24 February 1894. T. Palmer Newbould, *Pages from a Life of Strife. Being Some Recollections of William Henry Chadwick. The Last of the Manchester Chartists*, London, 1910.

178. E.P Thompson, 'Peculiarities of the English', in *The Poverty of Theory & Other Essays*, London, 1978, p. 281.

179. *Northern Star*, 1 February 1851.

180. *Ashton Reporter*, 26 December 1857 and 5 October 1861.

181. Ibid., 19 March 1859. Epstein, *Lion of Freedom*, p. 212.

182. *Rochdale Observer*, 12 July 1856. See also, *Manchester and Salford Advertiser*, 15 January 1842.

183. *People's Paper*, 27 February 1858; *Ashton Reporter*, 19 March 1859; Clark, *Reflections upon the Past Policy*, in Claeys (ed.), *Chartist Movement*, 6: 14-15.

184. *Ashton Reporter*, 5 October 1861.

185. *Northern Star*, 5 April 1851 and 11 June 1842.

186. *Ashton Reporter*, 26 December 1857.

187. This was how a West Riding Chartist described the situation in his town before the coming together of Chartism. See, Bates, *A Sketch of His Life*.

Conclusion

1. Hall and Roberts (eds.), *William Aitken*, pp. 40-41.
2. *Ashton News* and *Ashton Reporter*, 2 October 1869. Olive Anderson, *Suicide in Victorian and Edwardian England*, Oxford, 1987, pp. 218-21.
3. *Ashton News* and *Ashton Reporter*, 2 October 1869. Hall and Roberts (eds.), *William Aitken*, pp. 14, 18.
4. *Ashton News* and *Ashton Reporter*, 2 October 1869; Hall and Roberts (eds.), *William Aitken*, pp. 21-22. *PP* (Commons) 1867-68 [402] XIV: 382-83; TNA, PRO, HO 20/10, Interview of William Aitken. See also, Pickering, 'Trade of Agitation', pp. 221-37.
5. Hall and Roberts (eds.), *William Aitken*, p. 55. MCL, George Wilson Papers, M20/1868-69, Mason to Wilson, 19 November 1869.
6. Biagini and Reid (eds.), *Currents of Radicalism*, pp. 1-2. Biagini, *Liberty, Retrenchment and Reform*, pp. 2, 10-11. See also, Harrison and Hollis, 'Chartism, Liberalism, and the Life of Robert Lowery', pp. 503-35; Taylor, *Popular Politics in Early Industrial Britain*; Michael Winstanley, 'Oldham Radicalism and the Origins of Popular Liberalism, 1830-52', *Historical Journal* 36 (September 1993): 619-43.
7. Stedman Jones, *Languages of Class*, p. 104.
8. Joyce, *Visions*, pp. 37-38, 1-15.
9. Jerome Hamilton Buckley, *The Turning Key: Autobiography and the Subjective Impulse Since 1800*, Cambridge, 1984, vii and pp. 14-15, 19, 45. Charles Rycroft, 'Viewpoint: Analysis and the Autobiography', *Times Literary Supplement*, 27 May 1983: 541.
10. Buckley, *Turning Key*, p. 45.
11. Hall and Roberts (eds.), *William Aitken*, p. 28.
12. Ibid., pp. 28-29, 36. See also, Thompson, 'Who were "the People" in 1842?' in Chase and Dyck (eds.), *Living and Learning*, pp. 118-32. For a different perspective, see Joyce, *Visions*, pp. 37-38, 60, 103, 108; *idem, Democratic Subjects*, p. 132.
13. Harrison and Hollis, 'Chartism, Liberalism, and the Life of Robert Lowery', pp. 503-35.
14. Macaulay to Greig, 30 January [1846] and Macaulay to the Secretary of the Committee for the Liberation of Frost, Williams, and Jones, 16 February [1846], in Thomas Pinney (ed.), *The Letters of Thomas Babington Macaulay*, Vol. 4: *September 1841-December 1848*, Cambridge, 1977, 4: 291-93.
15. Hall and Roberts (eds.), *William Aitken*, p. 14.
16. Popular Memory Group, 'Popular Memory', in Johnson et al. (eds.), *Making Histories*, pp. 205-52; David Lowenthal, *The Past is a Foreign Country*, Cambridge, 1985, pp. 193-210; Alistair Thomson, 'The Anzac Legend: Exploring National Myth and Memory in Australia', in Samuel and Thompson (eds.), *Myths*, pp. 73-82; Pierre Nora (ed.), *Realms of Memory: Rethinking the French Past*, Vol 1: *Conflicts and Divisions*, translated by Arthur Goldhammer, New York, 1996; Emily Honig, 'Striking Lives: Oral History and the Politics of Memory', *Journal of Women's History* 9 (Spring 1997): 139-57.
17. Buckley, *Turning Key*, pp. vii, 3, 14-15, 19. Vincent, *Bread, Knowledge and Freedom*, pp. 1-38.

18. Hall and Roberts (eds.), *William Aitken*, p. 14. For the 1862 trip, see *Ashton Reporter*, 23 August 1862. Robert Folkenflik, 'Introduction: The Institution of Autobiography', in Robert Folkenflik (ed.), *The Culture of Autobiography: Constructions of Self-Representation*, Stanford, 1993, pp. 12-16.

19. Hall and Roberts (eds.), *William Aitken*, pp. 14, 17, 21, 40. William Aitken, 'Franklin's Maxims', *Oddfellows' Magazine* (April 1859): 79; Vincent, *Bread, Knowledge and Freedom*, pp. 14-15; Linda H. Peterson, *Victorian Autobiography: The Tradition of Self-Interpretation*, New Haven, 1986, pp. 1-3.

20. Aitken's 'Life of Hofer', quoted in Aitken's obituary, *Ashton Reporter*, 2 October 1869; TNA, PRO, HO 20/10, Interview of William Aitken; *McDouall's Chartist and Republican Journal*, 10 April 1841; Aitken, *Journey*, Preface and pp. 25-30, 34-35, 38, 46.

21. Samuel Bamford's autobiography was published as *Passages in the Life of a Radical* (1844) and *Early Days* (1849). The memoirs of Thomas Hardy came out in 1832; and the autobiographies of the Chartists John James Bezer and Robert Lowery were published, in serial form, respectively in 1851 and 1856-57. See, Vincent, *Bread, Knowledge and Freedom*, pp. 204-208.

22. Buckley, *Turning Key*, p. 45.

23. TNA, PRO, HO 20/10, Interview of William Aitken; *PP* (Commons) 1867-68 [402] XIV: 382-83; *Ashton News* and *Ashton Reporter*, 2 October 1869.

24. Hall and Roberts (eds.), *William Aitken*, p. 14. Vincent, *Bread, Knowledge and Freedom*, pp. 27-29; Eileen Janes Yeo, 'Will the Real Mary Lovett Please Stand Up? Chartism, Gender, and Autobiography', in Chase and Dyck (eds.), *Living and Learning*, pp. 163-64.

25. For his use of 'working men' and 'the working-classes', see Hall and Roberts (eds.), *William Aitken*, pp. 14, 19-22, 26, 28. In the last two instalments, which deal with Chartism, he avoided both constructions, with one exception, in favour of 'the people'. He twice referred to 'middle classes' on pp. 28 and 43.

26. Ibid., pp. 14, 19, 30, 39-40, 42-43.

27. Ibid., pp. 14, 27-28.

28. Ibid., p. 40.

29. Yeo, 'Mary Lovett', in Chase and Dyck (eds.), *Living and Learning*, pp. 164, 167.

30. *Ashton Reporter*, 2 October 1869. During his imprisonment in 1840 and flight to the United States during 1842-43, she had to manage on her own; the 1851 census listed her as a schoolmistress. See *Northern Star*, 15 July 1843; TNA, PRO, HO 107/2233.

31. Lowenthal, *The Past is a Foreign Country*, p. 210; Thomson, 'The Anzac Legend', in Samuel and Thompson (eds.), *Myths*, pp. 73-79.

32. Hall and Roberts (eds.), *William Aitken*, pp. 28, 14.

33. *Ashton Reporter*, 2 October 1869. Hall and Roberts (eds.), *William Aitken*, pp. 27-28.

34. Hall and Roberts (eds.), *William Aitken*, pp. 28, 40.

35. Ibid., pp. 19, 28, 30, 41. Walter E. Houghton, *The Victorian Frame of Mind, 1830-1870*, New Haven, 1957, pp. 27-53; Vincent, *Bread, Knowledge and Freedom*, pp. 197-200.

36. Hall and Roberts (eds.), *William Aitken*, pp. 39-40. For the cult of the hero, see Houghton, *Victorian Frame of Mind*, pp. 305-40; Thomas Carlyle, *On Heroes, Hero-Worship, & the Heroic in History*, London, 1841.

37. *Ashton News*, 2 October 1869; Hall and Roberts (eds.), *William Aitken*, pp. 15, 18, 22, 40.

38. William Aitken, 'Over the Atlantic, from the Mersey to the Mississippi', *Oddfellows' Magazine* (April 1864): 371. Vincent, *Bread, Knowledge and Freedom*, pp. 182, 186-87.

39. Adams, *Memoirs of A Social Atom*, pp. 211-12. See also, Ashton and Pickering, *Friends of the People*, pp. 7-28; Belchem and Epstein, 'Gentleman Leader Revisited', pp. 178-81; Joyce, *Visions*, pp. 34-40; Taylor, *Ernest Jones*, pp. 9-10, 79-80, 254-58.

40. Hall and Roberts (eds.), *William Aitken*, pp. 19-21, 24-25.

41. Ibid., p. 14.

42. Popular Memory Group, 'Popular Memory', in Johnson et al. (eds.), *Making Histories*, pp. 241-43; Thomson, 'The Anzac Legend', in Samuel and Thompson (eds.), *Myths*, pp. 77-79; Honig, 'Striking Lives', p. 140.

43. Maurice Halbwachs, *On Collective Memory*, edited and translated by Lewis A. Coser, Chicago, 1992, pp. 38-39.

44. *Ashton News* and *Ashton Reporter*, 2 October 1869; *Ashton Reporter*, 27 December 1862; *Oddfellows' Magazine* (July 1857): 129-32. Hall and Roberts (eds.), *William Aitken*, pp. 10-11; R.J.M. Blackett, *Divided Hearts: Britain and the American Civil War*, Baton Rouge, 2001, pp. 87, 115-17, 125-28, 173-77; Janet Toole, 'Workers and Slaves: Class Relations in South Lancashire in the Time of the Cotton Famine', *Labour History Review* 63 (Summer 1998): 160-81.

45. *Ashton Reporter*, 10 November 1855. See also, Aitken, *Journey*, p. 29.

46. William Aitken, 'A Story of the First French Revolution', *Oddfellows' Magazine* (July 1869): 203-204; *idem*, 'A Story of the First French Revolution', *Oddfellows' Magazine* (January 1870): 284, 289. In his autobiography Aitken also used the phrase 'liberty without licentiousness' on p. 27.

47. *Ashton Reporter*, 3 October 1868. See also, Ibid., 16 and 30 January 1869.

48. Ibid., 8 September 1860.

49. Ibid., 26 December 1857. For the war of the unstamped as part of the struggle for 'Liberal principles', see Ibid., 5 October 1861.

50. Ibid., 30 January 1869.

51. Ibid., 19 March 1859 and 20 September 1856.

52. Founded in January 1868, the *Ashton News* apparently received crucial financial backing from Hugh Mason. See Williams and Williams, *Extra, Extra, Read All About It*.

53. In the original text of his 'letters', obvious typographical errors and strange, erratic punctuation were common. The *News* only infrequently broke up the text into paragraphs. For instance, the 16 October instalment contained only two paragraph breaks. In the 1996 edition, the obvious errors have been corrected, and the text has been broken up into more frequent paragraphs. See Hall and Roberts (eds.), *William Aitken*, p. 56.

54. Vincent, *Bread, Knowledge and Freedom*, pp. 9-10. See also, John Butt and Kathleen Tillotson, *Dickens at Work*, London, 1957, pp. 15-16, 21-25, 202-203; John Sutherland, *Victorian Fiction: Writers, Publishers, Readers*, New York, 1995, pp. 55, 87, 115-16.

55. *PP* (Commons) 1851 [558] XVII: 388.

56. Frank Peel, *The Risings of the Luddites, Chartists, and Plug-Drawers*, fourth ed., with an Introduction by E.P. Thompson, New York, 1968, pp. viii-x. For dialect poets, see Samuel Hill, *Old Lancashire Songs and their Singers*, Ashton, n.d., pp. 51-52; Axon, *Black Knight*.

57. Hall and Roberts (eds.), *William Aitken*, p. 14.

58. Ibid., p. 24. *Ashton Reporter*, 16 and 30 January 1869.

59. Hall and Roberts (eds.), *William Aitken*, p. 36.

60. *Ashton Reporter*, 14 November 1857; 5 February and 20 August 1859; *National Reformer*, 13 February 1864.

61. *Ashton Reporter*, 27 October 1860 (local politics); *People's Paper*, 17 February 1855; *Ashton Reporter*, 10 March 1860 and 28 March 1868 (Chartist Institute); *Ashton Reporter*, 6 December 1862 and 26 September 1863; *National Reformer*, 30 January 1864 (Secularist Society).

62. Hall and Roberts (eds.), *William Aitken*, p. 28.

63. Ibid., p. 35. See Chapter Three.

64. Ibid., p. 30.

65. *Northern Star*, 2 February 1839. See also, *Manchester Guardian*, 24 April 1839; *Northern Star*, 27 April 1839; *Operative*, 31 March and 28 April 1839.

66. *Ashton Reporter*, 30 January 1869.

67. Hall and Roberts (eds.), *William Aitken*, pp. 15, 34, 16, 19.

68. Ibid., p. 19.

69. Ibid., pp. 24, 23. Gray, *Factory Question*, pp. 29-31, 36-37; Carolyn Malone, *Women's Bodies and Dangerous Trades in England, 1880-1914*, Woodbridge, 2003, pp. 9-14.

70. Hall and Roberts (eds.), *William Aitken*, pp. 31, 27-28.

71. Ibid., p. 27. For this same point, see Aitken, 'A Story of the First French Revolution', *Oddfellows' Magazine* (July 1869): 204.

72. Hall and Roberts (eds.), *William Aitken*, p. 30.

73. Ibid., p. 38. TNA, PRO, HO 40/37 Jowett to Your Lordship, 3 July 1839. See Chapter Three.

74. Thompson (ed.), *The Early Chartists*, pp. 16-27; Epstein, *Lion of Freedom*, pp. 124-26; Sykes, 'Physical-Force Chartism', pp. 211-17.

75. *Northern Star*, 18 May 1839; *Manchester and Salford Advertiser*, 27 October 1838; TNA, PRO, HO 40/37, Meeting of Chartists at Ashton-under-Lyne, 20 April 1839; *Northern Star*, 11 April 1840.

76. *Northern Star*, 17 November 1838.

77. Tameside, L322, Aitken, 'To the Non-Electors and Electors'.

78. Hall and Roberts (eds.), *William Aitken*, p. 36.

79. *Manchester and Salford Advertiser*, 22 June 1839; *Manchester Chronicle*, 10 August 1839. See also, BL, Place Papers, Add Mss 34,245B, Deegan to Fletcher, 6 August 1839.

80. See Chapter Three. *PP* (Commons) 1840 [600] XXXVIII: 10, 12, 8.
81. Hall and Roberts (eds.), *William Aitken*, p. 28.
82. Ibid., pp. 28, 42-43.
83. Thomas Wright, *Our New Masters*, London, 1873; reprint ed., New York, 1969, p. 62.
84. Hall and Roberts (eds.), *William Aitken*, p. 43.
85. Ibid., pp. 28-29.
86. Mill to Kinnear, 19 August and 25 September 1865, in Robson (ed.), *Collected Works*, Vol. 16: *The Later Letters of John Stuart Mill*, 16: 1093-94 and 1103-1104.
87. MCL, Charles Higson Mss (microfilm copy), H52 Omnibus Book by Arthur Mayall: 23.
88. Hall and Roberts (eds.), *William Aitken*, pp. 31, 35. Epstein, *Radical Expression*, pp. 70-71, 97-99; Thompson, 'Who were "the People" in 1842?' in Chase and Dyck (eds.), *Living and Learning*, pp. 118-19.
89. *Ashton News*, 2 October 1869.
90. *Ashton Reporter*, 30 January 1869.
91. Hall and Roberts (eds.), *William Aitken*, p. 34.
92. *Northern Star*, 18 May 1839. For other accounts, see TNA, PRO, HO 73/55, Mott to Poor Law Commissioners, 9 May 1839; *Manchester Guardian*, 8 May 1839.
93. *Manchester Examiner*, 11 April 1848.
94. Hall and Roberts (eds.), *William Aitken*, pp. 29, 36, 31, 35.
95. Ibid., pp. 14, 38, 28.
96. Ibid., pp. 14, 39-40.

Index

The Chartist Studies Series
from
The Merlin Press
available from www.merlinpress.co.uk

'… an invaluable series.' *The New Statesman*

'… has established a well-deserved reputation for publishing
so much new and innovative work.' *North East History*

CHARTISM AFTER 1848
The Working Class and the Politics of Radical Education
by Keith Flett

Based on original research, a study of the campaign for political and social democracy
and for workers education, after 1848.

This work looks at independent working-class radical education and politics in
England from the year of revolutions, 1848 to the passage of the 1870 Education Act.
It takes as its starting point Richard Johnson's analysis of really useful knowledge but
argues that radical ideas and radical working-class education and schools, far from
disappearing after 1848, in fact flourished.

The main source used is the late Chartist and radical working-class press focusing
on radical meetings and events and the ideas that informed them. The introductory
chapter situates the research in its theoretical, historical and particularly chronological
context, the following three chapters consider the events of 1848 and how these
influenced working-class ideas and education. The experience of radicals in the period
after 1848 is then considered, as support for Chartism declined and as Chartist ideas
moved further to the left. Two chapters look at the later 1850s and the little discussed
educational strategy for political change put forward by G.J. Holyoake and opposed by
W.E Adams. Two final chapters consider the development of radical education in the
post-Chartist period of the 1860s and, finally, suggest some conclusions from the work
in respect of the politics of the 1870 Education Act and beyond.

234 x 156 mm. index. 232 pages
ISBN.
paperback 9780850365399 £15.95
hardback 9780850365443

Chartist Studies Series No. 6

PAPERS FOR THE PEOPLE
A Study of the Chartist Press
Edited by Joan Allen and Owen R. Ashton

An original study of the role of the Chartist press in the campaign for democracy in Victorian Britain and overseas. Covering the period from 1838 to the late 1850s, it considers the press in England, Scotalnd, Wales, Ireland and Australia.
Most of the contributors are well-known specialists in the history of Chartism, writing from both innovative and revisionist perspectives.

'This collection of essays, uniformly well researched, well contextualized, and well written, opens up a field that journalism historians should not ignore, and is highly recommended reading.' *Journalism History*

234 x 156 mm. 12 plates, index, 245 pages.

ISBN.
paperback 0850365406 £15.95
hardback 0850365457 £45.00

Chartist Studies Series No. 7

FRIENDS OF THE PEOPLE
'Uneasy' Radicals in the Age of the Chartists
by Owen R. Ashton and Paul A. Pickering

This study of six Chartist Leaders portrays movements for democracy and social progress, and explores the role of the uneasy middle classes in movements for working-class rights. The comparative analysis provides insights in to the development of dissent, the nature of class and of radicalism in the nineteenth century and an introduction sketches the historical context.

'... the third in an invaluable series of Chartist studies from the Merlin Press'. *The New Statesman*

'A significant addition to scholarship on the subject … For those who teach Chartism, at whatever level, this will be a useful and instructive book to add to the reading lists. Each essay can be read on its own, and taken together they would provide a sound basis for a class discussion on the national and local dimensions of Chartism. Moreover, like the other books in the series published by Merlin Press, it is very reasonably priced.'
History

'… fills a gap in Chartist historiography and provides a valuable opportunity to

compare the backgrounds and contributions of six Chartist intellectuals in Britain.'
Labour History

'You need to read it to fully appreciate the richness of these studies.'
North East History

220x157mm, illustrations, index, 176 pp.
ISBN. 0850365198
2002 Paperback £14.95

Chartist Studies Series No. 3

The Chartist Legacy
Edited by Owen Ashton, Robert Fyson & Stephen Roberts

This volume comprises eleven essays written by leading scholars of the Chartist Movement.

Contents:
Asa Briggs: Introduction; Miles Taylor: The Prehistory of the Six Points c. 1760-1837; Joan Hugman: 'A Small Drop of Ink': Tyneside Chartism & the Northern Liberator; Owen Ashton: Orators and Oratory in the Chartist Movement 1840-47; Robert Fyson: The Transported Chartist: The Case of William Ellis 1842-47; Stephen Roberts: Feargus O'Connor in the House of Commons 1846-52; Paul Pickering: Feargus O'Connor and Ireland 1849-50; Jamie Bronstein: Chartism and Its Relationship With the United States; Tim Randall: Chartist Poetry and Song; Kelly Mays: Reading Chartist Autobiographies; Antony Taylor: Commemoration, Memorialisation and Political Memory in Post-Chartist Radicalism: The 1885 Halifax Chartist Reunion.

"thoroughly researched... uniformly clear and well written, and in some cases break new and exciting ground" English Historical Review

234 x156mm xvi, 297pp. 1999

ISBN: 0850364868 hardback £25.00
085036484 paperback £14.95

Chartist Studies Series No. 1

The People's Charter
Democratic Agitation in Early Victorian Britain
Edited by Stephen Roberts

A collection of essays – previously published in scholarly journals and therefore of limited availability – on aspects of Chartism
Hostile MPs, police spies, mass arrests, picked juries, jails that made prisoners ill and killed them- these were just some of the difficulties faced by working people who campaigned for the vote and some measure of equality before the law in the early Victorian period.
Much of the best scholarship on the Chartists has been published in scholarly journals and has therefore been unavailable to the general reader. This volume presents a selection of key essays.
The volume is introduced by the editor and is accompanied by a chronology. The glossary of historical references, and notes on further reading, make it easily accessible for the general reader.

Chartism is an option for a number of AS/A2 history courses, and teachers will find a selection of copyright free Chartist journalism which can be freely copied for use in schools.
234 x 156 mm 232 pp.

ISBN. 0850365147 Paperback £14.95

Chartist Studies series No. 4

Images of Chartism
Stephen Roberts and Dorothy Thompson

Seventy contemporary images of the Chartist Movement

This book draws together a pictorial record of the Chartist Movement: over seventy images, photographs, prints and drawings with portraits of Chartist leaders, illustrations of demonstrations and events, memorabilia and cartoons making lively political comment. All the pictures are explained and put into context making this a useful book for teachers wanting to illustrate what the Chartist movement was like.

245x185mm 112pp
ISBN. 0850364752
1998 Paperback £15.95

Chartist Studies series No. 2

Other Chartist interest titles:

DEMOCRATIC REVIEW
Chartist Reprints Series
Edited by G. Julian Harney

A facsimile reprint of a Chartist journal, printed originally in 1849-1850. It provides commentary on contemporary politics in Britain, and on events in Europe after the revolutions of 1848.
222x144mm viii, 632pp
ISBN. 0850360986
1968 Hardback £30.00

Chartist Reprints Series

NOTES TO THE PEOPLE
Chartist Reprints Series
Edited by Ernest Jones

A facsimile reprint of a Chartist journal, originally published in 1851-1852, containing fascinating articles on a variety of topics: colonies, historical notes, trade disputes, political polemic.
215x145mm xiv+1032pp
ISBN. 0850360978
2 volumes
1967 Hardbacks £50.00 the set

Chartist Reprints series
RED REPUBLICAN & FRIEND OF THE PEOPLE

Edited by G Julian Harney

A facsimile Chartist reprint of two newpapers, originally published in 1850-1851, with news, letters and articles on poetry, politics, etc.
Introduction by John Saville. 280x213mm xv+470pp
085036096X
2 volumes
1966 Hardbacks £50.00 the set

Chartist Reprint Series

All these and other Merlin Press titles can be ordered securely on the Merlin Press web site:
Merlin Press web site:
www.merlinpress.co.uk